Samuel Rutherford Crockett

The Men of the Moss-Hags

Samuel Rutherford Crockett

The Men of the Moss-Hags

ISBN/EAN: 9783337176570

Printed in Europe, USA, Canada, Australia, Japan

Cover: Foto ©ninafisch / pixelio.de

More available books at **www.hansebooks.com**

THE MEN OF THE MOSS-HAGS

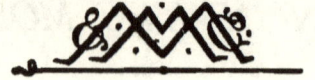

THE MEN OF THE MOSS-HAGS

BEING A HISTORY OF ADVENTURE TAKEN FROM THE PAPERS OF WILLIAM GORDON OF EARLSTOUN IN GALLOWAY AND TOLD OVER AGAIN BY

S. R. CROCKETT

New York
MACMILLAN AND CO.
AND LONDON
1895

All rights reserved

COPYRIGHT, 1895,
BY MACMILLAN AND CO.

Norwood Press
J. S. Cushing & Co. — Berwick & Smith
Norwood Mass. U.S.A.

To
ANDREW LANG
Poet, Romancer, Scholar, and Friend
of the goodly fellowship of the White Rose
I, born of the Hill-Folk
dedicate this attempt at a true history of
some who fought bravely beneath
the Banner of Blue

PREFATORY NOTE.

I desire to express grateful thanks to my researchers, Mr. James Nicholson of Kirkcudbright, who examined on my behalf all the local records bearing upon the period and upon the persons treated of in this book; and to the Reverend John Anderson of the Edinburgh University Library, who brought to light from among the Earlstoun Papers and from the long-lost records of the United Societies, many of the materials which I have used in the writing of this story.

I owe also much gratitude to the Library Committee of the University of Edinburgh, for permission to use the letters which are printed in the text, and for their larger permission to publish at some future time, for purposes more strictly historical, a selection from both the sets of manuscripts named above.

Most of all, I am indebted to my friend, Mr. John McMillan of Glenhead in Galloway, who has not only given me in this, as in former works, the benefit of his unrivalled local knowledge, but has travelled with me many a weary foot over those moors and moss-

hags, where the wanderers of another time had their abiding places. Let him accept this word of thanks. He is not likely to forget our stay together in the wilds of Cove Macaterick. Nor I our journey home.

S. R. CROCKETT.

Penicuik, Aug. 5, 1895.

CONTENTS.

CHAPTER		PAGE
I.	MY GOSSIP, MAISIE MAY	1
II.	GAY GARLAND CARRIES DOUBLE	8
III.	GAY GARLAND COMES HOME SADDLE EMPTY	15
IV.	SANDY GORDON COMES OVER THE HILL ALL ALONE	21
V.	THE CLASH OF WORDS	27
VI.	THE CLASH OF SWORDS	33
VII.	THE FIELD OF BOTHWELL BRIG	38
VIII.	THE CURATE OF DALRY	46
IX.	THROUGH DEATH'S DARK VALE	53
X.	THE GRAVE IN THE WILDERNESS	61
XI.	THE BLOOD OF THE MARTYRS	67
XII.	WE RIDE TO EDINBURGH	73
XIII.	WULLCAT WAT DARES HEAVEN AND HELL	79
XIV.	THE THING THAT FELL FROM TRAITOR'S GATE	86
XV.	THE BICKER IN THE SNOW	92
XVI.	THE GREY MOWDIEWORT	97
XVII.	OVER THE MUIR AMANG THE HEATHER	102
XVIII.	AULD ANTON OF THE DUCHRAE	107
XIX.	THE SWEET SINGERS OF THE DEER-SLUNK	113
XX.	THE HOME OF MY LOVE	125
XXI.	THE GREAT CONVENTICLE BY THE DEE WATER	130
XXII.	PEDEN THE PROPHET	137
XXIII.	BIRSAY THE COBBLER	143
XXIV.	THE SANQUHAR DECLARATION	154
XXV.	THE LAST CHARGE AT AYRSMOSS	161

CONTENTS.

CHAPTER		PAGE
XXVI.	HIDING WITH THE HEATHER-CAT	171
XXVII.	THE WATER OF THE WELL OF BETHLEHEM	180
XXVIII.	THE WELL-HOUSE OF EARLSTOUN	186
XXIX.	CUPBOARD LOVE	190
XXX.	THE BULL OF EARLSTOUN'S HOMECOMING	195
XXXI.	JEAN'S WA'S	202
XXXII.	PLAIN WORDS UPON MEN	207
XXXIII.	THE GARDENER OF BALMAGHIE	212
XXXIV.	THE TESTING OF THE TYKE	218
XXXV.	KATE OF THE DARK BROWS	224
XXXVI.	THE BLACK HORSE COMES TO BALMAGHIE	230
XXXVII.	A CAVALIER'S WOOING	237
XXXVIII.	IN COVE MACATERICK	243
XXXIX.	THE BOWER OF THE STAR	249
XL.	MARDROCHAT THE SPY	256
XLI.	THE HOUSE OF THE BLACK CATS	263
XLII.	THE NICK O' THE DEID WIFE	270
XLIII.	THE VENGEANCE OF "YON"	276
XLIV.	A DESIRABLE GENERAL MEETING	281
XLV.	THE OUTFACING OF CLAVERS	288
XLVI.	THE FIGHT AT THE CALDONS	296
XLVII.	THE GALLOWAY FLAIL	304
XLVIII.	THE FIGHT IN THE GUT OF THE ENTERKIN	311
XLIX.	THE DEATH OF MARDROCHAT	320
L.	THE BREAKING OF THE THIEVES' HOLE	326
LI.	THE SANDS OF WIGTOWN	334
LII.	THE MADNESS OF THE BULL OF EARLSTOUN	341
LIII.	UNDER SENTENCE OF DEATH	348
LIV.	ROBBERY ON THE KING'S HIGHWAY	351
LV.	THE RED MAIDEN	360
LVI.	THE MAID ON THE WHITE HORSE	365
	FOLLOWETH THE AUTHOR'S CONCLUSION	369

THE MEN OF THE MOSS-HAGS.

CHAPTER I.

MY GOSSIP, MAISIE MAY.

It was upon the fair green braes that look over the Black Water of Dee near by where it meets the clear Ken, that Maisie May and I played many a morning at Wanderers and King's men. I mind it as it were yesterday, for the dales and holms were pranked out with white hawthorn and broad gowans, and by our woodland hiding-places little frail wildflowers grew, nodding at us as we lay and held our breath.

Now Maisie Lennox (for that was her proper given name) was my cousin, and had been gossip of mine ever since we came to the age of five years; Sandy, my elder brother, making nothing of me because I was so much younger and he ever hot upon his own desires. Neither, if the truth must be told, did I wear great love upon him at any time. When we fell out, as we did often, he would pursue after me and beat me; but mostly I clodded him with pebble stones, whereat I had the advantage, being ever straight of eye and sure of aim. Whereas Sandy was gleyed* and threw stones like a girl, for all the stoutness of his arm.

But that is not to say like Maisie Lennox, who was

* Could not see straight.

Anthony Lennox's daughter, and could throw stones with any one. She lived at the Lesser Duchrae above the Black Water. As for me I lived at Earlstoun on the hillside above the Ken, which is a far step from the Duchrae. But our fathers were of the one way of thinking, and being cousins by some former alliance and friends of an ancient kindliness, it so happened, as I say, that Maisie Lennox and I played much together. Also my mother had great tenderness of heart for the bit lass that had no mother, and a father as often on the moors with the wildfowl, as at home with his one little maid.

For the times were very evil. How evil and contrary they were, we that had been born since 1660 and knew nothing else, could but dimly understand. For though fear and unrest abode in our homes as constant indwellers, with the fear of the troopers and plunderers, yet because it had always been so, it seemed not very hard to us. Indeed we bairns of these years played at Covenanting, as it had been the game of "Scots and English" on the hillside, even from the time when we first began to run alone.

Well do I mind that day when I pleaded and fleeched on my father to take me before him on Gay Garland, as he rode to the Duchrae. It was a brisk May day with an air vigorous as a draught of wine, yet cool, clear, and sweet as spring water is — a pearl of a day, such as hardly seems to come in these sullen later years.

So I cried out upon my father to take me. And as his manner was, he told me to inquire of my mother. But I desired rather that he should ask for me himself. So I lingered about the doors till he should ride forth upon his great black horse, that he might catch me up beside him on the cantle and cry in at the door, "Mother, I am taking William," as was his kindly wont. Never a man so brave and true and simple as my father.

While I bided there, Alexander my brother seeing me wait, called me to come with him to the hill. But because my heart was set to ride to the Duchrae with my father, I had no desire to go to the rabbit hunting. So when he saw that I would not company with him, he mocked me and called me "Lassie-boy!" Whereupon I smote him incontinent with a round pebble between the shoulder-blades, and he pursued me to the hallan door within which was my mother, looking to the maids and the ordering of the house.

From thence I mocked him, but under my breath, for fear that for ill-doing my mother would not permit me to go to the Duchrae.

"Stable-boy!" I called him, for he loved to be ever among the lowns of the wisp and currying comb, and as my mother said, grew like them even in manners. "Faugh, keep wide from me, mixen-varlet!"

These were no more than our well-accustomed greetings.

"Wait till I catch you, little snipe, down by the waterside!" Sandy cried, shaking his fist at me from the barn-end.

"And that will be a good day for your skin," answered I, "for I shall make you wash your face thoroughly — ay, even behind your ears."

For Sandy, even when in after days he went a-courting, was noways partial to having many comings and goings with a basin of cold water.

So he departed unsatisfied, because that in words I had the better of him.

Then came my father, and as I expected, stooping from the saddle he swung me up before him, supposing that I had already advised my mother. But indeed I had not said so, and happily he asked me nothing.

"A good day and an easy mind, sweetheart," he cried up the stairs to my mother, "I ride to the Duchrae for Conference. William goes with me for company."

And my mother came down the steps to see us ride off. For my father and she were like lad and lass after their years together, though not so as to make a show before strangers.

"Watch warily for the dragoons as you come to the narrows of the Loch," she said, "and bide not at Kenmuir. For if there be mounted muskets in all the neighbourhood, it is at the Kenmuir that they will be found."

And she watched us out of sight with her hand to her brows, before turning inward to the maids — a bonny woman in these years, fair as a blowing rose, was my mother. Or at least, so the picture rises before me as I write.

Thus my father, William Gordon of Earlstoun, rode away through these sweet holms and winding paths south toward the Duchrae. Nowhere is the world to my thinking so gracious as between the green woodlands of Earlstoun and the grey Duchrae Craigs. For the pools of the water of Ken slept, now black, now silver, beneath us. They were deep set about with the feathers of the birches, and had the green firs standing bravely like men-at-arms on every rocky knoll. Then the strath opened out and we saw Ken flow silver-clear between the greenest and floweriest banks in the world. The Black Craig of Dee gloomed on our right side as we rode, sulky with last year's heather. And the great Kells range sank behind us, ridge behind ridge of hills whose very names make a storm of music — Millyea, Milldown, Millfire, Corscrine, and the haunted fastnesses of the Meaull of Garryhorn in the head end of Carsphairn. Not that my father saw any of this, for he minded only his riding and his prayers; but even then I was ever taken up with what I had better have let alone. However, I may be held excused if the memory rises unbidden now, before the dimmer eye of one that takes a cast back into his youth, telling the tale as best he may, choosing here and there like a dorty child, only that which liketh him best.

In a little we clattered through the well-thatched roofs of New Galloway and set Gay Garland's head to the southward along the water-side, where the levels of the Loch are wont to open out upon you blue and broad and bonny. All that go that way know the place. Gay Garland was the name of my father's black horse that many a time and oft had carried him in safety, and was loved like another child by my mother and all of us. I have heard it said that in the Praying Society of which he was a grave and consistent member, my father was once called in question because he gave so light a name to his beast.

"Ye have wives of your own," was all the answer he made them, "I suppose they have no freits and fancies, but such as you are ready to be answerable for this day."

When my mother heard of this she said, "Ay, William, thy excuse was but old and lame, even that of our first father Adam — 'The woman thou gavest me she called my horse Gay Garland.'"

I suppose that to-day Ken flashes as clear and the heather blooms as bonny on the Bennan side. But not for me, for I have laid away so many that I loved in the howe of the Glen since then, and seen so many places of this Scotland red with a crimson the bell heather never made. Ay me for the times that were, and for all that is come and gone, whereof it shall be mine to tell!

But we came at long and last to the Duchrae, which is a sweet bit house, sitting on a south-looking braeface, though not a laird's castle like the tower of Earlstoun. Maisie Lennox met us at the loaning foot, whereat I begged that my father would put me down so that I might run barefoot with her. And I think my father was in nowise unwilling, for a twelve-year-old callant on the saddle before one is no comfort, though Gay Garland bore me like a feather.

So Maisie Lennox and I fell eagerly a-talking together after our first shy chill of silence, having many things to say. But as soon as ever we reached the Craigs we fell to our fantasy. It was an old game with us, like the sand houses we used to build in bairns' play. We drew lots, long stalk and short stalk, which of us should be the Wanderer. Maisie Lennox won the lot — as she always did, for I had no good fortune at the drawing of cuts. So she went to hide in some bosky bouroch or moss-hag, while I bode still among the hazels at the woodside, accoutring myself as a trooper with sword and pistol of tree.

Then I rode forth crying loud commands and sending my soldiers to seek out all the hidie-holes by the water-sides, and under all the tussocks of heather on the benty brows of the black mosses.

Soon Maisie Lennox began to cry after the manner of the hunted hill-folk — peeping like the nestlings of the muir-birds, craiking like the bird of the corn, laughing like the jack-snipe — and all with so clear a note and such brisk assurance that I declare she had imposed upon Tom Dalyell himself.

After seeking long in vain, I spied the fugitive hiding behind a peat-casting on the edge of the moss, and immediately cried on the men to shoot. So those that were men-at-arms of my command pursued after and cracked muskets, as the Wanderers jooked and fled before us. Yet cumbered with cavalry as I was on the soft bog land, the light-foot enemy easily escaped me.

Then when I saw well that catch her I could not, I sat me down on a heather bush and cried out to her that it was a silly game to play, and that we should begin something else. So she stopped and came back slowly over the heather. What I liked at all times about Maisie Lennox was that she never taunted back, but only took her own way when she wanted it — and she mostly did — silently and as if there were no other way in the world. For in all things she had an excellent humour óf silence, which, though I knew it not then, is rarer and worthier than diamonds. Also she knew, what it seems to me that a woman but rarely knows, when it is worth while making a stand to gain her will.

CHAPTER II.

GAY GARLAND CARRIES DOUBLE.

So after that we played yet another game, hiding together in the hags and crawling from bent bush to rush clump with mighty caution and discernment, making believe that the troopers sought us both. For this was the favourite bairns' play everywhere in the West and South.

Once when we came near to the house Gay Garland followed us, having been turned out on the Duchrae home park. He ran to me, as he ever did, for farings, and I fed him with crumblings out of my jacket pocket — "moolings" Maisie Lennox called them — which he ate out of my hand, a pretty thing to see in so noble a beast. Then he followed us about in our hidings, begging and sorning upon us for more. This made him not a little troublesome, till we would gladly have sent him back. But Gay Garland was a beast not easily turned.

After a while we came to the little wood of Mount Pleasant, where I saw some red rags fluttering on a bush. I was for going aside to see what they might be, but Maisie Lennox cried at me to turn back.

"There are people hereabouts that are not very chancy. My father saw the Marshalls go by this morning!"

Often and often I had heard of the tribe before, and they had a singular name for their ill-done deeds. Indeed the whole land was so overrun with beggars of the Strong Hand, and the times so unsettled, that nothing could be done to put a stop to their spoilings. For the King and his men were too busy riding down poor folk that carried Bibles and went to field-preachings, to pay attention to such as merely invaded homesteads and lifted gear.

As we set breast to the brae and came to the top of the little hill, I stumbled over something white and soft lying behind a heather bush. It was a sheep — dead, and with much of it rent and carried away. The ground about was all a-lapper with blood.

"A worrying dog has done this!" I said.

But Maisie Lennox came up, and as she caught sight of the carcase her face fell. She shook her head mighty seriously.

"Two-footed dogs," she said. "See here!" She lifted a piece of paper on which a bloody knife had been wiped. And she showed me, very wisely, how the best parts had been cut away by some one that had skill in dismemberment.

"'Tis Jock Marshall's band," she said; "an ill lot, but they shall not get off with this!"

And she went forward eagerly, keeping on the broad trail through the grass. We had not gone a hundred yards when we came upon another sheep in like case, and then by the ford of the Black Water we found yet another. I asked Maisie Lennox if we should not go home and lodge information.

"They'll get ower far away," was all she said.

"But you are not feared of them?" I asked, marvelling at the lassie. For even our Sandy that counted himself so bold, and could lift a bullock slung in a sheet with his teeth, would have thought twice before following up Jock Marshall and his band for the sake of an orra sheep or two.

But Maisie Lennox only turned to me in a curious way, in which there seemed mingled something of contempt.

"Feared!" she said. "What for should I be feared? The sheep are my faither's; but gang you back gin ye be feared."

So for very shame I answered that I was feared none — which was a great lie, for I had given a hundred pounds (Scots) to have been able to turn back with some credit. But we went along the broad trail boldly enough, and Gay Garland trotted loose-foot after us, sometimes stopping to crop the herbs by the way, and anon coming dancing to find us. At which I was glad, for it was at least some company besides the lassie.

Soon we came to a link of the path by the water-side, at a place that is called the Tinklers' Loup, where these sorners and limmers were mostly wont to congregate. There was blue smoke rising behind the knowe, and Maisie Lennox took a straight path over the heather toward it. I wondered to see the lass. She seemed indeed not to know fear.

"They are my faither's ain sheep," she said, as though that were sufficient explanation.

So to the top we came, and looked down. There was a whole camp beneath us. Dirty low reeky tans were set here and there amid a swarm of bairns and dogs. The children were running naked as they were born, and the dogs turning themselves into hoops to bite their tails. About a couple of fires with pots a-swing over them, bubbling and steaming, little clouds of wild-looking folk were gathered. Some had bones in their hands which they thrust into the fire for a minute and then took out again to gnaw at the burned portion. Tattered women looked within the pots. Once a man threw a knife at a boy, which struck him on the side. The boy cried out and the blood ran down, but none took any heed to his complaint or of the circumstance.

For a moment Maisie Lennox stood still and looked at me. Then she went a step or two forward, and her face was white and angered. I saw she was about to speak to them, yet for my life I could not keep her from it.

"Sheep stealers!" she cried; "vagabonds, ye shall hang for this! Not for naught shall ye harry an honest man's sheep. I ken you, Jock Marshall and all your crew. The Shirra shall hear of this before the morrow's morn!"

The encampment stood still at gaze looking up at us, fixed like a show painted on a screen, while one might slowly count a score. Then Babel brake loose.

With a wild rush, man, woman, child, and dog poured towards us. Of mere instinct I came up abreast of Maisie Lennox. Behind me came Gay Garland, and snuffed over my shoulder, scenting with some suspicion the tinklers' garrons* feeding in the hollow below.

We stood so still on the knowe-top that, I think, we must have feared them a little. We were by a gap in the bushes, and the ill-doers, seeing no more of us thought, no doubt, that there must be more behind, or two bairns had never been so bold. I think, too, that the very want of arms daunted them, for they drew back and seemed to consult together as though uncertain what to do.

Then a great scant-bearded unkempt man with long swinging arms, whom I took to be Jock Marshall, the chief tinkler and captain of their gang, pointed to them to scatter round the little knoll, no doubt with the purpose of making observations and cutting us off.

"Who may you be?" he cried, looking up at us.

"Right well you know," Maisie said, very loud and clear, speaking out like a minister in the tent at a field-preaching; "I am Anton Lennox of the Duchrae's daughter, whose sheep ye have boiling in your pots — and that after being well served with meal at the door, and louting low for thankfulness. And this is your thanks, ye robbers-behind-backs, gallow's thieves of Kelton Hill."

On my part I thought it was not good judgment so to anger

* Shaggy ponies.

the wild crew. But Maisie was not to be spoken to at such a time; so perforce I held my tongue.

"But ye shall all streek a tow for this," she said; "this day's wark shall be heard tell o' yet!"

By this time the word had been passed round the hill to Jock the tinkler that there were but two of us, and we unarmed. At which the loon became at once very bold.

"Have at them! Blood their throats! Bring the basin!" he cried. And the words were no vain things, for that was their well-accustomed way of killing — to let their victim's blood run into a basin, so that there might be no tell-tale stains upon the grass.

So from all sides they came speeling and clambering up the hill, loons yelling, dogs barking, till I thought my latest hour was come, and wished I had learned my Catechism better — especially the proofs. Gay Garland stood by with a raised look upon him, lifting his feet a little, as though going daintily over a bridge whose strength he was not sure of, and drawing all the while the wind upward through his nostrils.

Then though Maisie had been very bold, I can lay claim on this occasion to having been the wiser, for I caught her by the arm, taking Gay Garland's mane firmly with the other hand the while, lest he should startle and flee.

"Up with you," I cried, bending to take her foot in my hand, and she went up like a bird.

In a moment I was beside her, riding bare-back, with Maisie clasping my waist, as indeed we had often ridden before — though never so perilously, nor yet with such a currish retinue yowling at our tail.

I wore no weapon upon me — no, not so much as a bodkin. But stuck in my leather belt I had the two crooked sticks, which I had blackened with soot for pistols at our play of Troopers and Wanderers. I put my heels into Gay

Garland's sides, and he started down-hill, making the turf fly from his hoofs as he gathered way and began to feel his legs under him.

The gang scattered and rounded to close us in, but when Gay Garland came to his stride, few there were who could overtake him. Only Jock Marshall himself was in time to meet us face to face, a great knife in either hand. And I think he might have done us an injury too, had it not been for the nature of the ground where we met.

It was just at the spring of a little hill and the good horse was gathering himself for the upstretch. I held the two curved sticks at the tinkler's head, as though they had been pistols, at which I think he was a little daunted. Jock Marshall stopped in his rush, uncertain whether to leap aside; and in that very moment, Gay Garland spread his fore-feet for the spring, throwing up his head as if to clear the way. One of his iron-shod heels took the tinkler chief fair on the chest, and the breast-bone gave inwards with a crunch like the breaking of many farles of cake-bread. He fell down on the moss like one dead, and Gay Garland went over the moor with the whole tribe of whooping savages after him, spurning their fallen chief with his hoof as he passed.

Well it was for us that the noble horse carried us with such ease and that his feet were so sure. For a stumble in a rabbit hole and our throats were as good as slit.

But by the blessing of Providence and also by my good guiding of Gay Garland's mane, we passed the ford of the Black Water without hurt. Then was I very croose at the manner of our coming off, and minded not that the hardest blaff of downcome is ever gotten at the doorstep.

We were passing by the path that goes linking along the water-side, and talking to one another very cantily, when without warning a musket barked from the woodside, and as it were a red-hot gaud of iron ran into my thigh behind my knee. The world swayed round me and the green trees ran withershins about. I had fallen among the horse's feet, but that Maisie Lennox caught me, meeting Gay Garland's swerve with the grip of her knee — for she ever rode across and acrop like a King's horseman, till it was time for her to ride side-saddle and grow mim and prudent.

Haply just by the turn we met my father and old Anthony Lennox coming running at the sound of the shot. But as for me I never saw or heard them, for they ran past, hot to find the man who had fired at me. While as for me I came up the loaning of the Duchrae upon Gay Garland, with my head leaning back upon the young lassie's shoulder and the red blood staining her white skirt.

And this was the beginning of my lameness and sometime lack of vigour — the beginning also of my life friendship with Maisie Lennox, who was to me from that day as my brother and my comrade, though she had been but a bairn's playmate aforetime.

CHAPTER III.

GAY GARLAND COMES HOME SADDLE EMPTY.

THE night of the twenty-second of June, 1679, shall never be forgotten among us while Earlstoun House stands. It was the eve of the day whereon befell the weary leaguer of Bothwell when the enemy beset the Brig, and the good Blue Banner gat fyled and reddened with other dye-stuff than the brown moss-water. I mind it well, for I had grown to be man-muckle since the day on the Tinklers' Loup. After a day of heat there fell a night like pitch. A soughing wind went round the house and round the house, whispering and groping, like a forlorn ghost trying to find his way within.

If there was a shut eye in the great House of Earlstoun that night, it was neither mine nor my mother's. We lay and thought of them that were over the hill, striving for the Other King and the good cause. And our thoughts were prayers, though there was none to "take the Book" in Earlstoun that night, for I was never gifted that way. So we bedded without sound of singing or voice of prayer, though I think Jean Hamilton had done it for the asking.

I lay in my naked bed and listened all the night with unshut eye. I could hear in my mother's room the boards creak as she rose every quarter hour and looked out into the rayless dark. Maisie Lennox of the Duchrae, old Anton's daughter, now a well grown lass, lay with her. And Sandy's young wife, Jean Hamilton, with her sucking bairn, was in the little angled chamber that opens off the turret stair near by.

It befell at the back of one, or mayhap betwixt that and

two, that there came a sound at the nether door that affrighted us all.

"Rise, William! Haste ye," cried my mother with great eagerness in her voice, coming to my door in the dark. "Your father is at the nether door, new lichted doon from off Gay Garland. Rise an' let him in!"

And as I sat up on my elbow and hearkened, I heard as clearly as now I hear the clock strike, the knocking of my father's riding-boots on the step of the outer door. For it was ever his wont, when he came that way, to knap his toes on the edge of the step, that the room floorings might not be defiled with the black peat soil which is commonest about the Earlstoun. I have heard my father tell it a thousand times in his pleasantry, how it was when my mother was a bride but newly come home and notionate, that she learned him these tricks. For otherwise his ways were not dainty, but rather careless — and it might be, even rough.

So, as I listened, I heard very clear outside the house the knocking of my father's feet, and the little hoast he always gave before he tirled at the pin to be let in, when he rode home late from Kirkcudbright. Hearing which we were greatly rejoiced, and I hasted to draw on my knee-breeks, crying "Bide a wee, faither, an' briskly I'll be wi' ye to let ye in!"

For I was a little lame, halting on one foot ever since the affair of Tinkler Marshall, though I think not to any noticeable extent.

My mother at the door of her chamber cried, "Haste ye, William, or I must run mysel'!"

For my father had made her promise that she would not go out of her chamber to meet him at the return, being easily touched in her breast with the night air.

So I hasted and ran down as I was, with my points all untied, and set wide open the door.

"Faither!" I cried as I undid the bolt and pushed the leaves of the door abroad, "Faither, ye are welcome hame!" And I could hear my mother listening above, for his foot over the threshold. Yet he came not within, which was a wonder to me. So I went out upon the step of the nether door, but my father was not there. Only the same strange chill wind went round the house, soughing and moaning blindly as before, and a smoor of white fog blew like muirburn past the door.

Then my hair rose upon my head and the skin of my brow pricked, because I knew that strange portents were abroad that night.

"What for does your faither no come ben the hoose to me?" cried my mother impatiently from the stair-head. I could hear her clasping and unclasping her hands, for my ears are quick at taking sounds.

"I think he must be gone to the stable with Gay Garland, to stall him beside Philiphaugh," I answered, for so my father's old white horse was named, because in his young days my father had been at that place on the day when Montrose and his Highlandmen got their settling. This is what I said to my mother, but indeed my thought was far other.

I lifted a loaded pistol that lay ever in the aumrie by the door-cheek and went off in the direction of the stable. The door was shut, but I undid the pin and went within. *My father was not there.* The horses were moving restlessly and lifting their feet uneasily as they do on ice or other kittle footing. Then of a truth I knew there was something more than canny abroad about Earlstoun that night, and that we should hear ill news or the morning. And when a bundle of reins slipped from the shelf and fell on my shoulder like a man's hand clapping on me unaware, I cried out like a frighted fowl and dropped almost to the ground. Yet though I am delicate and not overly well grown in my body, I do not count myself a coward; even though my brother Sandy's courage be not mine. "Blind-eye, hard-head" was ever his sort, but I love to take my danger open-eyed and standing up — and as little of it as possible.

As I went back — which I did instantly, leaving the stable door swinging open — I heard my mother's voice again. She was calling aloud and the sound of her voice was yearning and full like that of a young woman.

"William!" she called, and again "William!"

Now though that is my name I knew full well that it was not to me, her son, that she called. For that is the voice a woman only uses to him who has been her man, and with her has drunk of the fountain of the joy of youth. Once on a time I shot an eagle on the Millyea, and his mate came and called him even thus, with a voice that was as soft as that of a cushie dove crooning in the tall trees in the early summer, till I could have wept for sorrow at my deed.

Then as I went in, I came upon my mother a step or two from the open door, groping with her arms wide in the darkness.

"Oh," she cried, "William, my William, the Lord be thankit!" and she clasped me to her heart.

But in a moment she flung me from her.

"Oh! it's you," she said bitterly, and went within without another word, her harshness jangling on my heart.

Yet I understood, for my mother was always greatly set on my father. And once when in jest we teased her to try her, telling her the story of the pious Æneas, and asking her to prophesy to us which one of us she would lift, if so it was that the house of Earlstoun were in a lowe.

"Faith," said my mother, "I wad tak' your faither on my back, gin a' the lave o' ye had to bide and burn!"

So it was ever with my mother. She was my father's sweetheart to her latest hour.

But when I went in I found her sitting, sheet-white and trembling on the settle.

"What's ta'en ye, mither?" I said to her, putting a shawl about her.

"O my man, my bonny man," she said, "there's nane to steek your e'en the nicht! An' Mary Gordon maun lie her leesome lane for evermair!"

"Hoot, mither," I said, "speak not so. My faither will come his ways hame i' the mornin' nae doot, wi' a' the lads o' the Kenside clatterin' ahint him. Sandy is wi' him, ye ken."

"Na," she said calmly enough, but as one who has other informations, "Sandy is no wi' him. Sandy gaed through the battle wi' his heid doon and his sword rinnin' reed. I see them a' broken — a' the pride o' the West, an' the dragoons are riding here an' there amang them, an' haggin' them doon. But your faither I canna see — I canna see my man ——"

"Mither," I said, mostly, I think, for something to say, "Mind the Guid Cause!"

She flung her hands abroad with a fine gesture as of scorn. "What cause is guid that twines a woman frae her ain man — an' we had been thegither three-an'-thirty year!"

In a little I got her to lie down, but the most simple may understand how much more sleep there was in Earlstoun that night. Yet though we listened with all our ears, we heard no other sound than just that blind and unkindly wind reestling and soughing about the house, groping at the doors and trying the lattices. Not a footstep went across the courtyard, not the cry of a bird came over the moors, till behind the barren ridges of the east the morning broke.

Then when in the grey and growing light I went down and again opened the door, lo! there with his nose against the latchet hasp was Gay Garland, my father's war-horse. He stood and trembled in every limb. He was covered with the lair of the moss-hags, wherein he had sunk to the girths. But on his saddle leather, towards the left side, there was a broad splash of blood which had run down to the stirrup iron; and in the holster on that side, where the great pistol ought to have been, a thing yet more fearsome — a man's bloody forefinger, taken off above the second joint with a clean drawing cut.

My mother came down the turret stair, fully dressed, and with her company gown upon her. Yet when she saw Gay Garland standing there at the door with his head between his knees, she did not seem to be astonished or afraid, as she had been during the night. She came near to him and laid a hand on his neck.

"Puir beast," she said, "ye have had sore travel. Take him to the stable for water and corn, and bid Jock o' the Garpel rise."

The dark shades of the night were flown away, and my mother now spoke quietly and firmly as was her wont. Much in times bygone had we spoken about sufferings in the House of Earlstoun, and, lo! now they were come home to our own door.

CHAPTER IV.

SANDY GORDON COMES OVER THE HILL ALL ALONE.

THE House of Earlstoun sits bonny above the water-side, and there are few fairer waters in this land than the Ken water. Also it looks its bonniest in the early morning when the dew is on all sides, and a stillness like the peace of God lies on the place. I do not expect the Kingdom of Heaven very much to surpass Earlstoun on a Sabbath morning in June when the bees are in the roses. And, indeed, I shall be well content with that.

But there was no peace in Earlstoun that morning — no, nor for many a morning to come. I was at the door watching for their coming, before ever a grouse cock stirred among the short brown heather on the side of Ardoch Hill. I told my mother over and over that without dŏubt Sandy was bringing father home.

"Gay Garland was aye a reesty beast!" I said. "Doubtless he started when my faither had his foot in the stirrup, and has come hame by himsel'!"

But I said nothing about the finger in the holster.

"Anither beast micht," said my mother, looking wistfully from the little window on the stair, from which she did not stir, "but never Gay Garland!"

And right well I knew she spake the truth. Gay Garland had carried my father over long to reest with him at the hinderend.

"Can ye no see them?" cried my mother again, from the room where ordinarily she sat.

Even Jean Hamilton, who had been but three years a wife, was not as restless that fair morning of midsummer as my mother, for she had her babe at her breast. In which she was the happier, because when he cried, at least she had something to think about.

Three weeks before, in the midst of the sunny days of that noble June, my father, William Gordon of Airds and Earlstoun, and my elder brother Alexander had ridden away to fight against King Charles. It took a long arm in those days to strive with the Stuarts. And as I saw them ride over the brae with thirty Glenkens blue bonnets at their tail, I knew that I was looking upon the beginning of the ruin of our house. Yet I went and hid my face and raged, because I was not permitted to ride along with them, nor to carry the Banner of Blue which my mother the Lady of Earlstoun, and Jean Hamilton, Sandy's wife, had broidered for them — with words that stirred the heart lettered fair upon it in threads of gold, and an Andrew's cross of white laid on the bonny blue of its folds.

My mother would have added an open Bible on the division beneath, but my father forbade.

"A sword, gin ye like, but no Bible!" he said.

So they rode away, and I, that was called William Gordon for my father, clenched hands and wept because that I was not counted worthy to ride with them. But I was never strong, ever since Maisie Lennox and I rode home from the Tinklers' Loup; and my mother said always that she had more trouble at the rearing of me than with all her cleckin'. By which she meant, as one might say, her brood of chickens.

To me my father cried out as he rode out of the yard:

"Abide, William, and look to your mother — and see that the beasts get their fodder, for you are the master of Earlstoun till I return."

"An' ye can help Jean to sew her bairn-clouts!" cried my brother Sandy, whom we called the Bull, in that great voice of his which could cry from Ardoch to Lochinvar over leagues of heather.

And I, who heard him with the water standing in my eyes because they were going out in their war-gear while I had to bide at home,— could have clouted him with a stone as he sat his horse, smiling and shaving the back of his hand with his Andrea Ferrara to try its edge.

O well ken I that he was a great fighter and Covenant man, and did ten times greater things than I, an ill-grown crowl, can ever lay my name to. But nevertheless, such was the hatred I felt at the time towards him, being my brother and thus flouting me.

But with us, as I have said, there abode our cousin Maisie Lennox from the Duchrae, grown now into a douce and sonsy lass, with hair that was like spun gold when the sun shone upon it. For the rest, her face rather wanted colour, not having in it — by reason of her anxiety for her father, and it may be also by the nature of her complexion — so much of red as the faces of Jean Hamilton and other of our country lasses. But because she was my comrade, I saw naught awanting, nor thought of red or pale, since she was indeed Maisie Lennox and my friend and gossip of these many years.

Also in some sort she had become a companion for my mother, for she had a sedate and dependable way with her, solate and wise beyond her years.

"She is not like a flichty young body aboot a hoose," said my mother.

But in this I differed, yet said nothing. For no one could have been to me what young Maisie of the Duchrae was.

After Sandy and my father had ridden away, and I that

was left to keep the house, went about with a hanging head because I had not ridden also, Maisie Lennox grew more than ordinarily kind. Never had a feckless lad like me, such a friend as Maisie of the Duchrae. It was far beyond that love which the maids chatter about, and run out to the stackyard in the gloaming to find — oft to their sorrow, poor silly hempies.

Yet Maisie May and I greeted in the morning without observance, but rather as brothers whom night has not parted. In the day we spoke but seldom, save to ask what might be needful, as the day's darg and duty drifted us together. But at even, standing silent, we watched the light fade from the hills of the west and gather behind those of the east. And I knew that without speech her heart was trying to comfort mine, because I had not been judged worthy to ride for the Covenants with her father and mine, and in especial because Sandy had openly flouted me before her. This was very precious to me and kept up my manhood in mine own eyes — a service far above rubies.

Thus they rode away and left the house of the Earlstoun as empty and unfriendly as a barn in hay harvest. From that day forward we spent as much time looking out over the moor from the house, as we did at our appointed tasks. I have already told of the happenings of the night of the twenty-second of June, and of my mother's strange behaviour — which, indeed, was very far from her wont. For she seldom showed her heart to my father, but rather faulted him and kept him at a stick's end, especially when he came heedlessly into her clean-swept rooms with his great moss-splashed riding-boots.

Of this time I have one thing more to tell. It was between the hours of ten and eleven of the day following this strange night, that my mother, having set all her house maidens to their tasks with her ordinary care and discretion, took down the bake-board and hung the girdle above a clear red fire of peat. Sometimes she did this herself, especially when my father was from home. For she was a master baker, and my father often vowed that he would have her made the deacon of the trade in Dumfries, where he had a house. He was indeed mortally fond of her girdle-cakes, and had wheaten flour ground fine at a distant mill for the purpose of making them.

"Mary Hope," he used to say to her in his daffing way, "your scones are better than your father's law. I wonder wha learned ye to bake aboot Craigieha' — tho', I grant, mony's the puir man the faither o' ye has keepit braw and het on a girdle, while he stirred him aboot wi' his tongue."

This he said because my mother was a daughter of my Lord Hope of Craigiehall, who had been President of the Court of Session in his time, and a very notable greatman in the State.

So, as I say, this day she set to the baking early, and it went to my heart when I saw she was making the wheaten cakes raised with sour buttermilk that were my father's favourites.

She had not been at it long before in came Jock o' the Garpel, hot-foot from the hill.

"Maister Alexander!" he cried, panting and broken-winded with haste, "Maister Alexander is comin' ower the Brae!"

There was silence in the wide kitchen for a moment, only the sound of my mother's roller being heard, "dunt-dunt-ing" on the dough.

"Is he by his lane?" asked my mother without raising her head from the bake-board.

"Ay," said Jock o' the Garpel, "a' by his lane. No a man rides ahint him."

And again there was silence in the wide house of Earlstoun.

My mother went to the girdle to turn the wheaten cakes that were my father's favourites, and as she bent over the fire, there was a sound as if rain-drops were falling and birsling upon the hot girdle. But it was only the water running down my mother's cheeks for the love of her youth, because now her last hope was fairly gone.

Then in the middle of her turning she drew the girdle off the fire, not hastily, but with care and composedness.

"I'll bake nae mair," she cried, "Sandy has come ower the hill his lane!"

And I caught my mother in my arms.

CHAPTER V.

THE CLASH OF WORDS.

A DOUBTFUL dawn had grown into a chosen day when I saddled in Earlstoun courtyard, to ride past the house of our kinswoman at Lochinvar on a sad and heavy errand. Sandy has betaken himself to his great oak on the border of the policies, where with his skill in forest craft he had built himself a platform among the solidest masses of the leaves. There he abode during the day, with a watch set on the Tod Hill and another on the White Hill above the wood of Barskeoch. Only at the even, when all things were quiet, would he venture to slip down and mix with us about the fire. But he swung himself swiftly back again to his tree by a rope, if any of the dragoons were to be heard of in the neighbourhood.

During all this time it comes back to me how much we grew to depend on Maisie Lennox. From being but "Anton Lennox's dochter" she came to be "Meysie, lass" to my mother, and indeed almost a daughter to her. Once, going to the chamber-door at night to cry ben some message to my mother, I was started and afraid to hear the sound of sobbing within — as of one crying like a young lass or a bairn, exceedingly painful to hear. I thought that it had been Maisie speaking of her sorrow, and my mother comforting her. But when I listened, though indeed that was not my custom, I perceived that it was my mother who grat and refused to be comforted.

"O my William!" she cried, moaning like a child that

would sob itself to sleep, "I ken, O I ken, I shall never see him mair. He's lyin' cauld and still at the dyke back that yince my airms keepit fast. O thae weary Covenants, thae weary, weary Covenants!"

"Hush thee, my dawtie, say not so!" I heard the voice of my cousin Maisie — I could not help but hear it, "The Lord calls us to do little for Him oursels, for we are feckless women, an' what can we do? But He bids us gie Him our men-folk, the desire o' our hearts. Brithers hae I gie'n, twa and three, and my last is my father that lies noo amang the moss-hags, as ye ken!"

But again I heard my mother's voice breaking through in a querulous anger.

"What ken ye, lassie? Brithers and faither, guids and gear, they arena muckle to loose. Ye never lost the man for wha's sake ye left faither an' mither, only just to follow him through the warl'!"

And in the darkness I could hear my mother wail, and Maisie the young lass hushing and clapping her. So, shamed and shaken at heart, I stole away a-tiptoe lest any should hear me, for it was like a crime to listen to what I had heard. But I am forgetting to tell of our riding away.

It was a morning so buoyant that we seemed verily upborne by the flood of sunlight, like the small birds that glided and sang in our Earlstoun woods. Yet I had small time to think of the beauty of the summer tide, when our father lay unburied at a dyke back, and some one must ride and lay him reverently in the earth.

Sandy could not go — that was plain. He was now head of the house and name. Besides the pursuit was hot upon him. So at my mother's word, I took a pair of decent serving men and wended my way over the hill. And as I went my heart was sore for my mother, who stood at the door to see us go. She had supplied with her own hands all the decent wrappings wherewith to bury my father. Sandy further judged it not prudent to attempt to bring him home. He had gotten a staw of the red soldiers, he said, and wished for that time to see no more of them.

But I that had seen none of them, was hot upon bringing my father to the door to lie among his kin.

"The driving is like to be brisk enough without that!" said Sandy.

And my mother never said a word, for now Sandy was the laird, and the head of the house. She even offered to give up the keys to Jean Hamilton, my brother's wife. But for all her peevishness Jean Hamilton knew her place, and put aside her hand kindly.

"No, mother," she said. "These be yours so long as it pleases God to keep you in the House of Earlstoun."

For which I shall ever owe Jean Hamilton a good word and kindly thought.

The names of the two men that went with me were Hugh Kerr and John Meiklewood. They were both decent men with families of their own, and had been excused from following my father and brother on that account.

Now as we went up the hill a sound followed us that made us turn and listen. It was a sweet and charming noise of singing. There, at the door of Earlstoun were my mother and her maidens, gathered to bid us farewell upon our sad journey. It made a solemn melody on the caller morning air, for it was the sound of the burying psalm, and they sang it sweetly. So up the Deuch Water we rode, the little birds making a choir about us, and young tailless thrushes of the year's nesting pulling at reluctant worms on the short dewy knowes. All this I saw and more. For the Lord that made me weak of arm, at least, did not stint me as to glegness of eye.

When we came to where the burn wimples down from

Garryhorn, we found a picket of the King's dragoons drawn across the road, who challenged us and made us to stand. Their commander was one Cornet Inglis, a rough and roystering blade. They were in hold at Garryhorn, a hill farm-town belonging to Grier of Lag, whence they could command all the headend of the Kells.

"Where away so briskly?" the Cornet cried, as we came riding up the road. "Where away, Whigs, without the leave of the King and Peter Inglis?"

I told him civilly that I rode to Carsphairn to do my needs.

"And what need may you have in Carsphairn, that you cannot fit in Saint John's Clachan of Dalry as well, and a deal nearer to your hand?"

I told him that I went to bury my father.

"Ay," he said, cocking his head quickly aslant like a questing cat that listens at a mouse-hole; "and of what quick complaint do fathers die under every green tree on the road to Bothwell? Who might the father of you be, if ye happen to be so wise as to ken?"

"My father's name was Gordon," I said, with much quietness of manner — for, circumstanced as I was, I could none other.

Cornet Inglis laughed a loud vacant laugh when I told him my father's name, which indeed was no name to laugh at when he that owned it was alive. Neither Peter Inglis not yet his uncle had laughed in the face of William Gordon of Earlstoun — ay, though they had been riding forth with a troop behind them.

"Gordon," quoth he, "Gordon — a man canna spit in the Glenkens without sploiting on a Gordon — and every Jack o' them a cantin' rebel!"

"You lie, Peter Inglis — lie in your throat!" cried a voice from the hillside, quick as an echo. Inglis, who had been hectoring it hand on hip, turned at the word. His black brows drew together and his hand fell slowly till it rested on his sword-hilt. He who spoke so boldly was a lad of twenty, straight as a lance shaft is straight, who rode slowly down from the Garryhorn to join us on the main road where the picket was posted.

It was my cousin and kinsman, Wat Gordon of Lochinvar — a spark of mettle, who in the hour of choosing paths had stood for the King and the mother of him (who was a Douglas of Morton) against the sterner way of his father and forebears.

The Wild-cat of Lochinvar they called him, and the name fitted him like his laced coat.

For Wullcat Wat of Lochinvar was the gayest, brightest, most reckless blade in the world. And even in days before his father's capture and execution, he had divided the house with him. He had rallied half the retainers, and ridden to Morton Castle to back his uncle there when the King's interest was at its slackest, and when it looked as if the days of little Davie Crookback were coming back again. At Wat Gordon's back there rode always his man-at-arms, John Scarlet, who had been a soldier in France and also in Brandenburg — and who was said to be the greatest master of fence and cunning man of weapons in all broad Scotland. But it was rumoured that now John Scarlet had so instructed his young master that with any weapon, save perhaps the small sword the young cock could craw crouser than the old upon the same middenstead.

"I said you lied, Peter Inglis," cried Wullcat Wat, turning back the lace ruffle of his silken cuff, for he was as gay and glancing in his apparel as a crested jay-piet. "Are ye deaf as well as man-sworn?"

Inglis stood a moment silent; then he understood who his enemy was. For indeed it was no Maypole dance to quarrel with Wat of Lochinvar with John Scarlet swaggering behind him.

"Did you not hear? I said you lied, man — lied in your throat. Have you aught to say to it, or shall I tell it to Clavers at the table to-night that ye have within you no throat and no man's heart, but only the gullet of a guzzling trencherman?"

"I said that the Gordons of the Glenkens were traitors. 'Tis a kenned thing," answered Inglis, at last mustering up his resolution, "but I have no quarrel with you, Wat Gordon, for I know your favour up at Garryhorn — and its cause."

"Cause —— " said Wullcat Wat, bending a little forward in his saddle and striping one long gauntlet glove lightly through the palm of the other hand, "cause — what knows Peter Inglis of causes? This youth is my cousin of Earlstoun. I answer for him with my life. Let him pass. That is enough of cause for an Inglis to know, when he chances to meet men of an honester name."

"He is a rebel and a traitor!" cried Inglis, "and I shall hold him till I get better authority than yours for letting him go. Hear ye that, Wat of Lochinvar!"

CHAPTER VI.

THE CLASH OF SWORDS.

THE two sat fronting one another on their horses. Inglis was the older and more firmly set man. But Wat of Lochinvar was slender and lithe as a bow that has not been often bent and quivers to the straight. It was a curious sight to see them passaging with little airs and graces, like fighting cocks matched in a pit.

The soldiers stood indifferently around. A pair of dragoons patrolled, turning and crossing as if on parade, within earshot of the quarrel of their officers. It was the first time I had ever seen what discipline meant. And in a moment I learned why they had broken us at Bothwell and Rullion Green. For I have heard my brother Sandy say that at any time in the Covenanting host, had three drawn together and spoken like men that are hot in questioning, the whole army would have run from their posts to hear and to take part in the controversy. But all the while these dragoons kept their noses pointing in the straight of their necks, and fronted and wheeled like machines. It was, in fact, none of their business if their officers cut each others' throats. But they knew that one John Graham would assuredly make it his business if they omitted their military service.

"Cornet Inglis," said Lochinvar, doffing lightly his feathered hat that had the King's colours in it, "hearken ye well. This is my cousin Will of Earlstoun, who took no part with his kin in the late rebellion, as I took no part with mine, but instead abode at home in peace. I require you to let him go upon his errand. I myself will be answerable for him to Colonel Graham of Claverhouse. After that we can arrange our little matter as to favour and its causes."

There was a keen leaping light in my cousin Wat's blue eyes, the light that I afterwards grew to know as the delight of battle. He was waxing coldly angry. For me I grow dourly silent as I become angered. My brother Sandy grows red and hot, but Wullcat Wat was of those more dangerous men to whom deadly anger, when it comes, at once quickens the pulses and stills the nerves.

"Think not I am afraid of a traitor's son, or of any of the name of Lochinvar," quoth Inglis, who was indeed no coward when once he had taken up a quarrel; "after all, ye are all no better than a bow-o'-meal-Gordon!"

It was the gage of battle. After that there was no more to be said. To call a man of our name "a-bow-o'-meal-Gordon" is equal to saying that he has no right to the name he bears. For it is said that a certain Lochinvar, wanting retainers to ride at his back, offered a snug holding and so many bolls of meal yearly to any lusty youth who would marry on his land, take his name, and set himself like a worthy sworder to breed well-boned loons to carry in their turns the leathern jack.

At the taunt, swift as flame Wat of Lochinvar rode nearer to his enemy on his quick-turning well-mouthed horse, and drawing the leather gauntlet through his fingers till the fingers were striped narrow like whip lashes, he struck Inglis with it upon the cheek.

"My father's head," he cried, "may be on the Netherbow. He had his way of thinking and died for it. I have mine and may die for it in my time. But in the meantime Lochinvar's son is not to be flouted by the son of a man who cried with all parties and hunted with none."

Two swords flashed into the air together, the relieved

scabbards jingling back against the horses' sides. The basket hilt of that of Cornet Inglis had the cavalry tassel swinging to it, while the crossbar and simple Italian guard of Wat Gordon's lighter weapon seemed as if it must instantly be beaten down by the starker weapon of the dragoon. But as they wheeled their horses on guard with a touch of the bridle hand, I saw John Scarlet, Wat's master of fence, flash a look at his scholar's guard-sword. Wat used an old-fashioned shearing-sword, an ancient blade which, with various hilt devices, many a Gordon of Lochinvar had carried when he ruffled it in court and hall. I caught John Scarlet's look of satisfaction, and judged that he anticipated no danger to one whom he had trained, from a fighter at haphazard like Cornet Peter Inglis. But yet the dragoon was no tyro, for he had proved himself in many a hard-stricken fray.

So without a word they fell to it. And, by my faith, it made a strange picture on the grassy track which wound itself through these wilds, to see the glossy black of Wat Gordon's charger front the heavier weight of the King's man's grey.

At the first crossing of the swords, the style of the two men was made evident. That of Inglis was the simpler. He fought most like a practical soldier, with the single purpose of making his adversary feel the edge of his weapon; while Wat, lighter and lither, had all the parade and pomp of the schools.

Lochinvar depended on a low tierce guard with a sloping point, and reined his horse near, that his enemy might be prevented from closing with him on his left, or side of disadvantage. The dragoon used the simpler hanging guard and pressed upon his adversary with plain dour weight of steel.

At the first clash of the iron the horses heaved their heads, and down from the hillside above there came a faint crying as of shepherds to their flocks. But the combatants were too intent to take notice. John Scarlet reined his horse at the side, his head a little low set between his shoulders, and his eyes following every thrust and parry with a glance like a rapier.

For the first five minutes Inglis tried all his powers of battering upon Wat Gordon's lighter guard, his heavy cavalry sword beating and disengaging with the fellest intent. He fought with a still and lip-biting fury. He struck to kill, hammering with strong threshing blows; Wat, more like a duellist of the schools — rather, as it seemed, to show his mastery of the weapon. But nevertheless the thin supple blade of the young laird followed every beat and lunge of the heavier iron with speed and certainty. Each moment it seemed as if Wat must certainly be cut down. But his black obeyed the rein at the moment of danger, and his sword twisted round that of his adversary as an adder winds itself about a stick.

More and more angry grew the dragoon, and a grim smile sat intent and watchful on the face of John Scarlet. But he spoke never a word, and the red sentries paced placidly to and fro along the burnside of Garryhorn. More and more wildly Cornet Inglis struck, urging his horse forward to force Lochinvar's black down the hill. But featly and gracefully the lad wheeled and turned, keeping ever his hand in tierce and his blade across his body, slipping and parrying with the utmost calm and ease.

"Click, click!" came the noise of the clashing sword-blades, flickering so swiftly that the eye could not follow them. In time Lochinvar found out his opponent's disadvantage, which was in the slower movement of his horse, but to this Inglis responded like a man. He kept his beast turning about within his own length, so that come where he would Wat had no advantage. Yet gradually and surely the dragoon was being tired out. From attacking he fell to guarding, and at last even his parry grew lifeless and feeble. Wat, on the other hand, kept his enemy's blade constantly engaged. He struck with certainty and parried with a light hammering movement that was pretty to watch, even to one who had no skill of the weapon.

At last, wearied with continual check, Inglis leaned too far over his horse's head in a fierce thrust. The beast slipped with the sudden weight, and the dragoon's steel cap went nearly to his charger's neck.

In a moment, seeing his disadvantage, Inglis attempted to recover; but Wat's lighter weapon slid under his guard as he threw his sword hand involuntarily up. It pierced his shoulder, and a darker red followed the steel upon his horseman's coat, as Wat withdrew his blade to be ready for the return. But of this there was no need, for Inglis instantly dropped his hand to his side and another sword suddenly struck up that of Wat Gordon, as the dragoon's heavy weapon clattered upon the stones.

CHAPTER VII.

THE FIELD OF BOTHWELL BRIG.

"Gentlemen," cried a stern, calm voice, "gentlemen, is it thus that ye amuse yourselves when ye are upon the King's service?"

I turned about, and lo! it was the voice of John Graham of Claverhouse, high-pitched to the carrying note of command — of the man whom all the South and West knew then as the great persecutor, and all the North afterwards as the great captain who stood for his master when all the others forsook him and fled. I admit that my heart beat suddenly feeble before him, and as for my lads who were with me, I think they gave themselves up for dead men. Though slender and not tall, Clavers nevertheless looked noble upon the black horse which had carried him at a gallop down the burnside from Garryhorn. His eyes were full of fire, his bearing of gallantry. Yet methought there was something relentless about the man — something that friend might one day feel the bite of as well as foe. For this was the man who, at his master's word, was now driving Scotland before him as sheep are driven into buchts on the hillside. But Scotland did not easily take to praying according to Act of Parliament, and I minded the witty old gentlewoman's word to Claverhouse himself, "Knox didna win his will without clavers, an' aiblins Clavers winna get his withoot knocks." It was a witty saying and a true, and many a day I lay in the moss-hags and wished that I had said it.

Yet I think we of the Ancient Province never felt so

keenly the bitterness of his oppression, though mostly it was without bowels of mercy, as we did the riding and driving of Robert Grier of Lag, of Douglas of Morton, of Queensberry and Drumlanrig, that were of ourselves — familiar at our tables, and ofttimes near kinsmen as well.

What John Graham did in the way of cess and exaction, and even of shooting and taking, was in some measure what we had taken our count and reckoning with. But that men who knew our outgoings and incomings, our strengths and fastnesses, who had companied with us at kirk and market, should harry us like thieves, made our hearts wondrously hot and angry within us. For years I never prayed without making it a petition that I might get a fair chance at Robert Grier — if it were the Lord's will. And indeed it is not yet too late.

But it was Claverhouse that had come across us now.

"You would kill more King's men!" he cried to Wat Gordon; "you that have come hither to do your best to undo the treason of your forebears. My lad, that is the way to get your head set on the Netherbow beside your father's. Are there no man-sworn Whigs in the West that true men must fall to hacking one another?"

He turned upon Inglis as fiercely:

"Cornet, are you upon duty? By what right do you fall to brawling with an ally of the country? Have we overly many of them in this accursed land, where there are more elephants and crocodiles in Whig-ridden Galloway than true men on whom the King may rely?"

But Inglis said never a word, being pale from the draining of his wound. I looked for him to denounce me as a rebel and a spy; but he was wholly silent, for the man after all was a man.

"How began ye this brawling?" quoth Claverhouse, looking from one to the other of them, minding me no more than I had been a tripping hedge-sparrow.

"We had a difference, and cast up our fathers to one another," at last said Inglis, half sullenly.

"It were best to let fathers a-be when you ride on his Majesty's outpost duty, Cornet Inglis. But you are wounded. Fall out and have your hurt examined."

"It is a flea-bite," quoth Peter Inglis, stoutly.

"A man this!" thought I. For I loved courage.

Yet nevertheless, he dismounted, and John Scarlet helped him off with his coat upon the short heather of the brae-face.

"And whom may we have here?" cried Claverhouse, as Inglis went stumblingly to the hillside upon the arm of John Scarlet. He turned his fine dark eyes full upon me as he spoke, and I thought that I had never seen any man look so handsome. Yet, for all that, fear of the great enemy of our house and cause sat cold in my vitals. Though I deny not that his surpassing beauty of person took my eye as though I had been a woman — the more perhaps because I had little enough of my own.

But my kinsman Wat Gordon was no whit dismayed. He dusted his silken doublet front, swept his white-feathered hat in the air in reverence, and introduced me to the formidable captain as one that has good standing and knows it well:

"My cousin, William Gordon, younger son of the House of Earlstoun!"

"Ah," said Claverhouse, smiling upon me not so ill-pleased, "I have heard of him — the home stayer, the nest-egg. He that rode not to Bothwell with 'the Earl'* and 'the Bull.' Whither rides he now thus early?"

"He rides, Colonel Graham, to bury his father."

I thought my cousin was too bold thus to blurt out my

---

* The laird of Earlstoun was often called in jest "the Earl."

mission, to the chief of them that had killed him whom I went to seek, but he was wiser than I in this matter.

Claverhouse smiled, and looked from the one to the other of us.

"You Gordons have your own troubles to get your fathers buried," he said. "I suppose you will claim that this cub also is a good King's man?"

"He is well affected, colonel," said Lochinvar gaily; "and there are none too many likeminded with him in these parts!"

"Even the affectation does him monstrous credit," quoth Clavers, clapping Walter on the shoulder; "it is much for a Gordon in this country to affect such a virtue as loyalty. I wonder," he went on, apparently to himself, "if it would be possible to transplant you Gordons, that are such arrant rebels here and so loyal in the North. It were well for the land if this could be done. In the North a few dozen Whigs would do small harm; here ten score King's men melled and married would settle the land and keep the King's peace."

Then he looked at my cousin with a certain uncommon gracious affection that sat well on him — all the more that he showed such a thing but rarely.

"Well, Wat, for your sake let young Earlstoun go bury his father in peace, an it likes him. The more Whigs buried the better pleased will John Graham be. If he will only bury his brother also when he is about it, he will rid the earth of a very pestilent fellow!"

"There is no great harm in Sandy," returned Lochinvar briskly and easily. From his whole demeanour I saw that he was in good estimation with Colonel Graham, and was accustomed to talk familiarly with him.

Perhaps the reason was that Claverhouse found himself much alone in Galloway. When he ordered a muster of the lairds and the well affected, only Grier of Lag and Fergusson of Craigdarroch came in, and even they brought but few at their back. Then again these rough-riding, hard drinkers of Nithside had little in common with John Graham. But Lochinvar was well trained by his mother, and had been some time about the court. It was, doubtless, a relief to the high-bred soldier to speak to him after the foul oaths and scurril jests of the country cavaliers.

"Why," said Claverhouse, "as you say, there is no great harm in Sandy; but yet Sandy hath a stout arm and can lay well about him when it comes to the dunts. Sandy's arm is stronger than Sandy's wit."

All this time I had not spoken, for so with a look my cousin Lochinvar had warned me to let him speak for me; but now I broke the silence.

"I am obliged to you, Colonel Graham," I said, "for your permission to go and bury my dead."

"Ay," said Claverhouse, with a certain courteous disdain that was natural to him, but which he dropped when he spoke to the young Lochinvar, "ay, you are no doubt greatly obliged to me; but your father, though a rebel, fought us fairly and deserves clean burial. A Whig is aye best buried at any rate," he continued, gathering up his reins as one that prepares to ride away.

"Lochinvar," he cried, in his voice of command, "take Cornet Inglis's post and duty, since you have disabled him. But mark me well, let there be no more tullying and brawling, or I shall send you all to bridewell. Hark you, young Wullcat of Lochinvar, I cannot have my officers cut up when they should be hunting Whigs — and" (looking at me) "preparing them for burial."

I think he saw the hatred in my eyes, when he spoke thus of my father lying stiff at a dyke back, for he lifted his hat to me quaintly as he went.

"A good journey to you, and a fair return, young Castle Keeper!" he said with a scorning of his haughty lip.

Yet I think that he had been greater and worthier had he denied himself that word to a lad on my errand.

Of our further progress what need that I tell? Hour after hour I heard the horses' feet ring on the road dully, as though I had been deep under ground myself, and they trampling over me with a rush. It irked me that it was a fine day and that my men, Hugh Kerr and John Meiklewood, would not cease to speak with me. But all things wear round, and in time we came to the place, where one had told Sandy as he fled that he had seen William Gordon of Earlstoun lie stark and still.

There indeed we found my father lying where he had fallen in the angle of a great wall, a mile or two south of the field of Bothwell. He had no fewer than six wounds from musket balls upon him. As I looked I could see the story of his end written plain for the dullest to read. He had been beset by a party of dragoons in the angle of a great seven-foot march dyke in which there was no break. They summoned him to surrender. He refused, as I knew he would; and, as his manner was, he had risked all upon a single-handed charge.

As we heard afterwards, he had come at the troopers with such fury that he killed three and wounded another, besides slaying the horse that lay beside him, before, with a storm of bullets, they stopped him in his charge. Thus died, not unworthily, even while I was bringing in the kye in the evening at Earlstoun, William Gordon, a father of whom, in life and death, no son need be ashamed.

And where we found him, there we buried him, wrapping him just as he was, in the shrouds my mother had sent for her well-beloved. Hugh Kerr was for taking his sword out of his hand to keep at home as an heirloom. But I thought no. For his hand was stiffened upon it where the blood had run down his wrist. And besides, it had been his friend while he lived and when he died, and it was hard to part him with that which had been to him as the sword of the Lord and of Gideon. So we buried his sword and him together, laying the little red Bible, stained and spotted with his blood, open upon his breast. Then we happed him up, and I, who could at that time fight but little, put up a short prayer over him — though not, of course, like a minister, or one bred to the trade. And I thought as I rode away that it was better to leave him the sword, than that Sandy should get it to prate about at his general meetings. Even as it was he could not let him be, but in the after days of quiet he must have him up to coffin him, and bury in the kirkyard of Glassford. Yet to do Sandy justice, he had the grace to leave him the sword in his hand.

Now my father had not fallen on the battlefield itself, but rather when hastening thither, for indeed he never saw the bridge, nor had hand in the guiding of the host, whose blood Robert Hamilton poured out as one that pours good wine upon the ground.

Yet because we were so near, we risked the matter and rode over to see the narrow passage of the Bridge where they had fought it so stoutly all day long. Here and there lay dead men yet unburied; but the countrymen were gradually putting the poor bodies in the earth. Some of them lay singly, but more in little clusters where they set their backs desperately to one another, and had it out with their pursuers that they might die fighting and not running. Still the pursuit had not been unmerciful, for there were few that had fallen beyond the long avenues of the Palace oaks.

But when we came to the banks of the river, and looked

down upon the bridge-head we saw the very grass dyed red, where the men had been shot down. And on the brae-sides where Hamilton had drawn them up when he called them from the bridge-end, they had fallen in swathes like barley. But it was not a heartsome sight, and we turned our rein and rode away, weary and sad within.

CHAPTER VIII.

THE CURATE OF DALRY.

WHEN I returned to Earlstoun I found the house in sad disorder. Maisie Lennox I found not, for she had ridden to the Duchrae to meet her father and to keep the house, which had had some unwonted immunity lately because of the friendship of the McGhies of Balmaghie. For old Roger McGhie was a King's man and in good favour, though he never went far from home. But only patrolled his properties, lundering such Whigs as came his way with a great staff, but tenderly withal and mostly for show. His daughter Kate, going the way of most women folk, was the bitterest Whig and most determined hearer of the field-preachers in the parish. Concerning which her father full well knew, but could neither alter nor mend, even as Duke Rothes himself could not change his lady's liking. Yet for Kate McGhie's sake the hunt waxed easier in all the headend of Balmaghie. And during this lown blink, old Anton came home from the hills to take the comforts of the bien and comfortable house of the Duchrae, for it promised to be a bitter and unkindly season. So the Earlstoun looked a little bare without Maisie Lennox, and I was glad that I was to be but a short time in it.

For another thing, the soldiers had been before me, and by order of the Council had turned the whole gear and plenishing over to find my brother Alexander — which indeed seeing what he had done at Bothwell, we can hardly wonder at. Even the intervention of our well-affected cousin of Lochinvar could not prevent this. The horses were driven away, the cattle lifted to be provender for the King's forces in the parish of Carsphairn and elsewhere. And it would go hard with us — if indeed we should even be permitted to keep the place that had been ours for generations.

My mother was strongly advised that, as I had not been mixed with the outbreaks, it was just scant possible that I might make something of an appeal to the Privy Council for the continuing of the properties, and the substituting of a fine. I was therefore to ride to Edinburgh with what attendance I could muster, and with Wat Gordon of Lochinvar to lead me as a bairn by the hand.

But it was with a sad heart and without much pleasure, save in having my father's silver mounted pistols (for I counted myself no mean marksman), that John Meiklewood, Hughie and I rode off from the arched door of the Earlstoun. My mother stood on the step and waved me off with no tear in her eye; and even poor Jean Hamilton, from the window whence she could see the great oak where my brother, her husband, was in hiding, caused a kerchief to show white against the grey wall of Earlstoun. I think the poor feckless bit thing had a sort of kindness for me. But when there was hardly the thickness of an eggshell between her man and death, it was perhaps small wonder that she cherished some jealousy of me, riding whither I listed over the wide, pleasant moors where the bumble bees droned and the stooping wild birds cried all the livelong day.

At St. John's Clachan of Dalry we were to meet with Wildcat Wat, who was waiting to ride forth with us to Edinburgh upon his own ploys. We dismounted at the inn where John Barbour, honest man, had put out the sign of his profession. It was a low, well-thatched change-house, sitting with its end to the road in the upper part of the village, with good offices and accommodation for man and horse about it — the same hostel indeed in which the matter of

Rullion Green took its beginning. Wat came down the street with his rapier swinging at his side, his feathered Cavalier hat on his head, and he walked with a grace that became him well. I liked the lad, and sometimes it almost seemed to me that I might be his father, though indeed our years were pretty equal. For being lame and not a fighter, neither craving ladies' favours, I was the older man, for the years of them that suffer score the lines deeper on a man's brow — and on his heart also.

When Wat Gordon mounted into the saddle with an easy spring his horse bent back its head and curveted, biting at his foot. So that I rejoiced to see the brave lad sitting like a dart, holding his reins as I hold my pen, and resting his other hand easily on his thigh. John Scarlet, his man-at-arms, mounted and rode behind him; and when I saw them up, methought there was not a pair that could match them in Scotland. Yet I knew that with the pistolets at paces ten or twenty, I was the master of both. And perhaps it was this little scrap of consolation that made me feel so entirely glad to see my cousin look so bright and bonny. Indeed had I been his lass — or one of them, for if all tales be true he had routh of such — I could not have loved better to see him shine in the company of men like the young god Apollo among the immortals, as the heathens feign.

At the far end of the village there came one out of a white house and saluted us. I knew him well, though I had never before seen him so near. It was Peter McCaskill, the curate of the parish. But, as we of the strict Covenant did not hear even the Indulged ministers, it was not likely that we would see much of the curate. Nevertheless I had heard many tales of his sayings and his humours, for our curate was not as most others — dull and truculent knaves many of them, according to my thinking — the scourings of the North. Peter was, on the other hand, a most humoursome varlet and excellent company on a wet day. Sandy and he used often to take a bottle together when they foregathered at John's in the Clachan; but even the Bull of Earlstoun could not keep steeks or count mutchkins with Peter McCaskill, the curate of Dalry.

On this occasion he stopped and greeted us. He had on him a black coat of formal enough cut, turned green with age and exposure to the weather. I warrant it had never been brushed since he had put it on his back, and there seemed good evidence upon it that he had slept in it for a month at least.

"Whaur gang ye screeving to, young sirs, so brave?" he cried. "Be canny on the puir Whiggies. Draw your stick across their hurdies when ye come on them, an' tell them to come to the Clachan o' Dalry, where they will hear a better sermon than ever they gat on the muirs, or my name's no Peter McCaskill."

"How now, Curate," began my cousin, reining in his black and sitting at ease, "are you going to take to the hill and put Peden's nose out of joint?"

"Faith, an' it's my mither's ain son that could fettle that," said the curate. "I'm wae for the puir Whiggies, that winna hear honest doctrine an' flee to the hills and hags — nesty, uncanny, cauldrife places that the very muir-fowl winna clock on. Ken ye what I was tellin' them the ither day? Na, ye'll no hae heard — it's little desire ye hae for either kirk or Covenant, up aboot the Garryhorn wi' red-wud Lag and headstrong John Graham. Ye need as muckle to come and hear Mess John pray as the blackest Whig o' them a'!"

"Indeed, we do not trouble you much, Curate," laughed my cousin; "but here is my cousin Will of Earlstoun," he said, waving his hand to me, "and he is nearly as good as a parson himself, and can pray by screeds."

Which was hardly a just thing to say, for though I could pray and read my Bible too when I listed, I did not trouble him or any other with the matter. Cain, indeed, had something to say for himself.— for it is a hard thing to be made one's brother's keeper. There are many ways that may take me to the devil. But, I thank God, officiousness in other men's matters shall not be one of them.

"He prays, does he?" quoth McCaskill, turning his shaggy eyebrows on me. " Aweel, I'll pray him ony day for a glass o' John's best. Peter McCaskill needs neither read sermon nor service-book. He leaves sic-like at hame, and the service ye get at his kirk is as guid and godly as gin auld Sandy himsel' were stelled up in a preaching tent an' thretty wizzened plaided wives makkin' a whine in the heather aneath ! "

"How do you and the other Peter up the way draw together?" asked my cousin.

The curate snapped his fingers.

" Peter Pearson o' Carsphairn — puir craitur, he's juist fair daft wi' his ridin' an' his schemin'. He will hear a pluff o' pouther gang blaff at his oxter some fine day, that he'll be the waur o' ! An' sae I hae telled him mony's the time. But Margate McCaskill's son is neither a Whig hunter nor yet as this daft Peter Pearson. He bides at hame an' minds his glebe. But for a' that I canna control the silly fowk. I was fearin' them the ither day," he went on. " I gied it oot plain frae the pulpit that gin they didna come as far as the kirkyaird at ony rate, I wad tak' no more lees on my conscience for their sakes. I hae plenty o' my ain to gar me fry. 'But,' says I, 'I'll report ye as attendin' the kirk, gin ye walk frae yae door o' the kirk to the ither withoot rinnin'. Nae man can say fairer nor that.'"

"An' what said ye next, Curate?" asked my cousin, for his talk amused us much, and indeed there were few merry things in these sad days.

"Ow," said Peter McCaskill, "I juist e'en said to them, 'Black be your fa'. Ye are a' off to the hills thegither. Hardly a tyke or messan but's awa' to Peden to get her whaulpies named at the Holy Linn! But I declare to ye a', what will happen in this parish. Sorra gin I dinna inform on ye, an' then ye'll be a' eyther shot or hangit before Yule!' That's what I said to them!"

Wat Gordon laughed, and I was fain to follow suit, for it was a common complaint that the curate of Dalry was half a Whig himself. And, indeed, had he not been ever ready to drink a dozen of Clavers's officers under the table, and clout the head of the starkest carle in his troop, it might have gone ill with him more than once.

"But I hae a bit sma' request to make of ye, Walter Gordon o' Lochinvar an' Gordiestoun," said the curate.

"Haste ye," said Wat, "for ye hae taigled us overly long already."

"An' it's this," said the curate, "I hae to ride to Edinburgh toon, there to tell mair lees than I am likely to be sained o' till I am a bishop an' can lee wi' a leecence. But it's the Privy Council's wull, an' sae I maun e'en lee. That tearin' blackguard, Bob Grier, has written to them that I am better affected to the Whigs than to the troopers of Garryhorn, and I am behoved to gang and answer for it."

"Haste ye, then, and ride with us," cried Walter, whose horse had stood long enough. "We ride toward the Nith with Colonel Graham, and after that to Edinburgh."

So in a little the curate was riding stoutly by our side. We were to travel by Dumfries and Lockerbie into Eskdale, whither Claverhouse had preceded us, obeying an urgent call from his acquaintance, Sir James Johnstone of Westerhall, who was still more eager to do the King's will than he — though, to begin with, he had been a Covenant man, and that of some mark too. But the fear of fines, and the bad example of his neighbours ever before his eyes, had brought out the hidden cruelty of the man. So now he rode at Claverhouse's bridle-rein, and the pair of them held black counsel on the state of the country. But the mood of Claverhouse was, at worst, only that of military severity, without heart of ruth or bowels of mercy indeed; but that of Westerhall was rather of roystering and jubilant brutality, both of action and intent.

So we rode and we better rode till we came to Eskdale, where we found Westerhall in his own country. Now I could see by the behaviour of the soldiers as we went, that some of them had small good will to the kind of life they led, for many of them were of the country-side and, as it seemed, were compelled to drive and harry their own kith and kin. This they covered with a mighty affectation of ease, crying oaths and curses hither and thither tempestuously behind their leaders — save only when John Graham rode near by, a thing which more than anything made them hold their peace, lest for discipline's sake he should bid them be silent, with a look that would chill their marrows.

CHAPTER IX.

THROUGH DEATH'S DARK VALE.

Now this Eskdale was the Johnstone's own country, and one in which I was noways at home — a country of wide green holms and deep blind "hopes" or hollows among the mountains, where the cloud shadows bide and linger, and whence they come out again to scud swiftly over the hips of the hills. I had been trained to be pleasant and prudent in my conversation, and there was little to take me out of myself in the company I had perforce to keep. Yet I dared not withdraw myself from their train, lest the jealousy of our band, which was latent among the more scurril of them, should break out. So I rode mostly silent, but with a pleased countenance which belied my heart.

Indeed, had it not been for the good liking which everywhere pursued my cousin Lochinvar, I cannot tell what might have come out of the dislike for us "Glenkens Whiggies," which was their mildest word for us. Yet my man Hugh never said a word, for he was a prudent lad and slow of speech; while I, being no man of war, also looked well to my words, and let a wary tongue keep my head. As for John Meiklewood, honest man, he took suddenly one morning what he termed a "sair income in his wame," and leave being scantily asked, he hied him home to his wife and weans at the Mains of Earlstoun.

Now this was the manner of our march. Claverhouse sent his horse scouring up on the tops of the hills and along the higher grounds, while his foot quartered the lower districts, bringing all such as were in any way suspicious to the kirkyards to be examined. Old and young, men and women alike, were taken; and often — chiefly, it is true, behind Claverhouse's back — the soldiers were most cruel at the business, making my blood boil, till I thought that I must fly out and strike some of them. I wondered not any longer that my father had taken to the hill, sick to death of the black terror which Charles's men caused daily to fall upon all around them, wherever in Scotland men cared enough about their religion to suffer for it.

How my cousin Lochinvar stood it I cannot tell. Indeed I think that but for the teaching of his mother, and the presence of John Scarlet, who at this time was a great King's man and of much influence with Wat Gordon, he had been as much incensed as I.

One morning in especial I mind well. It was a Tuesday, and our company was under the command of this Johnstone of Westerha', who of all the clan, being a turncoat, was the cruellest and the worst. For the man was in his own country, and among his own kenned faces, his holders and cottiers — so that the slaughter of them was as easy as killing chickens reared by hand.

And even Claverhouse rather suffered, and shut his eyes to it, than took part in the hard driving.

"Draw your reins here," the Johnstone would say, as we came to the loaning foot of some little white lime-washed house with a reeking lum. "There are some Bible folk here that wad be none the worse o' a bit ca'!"

So he rode up to the poor muirland housie sitting by itself all alone among the red heather. Mostly the folk had marked us come, and often there was no one to be seen, but, as it might be, a bairn or two playing about the green.

Then he would have these poor bits of things gathered up and begin to fear them, or contrariwise to offer them fair things if only they would tell where their parents were, and who were used to come about the house.

There is a place, Shieldhill by name, that sits blithely on the brae-face at the entering in of Annandale. The country thereabouts is not very wild, and there are many cotter houses set about the holms and dotted among the knowes. Westerha' enclosed the whole with a ring of his men, and came upon them as he thought unawares, for he said the place was like a conventicle, and rife with psalm-singers. But he was a wild man when he found the men and women all fled, and only the bairns, as before, feared mostly out of their lives, sitting cowering together by the ingle, or hiding about the byres.

"I'll fear them waur," said Westerha', as he came to the third house and found as before only two-three weans, "or my name is no James Johnstone."

So what did this ill-set Johnstone do, but gather them all up into a knot by a great thorn-tree that grows on the slope. This Tuesday morn was clear and sunny — not bright, but with a kind of diffused light, warm and without shadows, as if the whole arch of the lift were but one sun, yet not so bright as the sun we mostly have.

There were some thirty bairns by the tree, mostly of Westerha's own name, save those that were Jardines, Grahams, and Charterises, for those are the common names of that country-side. The children stood together, huddled in a cloud, too frightened to speak or even to cry aloud. And one thing I noticed, that the lassie bairns were stiller and grat not so much as the boys — all save one, who was a laddie of about ten years. He stood with his hands behind his back, and his face was very white; but he threw back his head and looked the dragoons and Annandale's wild riders fair in the face as one that has conquered fear.

Then Westerha' rode forward almost to the midst of the

cloud of bairns, "gollering" and roaring at the bit things to frighten them, as was his custom with such. They were mostly from six to ten years of their age; and when I saw them thus with their feared white faces, I wished that I had been six foot of my inches, and with twenty good men of the Glen at my back. But I minded that I was but a boy —"stay-at-home John," as Sandy called me — and worth nothing with my hands. So I could only fret and be silent. I looked for my cousin Lochinvar, but he was riding at the Graham's bridle rein, and that day I saw nothing of him. But I wondered how this matter of the bairns liked him.

So Westerha' rode nearer to them, shouting like a shepherd crying down the wind tempestuously, when his dogs are working sourly.

"Hark ye," he cried, "ill bairns that ye are, ye are all to dee, and that quickly, unless ye answer me what I shall ask of you."

Then I saw something that I had never seen but among the sheep, and it was a most pitiful and heart-wringing thing to see, though now in the telling it seems no great matter. There is a time of the year when it is fitting that the lambs should be separated from the ewes; and it ever touches me nearly to see the flock of poor lammies when first the dogs come near to them to begin the work, and wear them in the direction in which they are to depart. All their little lives the lambs had run to their mothers at the first hint of danger. Now they have no mothers to flee to, and you can see them huddle and pack in a frightened solid bunch, quivering with apprehension, all with their sweet little winsome faces turned one way. Then as the dogs run nearer to start them, there comes from them a little low broken-hearted bleating, as if terror were driving the cry out of them against their wills. Thus it is with the lambs on the hill, and so also it was with the bairns that clung together in a cluster on the brae-face.

A party of soldiers was now drawn out before them, and the young things were bid look into the black muzzles of the muskets. They were indeed loaded only with powder, but the children were not to know that.

"Now," cried Westerha', "tell me who comes to your houses at night, and who goes away early in the morning!"

The children crept closer to one another, but none of them answered. Whereupon Westerha' indicated one with his finger — the lad who stood up so straightly and held his head back.

"You, young Cock-of-the-heather, what might be your black Whig's name?"

"Juist the same as your honour's — James Johnstone!" replied the boy, in no way abashed.

Methought there ran a titter of laughter among the soldiers, for Westerha' was noways so well liked among the soldiers as Claverhouse or even roaring Grier of Lag.

"And what is your father's name?" continued Westerha', bending just one black look upon the lad.

"James Johnstone!" yet again replied the boy.

Back in the ranks some one laughed.

Westerhall flung an oath over his shoulder.

"Who was the man who laughed? I shall teach you to laugh at the Johnstone in his own country!"

"It was Jeems Johnstone of Wanphray that laughed, your honour," replied the calm voice of a troop-sergeant.

Then Westerha' set himself without another word to the work of examination, which suited him well.

"You will not answer, young rebels," he cried, "ken you what they get that will not speak when the King bids them?"

"Are you the King?" said the lad of ten who had called himself James Johnstone.

At this Westerhall waxed perfectly furious, with a pale

and shaking fury that I liked not to see. But indeed the whole was so distasteful to me that sometimes I could but turn my head away.

"Now, ill bairns," said Westerha', "and you, my young rebel-namesake, hearken ye. The King's command is not to be made light of. And I tell you plainly that as you will not answer, I am resolved that you shall all be shot dead on the spot!"

With that he sent men to set them out in rows, and make them kneel down with kerchiefs over their eyes.

Now when the soldiers came near to the huddled cluster of bairns, that same little heart-broken bleating which I have heard the lambs make, broke again from them. It made my heart bleed and the nerves tingle in my palms. And this was King Charles Stuart making war! It had not been his father's way.

But the soldiers, though some few were smiling a little as at an excellent play, were mostly black ashamed. Nevertheless they took the bairns and made them kneel, for that was the order, and without mutiny they could not better it.

"Sodger-man, wull ye let me tak' my wee brither by the hand and dee that way? I think he wad thole it better!" said a little maid of eight, looking up.

And the soldier let go a great oath and looked at Westerha' as though he could have slain him.

"Bonny wark," he cried, "deil burn me gin I listed for this!"

But the little lass had already taken her brother by the hand.

"Bend doon bonny, Alec my man, doon on your knees!" said she.

The boy glanced up at her. He had long yellow hair like Jean Hamilton's little Alec.

"Wull it be sair?" he asked. "Think ye, Maggie? I houp it'll no be awfu' sair!"

"Na, Alec," his sister made answer, "it'll no be either lang or sair."

But the boy of ten, whose name was James Johnstone, neither bent nor knelt.

"I hae dune nae wrang. I'll juist dee this way," he said; and he stood up like one that straightens himself at drill.

Then Westerha' bid fire over the bairns' heads, which was cruel, cruel work, and only some of the soldiers did it. But even the few pieces that went off made a great noise in that lonely place. At the sound of the muskets some of the bairns fell forward on their faces as if they had been really shot. Some leapt in the air, but the most part knelt quietly and composedly.

The little boy Alec, whose sister had his hand clasped in hers, made as if he would rise.

"Bide ye doon, Alec," she said, very quietly, "it's no oor turn yet!"

At this the heart within me gave way, and I roared out in my helpless pain a perfect "gowl" of anger and grief.

"Bonny Whigs ye are," cried Westerha', "to dee withoot even a prayer. Put up a prayer this minute, for ye shall all dee, every one of you."

And the boy James Johnstone made answer to him:

"Sir, we cannot pray, for we be too young to pray."

"You are not too young to rebel, nor yet to die for it!" was the brute-beast's answer.

Then with that the little girl held up a hand as if she were answering a dominie in a class.

"An it please ye, sir," she said, "me an' Alec canna pray, but we can sing 'The Lord's my Shepherd,' gin that wull do! My mither learned it us afore she gaed awa'."

And before any one could stop her, she stood up like one that leads the singing in a kirk. "Stan' up, Alec, my wee mannie," she said.

Then all the bairns stood up. I declare it minded me of Bethlehem and the night when Herod's troopers rode down to look for Mary's bonny Bairn.

Then from the lips of the babes and sucklings arose the quavering strains:

> "The Lord's my Shepherd, I'll not want.
> He makes me down to lie
> In pastures green; He leadeth me
> The quiet waters by."

As they sang I gripped out my pistols and began to sort and prime them, hardly knowing what I did. For I was resolved to make a break for it, and, at the least, to blow a hole in James Johnstone of Westerha' that would mar him for life before I suffered any more of it.

But as they sang I saw trooper after trooper turn away his head, for, being Scots bairns, they had all learned that psalm. The ranks shook. Man after man fell out, and I saw the tears happing down their cheeks. But it was Douglas of Morton, that stark persecutor, who first broke down.

"Curse it, Westerha'," he cried, "I canna thole this langer. I'll war nae mair wi' bairns for a' the earldom i' the North."

And at last even Westerha' turned his bridle rein, and rode away from off the bonny holms of Shieldhill, for the victory was to the bairns. I wonder what his thoughts were, for he too had learned that psalm at the knees of his mother. And as the troopers rode loosely up hill and down brae, broken and ashamed, the sound of these bairns' singing followed after them, and soughing across the fells came the words:

> "Yea, though I walk in Death's dark vale,
> Yet will I fear none ill:
> For Thou art with me; and Thy rod
> And staff me comfort still."

Then Westerha' swore a great oath and put the spurs in his horse to get clear of the sweet singing.

CHAPTER X.

THE GRAVE IN THE WILDERNESS.

BUT on the morrow I, who desired to see the ways of the Compellers, learned a lesson that ended my scholarship days with them. James Johnstone seemed somewhat moved by the matter of the bairns, but by the morning light he had again hardened his heart, like Pharaoh, more bitterly than before. For he was now on his own land, and because his thought was that the King would hold him answerable for the behaviour and repute of his people, he became more than ordinarily severe. This he did, being a runnagate from the wholesome ways of the Covenant; and, therefore, the more bitter against all who remained of that way.

He drove into the yards of the farm-towns, raging like a tiger of the Indies, now calling on the names of the goodman of the house, and now upon other suspected persons. And if they did not run out to him at the first cry, he would strike them on the face with the basket hilt of his shable till the blood gushed out. It was a sick and sorry thing to see, and I think his Majesty's troopers were ashamed; all saving the Johnstone's own following, who laughed as at rare sport.

But I come now to tell what I saw with my own eyes of the famous matter of Andrew Herries, which was the cause of my cousin of Lochinvar leaving their company and riding with me and Hugh Kerr all the way to Edinburgh. As, indeed, you shall presently hear. And the manner of its happening was as follows. We were riding full slowly along the edge of a boggy loch in the parish of Hutton, and, as usual, quartering the ground for Whig refugees, of whom it was suspected that there were many lurking in the neighbourhood. We had obtained no success in our sport, and Westerhall was a wild man. He ran about crying "Blood and wounds!" which was a favourite oath of his, and telling what he would do to those who dared to rebel, and harbour preachers and preachers' brats on his estate. For we had heard that the lass who had bearded us on the braeface by the school, with her little brother Alec in her hand, was the daughter of Roger Allison, a great preacher of the hill-folk who had come to them over from Holland, to draw them together into some of their ancient unity and power.

Westerhall, then, knew not as yet in whose house she was dwelling, but only that she had been received by one of his people. But this, if it should come to Claverhouse's ears, was enough to cause him to set a fine upon the Johnstone — so strict as against landlords were the laws concerning intercommuning with rebels or rebels' children on their estates. This was indeed the cause of so many of the lairds, who at first were all on the side of the Covenant, turning out Malignants and persecutors. And more so in the shire of Dumfries than in Galloway, where the muirs are broader, the King's arm not so long, and men more desperately dour to drive.

All of a sudden, as we went along the edge of a morass, we came upon something that stayed us. It was, as I say, in Hutton parish, a very pleasant place, where there is the crying of many muirfowl, and the tinkle of running water everywhere. All at once a questing dragoon held up his arm, and cried aloud. It was the signal that he had found something worthy of note. We all rode thither — I, for one, praying that it might not be a poor wanderer, too wearied to run from before the face of the troopers' widespreading advance.

However, it was but a newly-made grave in the wilderness, hastily dug, and most pitifully covered with green fresh-cut turves, in order to give it the look of the surrounding morass. It had very evidently been made during the darkness of the night, and it might have passed without notice then. But now, in the broad equal glare of the noontide, it lay confessed for what it was — a poor wandering hill-man's grave in the wild.

"Who made this?" cried Westerhall. "Burn me on the deil's brander, but I'll find him out!"

"Hoot," said Clavers, who was not sharp set that day, perhaps having had enough of Westerhall's dealing with the bairns yesterday, "come away, Johnstone; 'tis but another of your Eskdale saints. Ye have no lack of them on your properties, as the King will no doubt remember. What signifies a Whig Johnstone the less? There's more behind every dyke, and then their chief is aye here, able and willing to pay for them!"

This taunt, uttered by the insolent scorning mouth of Claverhouse, made Westerhall neither to hold nor bind. Indeed the fear of mulct and fine rode him like the hag of dreams.

"Truth of God!" cried he; for he was a wild and blasphemous man, very reckless in his words; "do so to me, and more also, if I rack not their limbs, that gied the clouts to wrap him in. I'se burn the bed he lay in, bring doon the rafter and roof-tree that sheltered him — aye, though it were the bonny hoose o' St. Johnstone itsel', an' lay the harbourer of the dead Whig cauld i' the clay, gin it were the mither that bore me! Deil reestle me gin I keep not this vow."

Now, the most of the men there were upon occasion bonny swearers, not taking lessons in the art from any man; but to the Johnstone they were as children. For, being a runnagate Covenanter, and not accustomed in his youth to swear, he had been at some pains to learn the habit with care, thinking it a necessary accomplishment and ornament to such as did the King's business, especially to a captain of horse. Which, indeed, it hath ever been held, but in moderation and with discretion. Westerhall had neither, being the man he was.

"Fetch the Whig dog up!" he commanded.

The men hesitated, for it was a job not at all to their stomachs, as well it might not be that hot day, with the sun fierce upon them overhead.

"Tut, man," said Clavers, "let him lie. What more can ye do but smell him? Is he not where you and I would gladly see all his clan? Let the ill-favoured Whig be, I say!"

"I shall find out who sheltered him on my land. Howk him up!" cried Westerhall, more than ever set in his mad cruelty at Colonel Graham's words. So to the light of the merciless day they opened out the loose and shallow grave, and came on one wrapped in a new plaid, with winding sheets of pure linen underneath. These were all stained and soaked with the black brew of the moss, for the man had been buried, as was usual at the time, hastily and without a coffin. But the sleuthhound instinct of the Johnstone held good. "Annandale for the hunt, Nithsdale for the market, and Gallowa' for the fecht!" is ever a true proverb.

"Let me see wha's aucht the sheet?" he said.

So with that, Westerhall unwound the corner and held it up to the light.

"Isobel Allison!" he exclaimed, holding the fine linen up to the light, and reading the name inwoven, as was then the custom when a bride did her providing. "The widow Herries, the verra woman — ain dam's sister to the Whig preacher — sant amang the hill-folk. Weel ken I the kind o' her. To the hill, lads, and we will burn the randy oot, even as I said. I'll learn the Hutton folk to play wi' the beard o' St. Johnstone."

"Foul Annandale thief!" said I, but stilly to myself, for who was I to stand against all of them? Yet I could see that, save and except the chief's own ragged tail, there were none of the soldiers that thought this kind of work becoming.

Ere he mounted, Westerhall took the poor, pitiful body, and with his foot despitefully tumbled it into a moss-hole.

"I'll show them what it is to streek dead Whigs like honest men, and row them dainty in seventeen hunder linen on my land!" cried Westerhall.

And indeed it seemed a strange and marvellous Providence to me, that young Isobel Allison, when she wove in that name with many hopes and prayers, the blood of her body flushing her cheek with a maiden's shy expectation, should have been weaving in the ruin of her house and the breaking of her heart.

Now the cot of the widow Herries was a bonny place. So I believe, but of its beauty I will not speak. For I never was back that way again — and what is more, I never mean to be.

We came to the gavel end of the house. Westerhall struck it with his sword.

"We'll sune hae this doon!" he said to us that followed. Then louder he cried, "Mistress, are ye within?" as the custom of the country is.

A decent woman with a white widow's cap on her head was scraping out a dish of hen's meat as we rode to the door. When she saw us on our horses about the close, the wooden bowl fell from her hands and played clash on the floor.

"Aye, my bonny woman," quoth Westerhall, "this comes o' keeping Whigs aboot your farm-toon. Whatna Whig rebel was it ye harboured? Oot wi't, Bell Allison! Was it the brither o' ye, that cursed spawn o' the low country?

F

Doon on your knees an' tell me, else it is your last hour on the earth."

The poor woman fell on her knees and clasped her hands.

"O Westerha'!" she stammered, "I'll no lee till ye. It was but a puir Westland man that we kenned not the name o'. We fand him i' the fields, and for very God's pity brocht him hame to our door and laid him on the bed. He never spak' 'yea' or 'nay' to us all the time he abode in our hoose-place, and so passed without a word late yestreen."

"Lying Whig!" cried Westerhall, "who was it that found him? Whatna yin o' your rebel sons — chasing up hill and doon dale after your blackguard brither, was it that brocht him hame?"

"I kenna wha it was that brocht him. It was a wee bit lass that fand him when she was playin' i' the moss wi' her brither."

"I ken your wee bit lasses," said Westerhall; "she's a bonny sprig o' that braw plant o' grace, Roger Allison, wha's heid shall yet look blythe on the West Port o' Edinburgh, wi' yin o' his cantin' thief's hands on ilka side o't."

The poor woman said no word, but out from the chamber door came our little lass of yesterday and stood beside her.

"Wha's plaidie is this?" again quoth Westerhall, holding up the plaid in which the dead man had been wrapped, like an accusation in his hand; "to the hill, boys, and lay hand on this honest woman's honest sons. King Charles wull hae something to say to them, I'm thinkin'."

With that he leapt from his horse, throwing the reins to the widow.

"Hae, haud my horse," he said, "an' gin ye stir an inch, ye'll get an ounce o' lead in you, ye auld shakin' limb o' Sawtan."

CHAPTER XI.

THE BLOOD OF THE MARTYRS.

WITH that, like a loch broken loose, Johnstone's tail of Annandale thieves rushed within the house and dang all things here and there at their liking. Some came forth carrying good house gear, some table furniture, and some the plenishing of bed and wardrobe. They turned all that they could not carry into the midst of the floor to burn at their leisure. They drove away the cattle from off the brae-face. They gathered the widow's poor head of sheep off the hill. And all the time Isobel Herries stood trembling for her lads and holding the chief's horse. As the men passed, one after another, they flung words at her that will not bear writing down. And I was glad that the little maid who stood by with her brother in her hand, understood not their import.

When all was done, Westerhall set to work and pulled down the whole house, for the rigging and walls were but of baked clay and crumbled before them. Yet the poor woman wailed for them bitterly, as they had been a palace.

"The bonny bit, O the bonny bit!" she cried. "Where I had sic a sweet bairn-time. I was that happy wi' a' my tottlin' weans aboot my hand. But I kenned it couldna last — it was ower sweet to last."

So they turned her out to the bare hillside with the bairns in her hand. It did not, to my thinking, make the case any better that her brother was a rebel. But in those days it was treason to succour the living or honour the dead — ay, even if they had lain in your bed and stirred in your side. It was forbidden on pain of death to give them so much as a bed or a meal of meat. For such was the decree of just and pious Charles, King at Whitehall, who alone had the right to say in what fashion the poor ignorant folk of Scotland should worship the God of their fathers.

We had not ridden far after leaving the house a heap of ruins, before we met Claverhouse and his troop, riding slow, with a prisoner in the midst of them.

"What luck!" cried he; "good sport in your ain coverts, Westerha'?"

He had a delicately insolent contempt for the Johnstone that set well on him, though as I knew well he could be as cold and bloody as any of them when the humour drove him. Yet mostly he killed like a gentleman after all, and not like a border horse thief—save only in the case of honest John Brown of Priesthill.

But Westerhall had caught sight of Clavers's prisoner. He rode up to him and struck him a buffet in the face, though the lad's hands were tied before him. He was a youth of eighteen, as near as one might guess, a boy of a pleasant and ruddy countenance, such as one may chance to see on any brae-face in Scotland where there are sheep feeding, with a staff in his hand and a dog at his heels.

"My Whiggie, I have you now," he cried. "I'll e'en learn you to row dead rebels in your plaidie, and harbour hill preachers on my land. Could I get at your brothers, I declare I wadna leave a Herries birkie on the lands o' Westerha'. Have him down, men," he cried, "and shoot him here."

But Clavers interposed.

"No," he said, "he is now my prisoner. Ride ye on to Westerha'; and there, Johnstone, I shall give ye a present of him to make a kirk or a mill of. It'll be you that will have to pay the harbourage cess for this day's work at ony gate!"

So to Westerhall Johnstone rode, very gloomy and ill at ease — for the black dog was sitting heavy on him at the thought of the fine anent harbourers of rebels being found on his land. Again and again he broke out on the poor youth Andrew Herries, threatening what he would do with him when he got him to Westerhall. But the youth never so much as answered back, only cast down his head and looked on the moss before him. Yet he walked carefully and without stumbling as one that takes heed to his going.

Now at a bonny spot where there is much green grass, it so happened that we halted. You will find the place readily if ever you pass that way. It is just on that tongue of land where the Rig Burn meets the Esk Water and close by the house of Westerhall. There, where the Great Hill of Stennies Water pushes down a spur to the water-side, was our halting place. Here, as soon as we alighted down, Westerhall passed sentence on Andrew Herries, saying that he had due authority from the Council as King's Justicer for the parts about the Esk and Annan.

Claverhouse was noways keen for the lad's shooting, and strove to put him off. Yet he was not over-earnest in the matter, for (as he often said) to John Graham a dead Whig was always greatly better than a living.

But for all that, he waved his hand and cried aloud:

"The blood of this poor man, Westerha', be upon you. I am free from it."

Nevertheless, since Westerhall had given the sentence and for example's sake it could not be departed from, Claverhouse ordered a Highland gentleman, the captain of a free company that was traversing the country with him, to shoot the lad and get it over. But Donald Dhu cocked his bonnet till the eagle's feather in it stood erect, and in high dudgeon drew off his clansmen.

"Hursel cam', frae the Heelants to fecht men, and no to be pluff-pluffin' poother at poor lads that are no lang frae the mither's milk."

This was the statement of Donald Dhu, and I that had no love for Highlandmen, nor any cause to love them, remembering the hand they made of my father's house of Earlstoun, could have cheered him where I stood. But I remembered the errand I was on, and for my mother's sake forbore.

"What!" cried Westerhall, glowering at him and riding up close, as if to strike him, "would you disobey the General's orders!"

"Donald Dhu has no General but his King," cried the bold Highlandman. "Call up your row-footed messans, and bid them do your nain dirty work."

Then Claverhouse, who of all things loved not to be outfaced, ordered him peremptorily to obey.

"Indeed, John Graham, hursel will fecht ye first — you and a' your troop."

Then seeing that Clavers was about to raise his hand in command, as though to take him unawares —

"Claymores!" suddenly cried Donald Dhu, and behind him fifty Highland brands flashed in air as the wild clansmen threw back their plaids to clear the sword-arm.

"This I shall report to the Privy Council," said Clavers very gravely, turning on him a black and angry countenance.

But the brave Highlander was noways affected.

"Hooch!" he said, giving his fingers a snap, "a fig for your Preevies — Donald Dhu wull hae small notion o' Preevy Cooncils on Ben Muick. Gin Preevies come to veesit Donald Dhu on Spey side, it's just hursel that wull be the prood man to see the Preevies — aye, or you yersel' either, John Graham!"

Thus much Donald Dhu, and he was a good man and died linking down the brae with his men true, behind John Graham at Killiecrankie in the fulness of time — which was better work than, as he said, "pluff-pluffin' poother at puir lawlan tykes."

But when Westerhall saw that the Highland birses were up, and that he would in no wise obey orders, he ordered some of his own scoundrels to do the thing. For his black heart was set on the shooting of the lad.

Then I could endure no longer, but ran forward as if to save him, crying out to them that he was innocent, and but a lad at any rate, which mightily angered Westerhall.

"Stell up the yae rebel whelp beside the other!" he said; and I believe that had we been alone with the Annandale men, they would have done it.

But Clavers said: "Let be! Take away young Earlstoun to the knowe-tap!"

So they led me off, fairly girning with anger and impotence. For once I longed for Sandy's brute strength to charge at them like a bull with the head down.

"Lochinvar!" I cried, as they forced me away. "To me, Lochinvar!"

But, alas! my cousin was off on some of his own ploys, and came not till too late. As you shall hear.

Then when the men were in rank to fire, Westerhall bid Andrew Herries draw down his blue bonnet over his eyes. But he was a lad of most undaunted courage, and though he had come so meekly to the slaughter, now he spoke out boldly enough.

"I wad raither dee," he said, "in the face o' a' men and the plain licht o' God. I hae dune nocht to make me shamed afore my death-bringers. Though, being but young,

I hae but little testimony to gie, an' nae great experience o' religion to speak aboot. The end has come ower quick on me for that!"

Then they asked him, as was their custom, if he had aught to say before sentence should take effect upon him.

"Nocht in particular," he said, "but there's a book here (and he pulled a little Bible out of his breast) that you an' me will be judged by. I wish I had read mair earnestly in it an' profited better by it. But at ony rate I aye carried it to read at the herdin', and my time has been cut short."

"Make haste," they said, "we haena time to taigle wi' ye."

"And I hae as little desire to taigle you," he said, "but I am glad that I didna grudge the puir Westland man my best plaid for his last covering, though there be none to do as muckle for me."

The fire rang out. The blue wreaths of smoke rose level, and there on the green sward, with his face to the sky, and his Bible yet in his hand, lay the widow's son, Andrew Herries, very still.

"So perish all the King's rebels," cried Westerhall loudly, as it were, to give the black deed a colour of law.

But John Graham said never a word, only lifted his hat and then rode away with a countenance like the granite stone of the mountain.

CHAPTER XII.

WE RIDE TO EDINBURGH.

When my cousin Lochinvar heard what had been done in the matter of the lad, Andrew Herries, his anger burned fiercely within him. He sought Westerhall on the instant.

"Foul Annandale thief!" he cried, "come out and try the length of thy sword on the heather. Down with thee and see if thou canst stand up to a man, thou great stirk. 'Tis easy putting thy wolf's spite on helpless bairns, but this sword-arm shall tickle thy midriff to an unkenned tune."

But Colonel Graham would not let them fight. .

"Aroint thee," he said to Lochinvar, "for a young ruffler and spitfire. Well may they call thee Wullcat. But you shall not decimate my troop, or I must put you in irons, for all those bright eyes which the ladies love."

Lochinvar turned to him.

"Colonel Graham, did you yourself not say, 'I am guiltless of this poor man's life!' So, at least, I have been informed."

Claverhouse nodded grimly. It was not a weakness he often showed.

"Then why not let me have it out with this bairn-slayer? I had e'en garred the guard o' my sword dirl again his ribs."

In another the boast had seemed like presumption, but so noble a sworder was Wat Gordon that he but stated a truth. And all that were present knew it for such.

"Westerhall will be the more grateful to me, in that

case," said Clavers, "but hark ye, Lochinvar! there must be no more of this. Ye would reduce the number of his Majesty's forces effective in one way. The Reverend Richard Cameron (with whom Providence send me a good and swift meeting) in another. But in the end it comes to the same thing. Now I opine, it will fit you well to hie to Edinburgh with despatches. And I prithee take your noble and peaceful cousin of Earlstoun with thee. Gin thou canst exchange him there for his brother Sandy, I shall be the more glad to see thee back."

So in a little Wat Gordon and I (Hugh Kerr and John Scarlet being with us) were riding with Claverhouse's despatches to the Privy Council.

Northward we travelled through infinite rough and unkindly places, vexed ever with a bitter wind in our faces. As we passed many of the little cot houses on the opposite hillsides, we would see a head look suddenly out upon us. Then the door fell open, and with a rush like wild things breaking from their dens, a father and a son, or such-like, would take the heather. And once, even, we saw the black coat of a preacher. But with never a halt we went on our way, sharp-set to reach Edinburgh.

As we went, Wat Gordon spoke to me of the great ones of the town, and especially of the Duchess of Wellwood, with whom, as it appeared, he was high in favour. But whether honestly or no, I had no means of judging. It was passing strange for me, who indeed was too young for such love, even had I been fitted by nature for it — to hear Wat speak of the gallantry of the great ladies of the Court, and of the amorous doings at Whitehall. For I had been strictly brought up — a thing which to this day I do not regret, for it gives even ill-doing a better relish. But in these times when there are many new-fangled notions about the upbringing of children and the manner of teaching them, I ever declare I do not know any better way than that which my father used. Its heads and particulars were three — the Shorter Catechism for the soul, good oatmeal porridge for the inward man — and for the outward, some twigs of the bonny birk, properly applied and that upon the appointed place.

So that to hear of the gay French doings at the Court, which by Wat's telling were greatly copied in Edinburgh, was to me like beholding the jigging and coupling of puggy monkeys in a cage to make sport for the vulgar.

"The Lord keep me from the like of that!" I cried, when he had told me of a ploy that my Lady Castlemaine and my pretty Mistress Stuart had carried through together — the point of which was that these two quipsome dames were wedded, like man and wife, and eke bedded before the Court.

And at this Wat Gordon, who had not much humour at the most of times, turned on me with a quizzical look on his face, saying, "I think you are in no great danger, Cousin William."

Which I took not ill, for at that time I cared not a jot about the appearance of my body, nor for any lady's favour in the land.

When we reached Edinburgh, I went immediately to decent lodgings in the West Bow, to which I had been directed by my mother; but Walter, saying that the West Bow was no fit lodging for a gentleman, went on to settle himself in one of the fashionable closes off the Lawnmarket.

As soon as we were by ourselves, my man, Hugh Kerr, came to me, and began to ask if I knew anything of John Scarlet, the serving man that accompanied my cousin.

I replied that I knew nothing of him, save that my cousin had past all endurance cried him up to me as a mighty sworder.

"Weel," said Hugh Kerr, "it may be, but it's my opeenion, that he is a most mighty leer, an' a great scoundrel forbye."

I asked him why, and at the first go-off he would give me no better answer than that he opined that his name was not John Scarlet but John Varlet, as better denoting a gentleman of his kidney.

But when I pressed him, he told me that this serving man had told him that he had committed at least half-a-dozen murders — which he called slaughters and justified, that he had been at nigh half a hundred killings in the fields, yet that he could pray like Mr. Kid himself at a Societies' Meeting, and be a leader among the hill-folk when it seemed good to him.

"An' the awesome thing o't a' is that the ill deil declared that he had half-a-dizzen wives, and that he could mainteen the richts o' that too. So I reasoned with him, but faith! the scoundrel had the assurance to turn my flank wi' Abraham and the patriarchs. He said that he wadna cast up Solomon to me, for he wasna just prepared to uphaud the lengths that Solomon gaed to i' the maitter o' wives."

But I told Hugh to give his mind no concern about the sayings or doings of Master John Scarlet or Varlet, for that it was all most likely lies; and if not, neither he nor I was the man's master, to whom alone he stood or fell.

But for all that I could see that Hughie was much dashed by his encounter with my cousin's follower, for Hughie accounted himself a great hand at the Scripture. We heard afterwards that John Scarlet had been a sometime follower of Muckle John Gib, and that it was in his company that he learned notions, which is a thing exceedingly likely. But this was before Anton Lennox of the Duchrae took John in hand and sorted him to rights, that day in the moss of the Deer-Slunk between Lowthian and Lanark.

Then with my cousin's interest to back me, and especially that which he made with the Duchess of Wellwood, I wore out the winter of the year 1679 in petitions and embassies, praying that the estates should not be taken from us, and biding all the time in my lodging in the West Bow. I had James Stewart, then in hiding, to make out my pleas, and right ably he drew them. It was a strong point in our favour that my father had not been killed at Bothwell, but only when advancing in the direction of the combatants. And besides, I myself had bidden at home, and not ridden out with the others. As for Sandy, he had not the chance of a lamb in the wolf's maw, having been on the field itself with a troop; so I stood for my own claim, meaning with all my very heart to do right by my elder brother when the time came — though, indeed, I had but small reason to love him for his treatment of me. Yet for all that, I shall never say but what he was a stupid, honest lown enough.

Mayhap if he had been other than my brother, I had loved him better; but he tortured me as thoughtlessly when I was a weakly lad as if I had been a paddock or a fly, till the instinct of dislike infected my blood. And after that there could be no hope of liking, hardly of tolerance. This is the reason of most of the feuds among brothers the world over. For it is the fact, though there are few fathers that suspect it, that many elder brothers make the lives of the youngers a burden too heavy to be borne — which thing, together with marrying of wives, in after years certainly works bitterness.

More than anything, it struck me as strange that my cousin Lochinvar could make merry in the very city — where but a few months before his father had been executed and done to death. But Hughie Kerr told me one evening, when we were going over Glenkens things, how Wat's father had used him — keeping him at the strap's end. For Wat was ever his mother's boy, who constantly took his part as he needed it, and made a great cavalier and King's man of him. This his father tried to prevent and drive out of him with blows, till the lad fairly hated him and his Covenants. And so it was as it was. For true religion comes not by violence, but chiefly, I think, from being brought up with good men, reverencing their ways and words.

CHAPTER XIII.

WULLCAT WAT DARES HEAVEN AND HELL.

IT was about the end of February, when the days are beginning to creep out quickly from their shortest, that my aunt, the Lady Lochinvar, came to town. I, that asked only meat and house-room, companied not much with the braver folk who sought the society of my cousin of Lochinvar. Wat glanced here and there in some new bravery every day, and I saw him but seldom. However, my lady aunt came to see me when she had been but three days in town. For she was punctilious about the claims of blood and kinship, which, indeed, women mostly think much more of than do men.

"A good morning, cousin," said she, "and how speeds the suit?"

Then I told her somewhat of the law's delays and how I had an excellent lawyer, albeit choleric and stormy in demeanour,— one of mine own name, Mr. William Gordon, though his pleas were drawn by James Stewart, presently in hiding. What Gordon said went down well with my Lords of the Council meeting in Holyrood, for he was a great swearer and damned freely in his speech. But Hugh Wallace, that was the King's cash-keeper, claimed the fine because that my father was a heritor — conform to the Acts of Parliament made against these delinquencies and conventicles in 1670 and 1672, appointing the fines of heritors being transgressors to come into the treasury. But Sir George Mackenzie said, "If this plea be not James Stewart's drawing I have no skill of law. Tell me, Gordon, gin ye drew this yoursel' or is James Stewart in Scotland?"

Then my lady of Lochinvar asked of me when I thought my matters might be brought to an end.

"That I know not," said I; "it seems slow enough."

"All law is slow, save that which my man and your father got," said she.

I was astonished that she should mention her man, with that courage and countenance, and the story not six months old; indeed, his very head sticking on the Netherbow, not a mile from us as we talked. But she saw some part of this in my face, and quickly began to say on.

"You Gordons never think you die honest unless you die in arms against the King. But ye stand well together, though your hand is against every other man. And that is why I, that am but a tacked-on Gordon, come to help you if so be I can; though I and my boy stand for the King, and you and your rebel brother Sandy for the Covenants. Weary fa' them — that took my man from me — for he was a good man to me, though we agreed but ill together concerning kings and politics."

"Speak for my brother Sandy," I said, "I am no strong sufferer, and so shall get me, I fear me, no golden garments."

Thus I spoke in my ignorance, for the witty lown-warm air of Edinburgh in spiritual things had for the time being infected me with opinions like those of the Laodicians.

Now this was a favourite overword of my mother's, that suffering was the Christian's golden garment. But to my aunt, to whom religion was mostly family tradition (or so I thought), I might as well have spoken of fried fish.

"But concerning Walter," she went on, as one that comes to a real subject after beating about the bush, "tell me of him. You have been here with him in this city the best part of three months."

Now indeed I saw plainly enough what it was that had procured me the honour of a visit so early from my lady of Lochinvar.

"In this city I have indeed been, my aunt," I replied, "but not with Walter. For I am not Lord of Lochinvar, but only the poor suitor of the King's mercy. And I spent not that which I have not, nor yet can I afford further to burden the estate which may never be mine."

She waved her hand as at a Whig scruple, which good King's folk made light of.

"But what of Walter — you have seen — is it well with the lad?"

She spoke eagerly and laid her hand on my arm.

But after all the business was not mine, and besides, a Gordon — Covenant or no Covenant — is no tale-piet, as my lady might well have known.

"Wat Gordon," said I, "is the gayest and brightest young spark in town, like a Damascus blade for mettle, and there are none that love not his coming, and grieve not at his going."

"Ay — ladies, that I ken," said my aunt. "What of my Lady Wellwood?"

Now I had a very clear opinion of my Lady Wellwood, though I knew her not; for indeed she would not have waved the back of her lily hand to me in the street. But she was a handsome woman, and I admired her greatly for the fairness of her countenance as she went by. Besides, the business of Wat and my Lady Wellwood was none of mine.

"My lady is in truth a fine woman," I said calmly, looking up as if I were saying what must please my visitor.

The Lady Lochinvar struck one hand on the other hastily and rose.

"Attend me home," she said; "I see after all that you are a man, and so must defend all men and admire all women."

G

"The last, for your ladyship's sake, I do," I made answer. For in those days we were taught to be courteous to the elder ladies, and to make them becoming compliments, which is in danger of being a forgotten art in these pettifogging times.

"What takes you to the Covenant side?" asked Lady Lochinvar, "Certes, the Falkland dominie had not made that speech."

"The same that took your husband, Lady Lochinvar," I returned, somewhat nettled. For she spake as if the many honest folk in Scotland were but dirt beneath the feet of the few. But that was ever the way of her kind.

"Kenned ye ever a Gordon that would be driven with whips of scorpions, or one that could not be drawn with the light of ladies' eyes?"

She sighed, and gathered up her skirts.

"Ay, the last all too readily," she said, thinking, I doubt not, of Walter Gordon and my lady of Wellwood.

It was dusking when we stepped out. My aunt took my arm and desired that we should walk home, though already I had called a chair for her. So we went up the narrow, dirty street and came slowly to her lodgings. Walter met us on the stair of the turnpike. He was shining in silk and velvet as was recently his constant wont. Lace ruffles were at his wrists. He had a gold chain about his neck, and a jewelled rapier flashed and swung in a gold-broidered velvet sheath at his side.

He seemed no little dashed by our coming in together. I quickly understood that he had thought his mother safely out of the way, and wondered how I should keep the peace between them. For by the tremble of her hand on my arm I felt that the storm was nigh the breaking.

Yet for all that he stopped and kissed her dutifully, standing on the step with his hat in his hand, to let her pass within.

The flickering light of the cruisie lamp in the stairhead fell on him, and I thought he had the noblest figure of a youth that ever my eyes had rested upon.

But his mother would not let him go.

"Attend me to my chamber, Walter," she said. "I have that concerning which I would speak with you."

So we went upward, turning and twisting up the long stairs, till we came to the door where my lady lodged. She tirled fretfully at the pin, the servant-maid opened, and we went within. The window stood wide to give a draft to the fire of wood that burned on the firegrate. I went over to close it, and, as I did so, a broad flake of snow swirled down, and lay melting on my wrist. It told me that it was to be a wild night — the last snowstorm of the year, belike.

My lady came back from her own bed-chamber in a moment. She had merely laid aside her plaid, waiting not to change her gown lest her son should be gone.

Walter Gordon stood discontentedly enough at the side of the firegrate, touching the glowing embers with his French shoe, careless of how he burnt it.

"Walter," said my aunt, "will you not pleasure us with your company to-night?"

"I cannot, my lady," said Lochinvar, without looking up; "I have made an engagement elsewhere."

He spoke baldly and harshly, as one that puts a restraint on himself.

His mother looked at him with her eyes like coals from which the leaping flame has just died out. For a moment she said nothing, but the soul within her flamed out of the windows of her house of clay, fiery and passionate. It had come to the close and deadly pinch with her, and it was on the dice's throw whether she would lose or keep her son.

"Walter Gordon," she said at last, "has your mother journeyed thus far to so little purpose, that now she is here, you will not do her the honour to spend a single night in her company? Since when has she become so distasteful to you?"

"Mother," said Wat, moved in spite of himself, "you do not yourself justice when you speak so. I would spend many nights with you, for all my love and service are yours; but to-night I cannot fail to go whither I have promised without being mansworn and tryst-breaker. And you have taught me that the Gordons are neither."

"Wat," she said, hearing but not heeding his words, "bide you by me to-night. There be sweet maids a many that will give their lives for you. You are too young for such questing and companionry. Go not to my Lady Wellwood to-night. O do not, my son! 'Tis your mother that makes herself a beggar to you!"

At the name of my Lady Wellwood Walter Gordon started from his place as though he had been stung and glanced over at me with a sudden and fiery anger.

"If my cousin —— "

But I kept my eyes clear upon him, as full of fire mayhap as his own. And even in that moment I saw the thought pass out of his mind in the uncertain firelight.

"Your cousin has told me nothing, though I deny not that I asked him," said my lady curtly. "Young men hang together, like adder's eggs. But Wat, dear Wat, will you not put off your gay apparelling and take a night at the cartes with us at home. See, the fire is bright and the lamp ready. It will be a wild night without presently!"

"To-morrow, mother, to-morrow at e'en shall be the night of my waiting upon you. To-night, believe me, I cannot — though, because you ask me, with all my heart I would that I could."

Then his mother rose up from her seat by the fire, and went up to him. She laid her hand on his arm and looked into his eyes.

"O Walter, my boy, go not forth to-night"—(here I declare to God the proud woman knelt to her own son)——"See, I have put off my pride, and I pray you not to go for my sake—for your mother's sake, that never denied you anything. There is evil boding in the air."

She shuddered and, in rising, threw an arm over his shoulder, as though she had been his sweetheart and were fleeching with him.

For a moment I saw Wat Gordon waver. Then he took her hand gently and drew it down from his shoulder.

"Mother, for you I would do all, save set a stain upon my honour. But this thing I cannot, for I have plighted my word deep and fast, and go I must to-night."

"Tell me," said my aunt, "is it a matter of treason to the King?"

Her eyes were eager, expectant. And for very pity of her I hoped that Walter could give her satisfaction on the point. But it was not as I thought, for who can track a woman's heart?

"God forbid," said Wat Gordon heartily, as one that is most mightily relieved.

But his mother fell back and her hands dropped to her side.

"Then," she said, "it is my Lady Wellwood!—I had rather a thousand times it had been treason and rebellion—aye, though it had set your head on high beside your father's."

"Lady Wellwood or another!" cried Wat, "nor heaven nor hell shall gar me break my tryst this nicht!"

And without another word Walter Gordon went down the stairs as one that runs defiantly to death, daring both God and man—and, alas! the mother also that bore him.

CHAPTER XIV.

THE THING THAT FELL FROM TRAITOR'S GATE.

THE Lady Lochinvar stood a moment still by the fire, listening, her hand raised as if to command silence. Then she ran to the door like a young lass, with a light foot and her hand on her heart. The steps came fainter up the stair, and in another moment we heard the clang of the outer door.

My lady turned to me.

"Have you your pistols by you?" she whispered in a hoarse and angry voice, clutching me by the lapels of my coat. "Go, man! Go, follow him! He rushes to his death. And he is all that I have. Go and save him!"

She that had fleeched with her son, like a dove succouring its young, laid harshly her commands upon me.

"I am no fighter, aunt," I said. "What protection can I be to Walter Gordon, the best sworder in Edinburgh town this night from Holyrood to the Castle?"

My lady looked about her as one that sees a stealthy enemy approach. Her hand trembled as she laid it on my arm.

"What avails good swordsmanship, when one comes behind and one before, as in my dream I saw them do upon my Walter, out of the house of my Lord Wellwood. They came upon him and left him lying on the snow.— Ah, go, dear cousin William!" she said, breaking into a sharp cry of entreaty lest I should fail her. "It is you that can save him. But let him not see you follow, or it will make him more bitter against me. For if you cannot play with the sword, you can shoot with the pistol; so I have heard, and they tell me that no one can shoot so truly as thou. They would not let thee shoot at Kirkcudbright for the Siller Gun though thou art a burgess, because it were no fair game. Is it not true?"

And so she stroked and cuitled me with flattery till I declare I purred like our Gib cat. I had begun there and then to tell her of my prowess, but that she interrupted me.

"He goes toward the High Street. Hasten up the South Wynd, and you will overtake him yet ere he comes out upon the open road."

She thrust two pistols into my belt, which I laid aside again, having mine own more carefully primed with me, to the firing of which my hand was more accustomed — and that to a marksman is more than half the battle.

When I reached the street the wildness of the night justified my prophecy. The snow was falling athwart the town in broad wet flakes, driving flat against the face with a splash, before a gusty westerly wind that roared among the tall lums of the steep-gabled houses — a most uncomfortable night to run the risk of getting a dirk in one's ribs.

I saw my cousin before me, linking on carelessly through the snow with his cloak about his ears and his black-scabbard rapier swinging at his heels.

But I had to slink behind backs like a Holyrood *dyvour* — a bankrupt going to the Sanctuary, jooking and cowering craftily in the lee-side shadow of the houses. For though so wild a night, it was not very dark. There was a moon up there somewhere among the smother, though she could not get so much as her nose through the wrack of banked snow-cloud which was driving up from the west. Yet Wat could have seen me very black on the narrow strip of snow, had he ever once thought of looking over his shoulder.

But Wat the Wullcat of Lochinvar was not the one to look behind him when he strode on to keep tryst. I minded his bitter reckless words to his mother, "Heaven and hell shall not make me break my tryst to-night!" Now Heaven was shut out by the storm and the tall close-built houses, and Walter Gordon had an excellent chance of standing a bout with the other place.

No doubt my Lady Wellwood bided at the window and looked out for him to come to her through the snow. And I that had for common no thought of lass or lady, cannot say that I was without my own envying that the love of woman was not for me. Or so at least I thought at that time, even as I shielded my eyes under my bonnet and drave through the snow with the pistols loose in my belt. But Wat of Lochinvar walked defiantly through the black storm with a saucy swing in his carriage, light and careless, which I vouch drew my heart to him as if I had been a young girl. I had given ten years of my life if just so I could have taken the eyes of women.

As clear as if I had listened to the words, I could hear him saying over within himself the last sentence he had used in the controversy with his mother—"Heaven and hell shall not cause me to break my tryst to-night!"

Alack! poor lad, little understood he the resources of either. For he had yet to pass beneath Traitor's Gate.

For once the narrow High Street of Edinburgh was clean and white—sheeted down in the clinging snow that would neither melt nor freeze, but only clung to every joint, jut, stoop, and step of the house-fronts, and clogged in lumps on the crockets of the roof. The wind wrestled and roared in great gusts overhead in the black, uncertain, tumultuous night. Then a calm would come, sudden as a curtain-drop in the play-house, and in the hush you could hear the snow sliddering down off the high-pitched roofs of tile. The light of the moon also came in varying wafts and flickers, as the wind blew the clouds alternately thicker and thinner across her face.

Now I felt both traitor and spy as I tracked my cousin down the brae. Hardly a soul was to be seen, for none loves comfort more than an Edinburgh burgher. And none understands his own weather better. The snow had swept ill-doer and well-doer off the street, cleaner than ever did the city guard — who, by the way, were no doubt warming their frozen toes by the cheerful fireside in some convenient house-of-call.

So meditating, for a moment I had almost forgotten whither we were going.

Before us, ere I was aware, loomed up the battlements and turrets of the Netherbow. 'Twas with a sudden stound of the heart, that I remembered what it was that ten months and more ago had been set up there. But I am sure that, sharp-set on his love matter, like a beast that hunts nose-down on a hot trail, Wat Gordon had no memory for the decorations of the Netherbow. For he whistled as he went, and stuck his hand deeper into the breast of his coat. The moon came out as I looked, and for a moment, dark and grisly against the upper brightness, I saw that row of traitors' heads which the city folk regarded no more in their coming and going, than the stone gargoyles set in the roof-niches of St. Giles.

But as soon as Wat went under the blackness of the arch, there came so fierce a gust that it fairly lifted me off my feet and dashed me against the wall. Overhead yelled all the mocking fiends of hell, riding slack-rein to a new perdition. The snow swirled tormented, and wrapped us both in its grey smother. Hands seemed to pull at me out of the darkness, lifted me up, and flung me down again on my face in the smoor of the snow. A great access of fear fell on me. As the gust overpassed, I rose, choked and gasping. Overhead I could hear the mighty blast go roaring and howling away among the crags and rocks of Arthur's Seat.

Then I arose, shook the snow from my dress, glanced at the barrels and cocks of my pistols to see that they were not stopped with snow, and stepped out of the angle of the Bow to look after my cousin. To my utter astonishment, he was standing within four feet of me. He held some dark thing in his hand, and stared open-mouthed at it, as one demented. Without remembering that I had come out at my lady's bidding to follow Wat Gordon secretly, I stepped up to him till I could look over his shoulder.

"Walter!" I said, putting my hand on his arm.

But he never minded me in the least, nor yet appeared surprised to find me there. Only a black and bitter horror sat brooding on his soul.

He continued to gaze, fascinated, at the dark thing in his hand.

"GOD — GOD — GOD!" he sobbed, the horror taking him short in the throat. "Will, do you see THIS?"

Such abject terror never have I heard before nor since in the utterance of any living man.

"Do you see This?" he said. "See what fell at my feet as I came through the arch of the Bow upon mine errand! The wind brought it down."

Above the moon pushed her way upwards, fighting hard, breasting the cloud wrack like a labouring ship.

Her beams fell on the dark Thing in Wat Gordon's hand.

"GREAT GOD!" he shouted again, his eyes starting from their sockets, "IT IS MINE OWN FATHER'S HEAD!"

And above us the fitful, flying winds nichered and laughed like mocking fiends.

It was true. I that write, saw it plain. I held it in this very hand. It was the head of Sir John of Lochinvar, against whom, in the last fray, his own son had donned the war-gear. Grizzled, black, the snow cleaving ghastly about the empty eye-holes, the thin beard still straggling snow-clogged upon the chin — it was his own father's head that had fallen at Walter Gordon's feet, and which he now held in his hand.

Then I remembered, with a shudder of apprehension, his own words so lately spoken — "Heaven and hell shall not cause me to break my tryst to-night."

Walter Gordon stood rooted there, dazed and dumbfoundered, with the Thing in his hand. His fine lace ruffles touched it as the wind blew them.

I plucked at him.

"Come," I said, "haste you! Let us bury it in the Holyrood ere the moon goes down."

Thus he who boasted himself free of heaven and hell, had his tryst broken by the Thing that fell from the ghastly gate on which the traitors' heads are set in a row. And that Thing was the head of the father that begat him.

CHAPTER XV.

THE BICKER IN THE SNOW.

THEN, seeing Walter Gordon both agitated and uncertain which way to turn, I took out of his shaking hands the poor mishandled head, wrapping it in my plaid, and so led the way down the Canongate towards the kirkyard of the Chapel of Holyroodhouse, where it seemed to me most safe to bury the Thing that had fallen in such marvellous fashion at our feet that night.

The place I knew well enough. I had often meditated there upon the poor estate of our house. It was half ruinous, and I looked to meet with no man within the precincts on such a night. But short, deceiving, and ostrich-blind are all our hopes, for by going that way I brought us into the greatest danger we could possibly have been in.

For, as we came by the side port of Holyroodhouse, and took the left wynd which leads to the kirkyard, it seemed that I heard the sound of footsteps coming after me. It was still a night of snow, but the blast of flakes was wearing thinner and the wind less gusty. The moon was wading among great white-edged wreaths as though the snows had been driven right up to heaven and were clogging the skies.

It was I who led, for my cousin, Wat Gordon, being stopped dead in his heart's desire, like a dog quivering for the leap that suddenly gets his death-wound, now went forward as one blind, and staggered even in the plain places. Also, it was well that I must guide him, for thus I was kept from thinking of the horrid burden I carried.

We were at the angle of the wall, and going slowly down among the cumbering heaps of rubbish by the dyke-side, when I certainly heard, through the soughing of the wind, and the soft swirl of the snow-flakes, the quick trampling of footsteps behind us. It seemed to me that they came from the direction of the Queen's Bathhouse, by which, as I now minded, my Lord Wellwood had built his new house.

I turned in my tracks, and saw half a dozen of fellows running towards us with their swords drawn; and one who seemed short of stature and ill at the running, following after them. Then I pulled quickly at Walter's sleeve, and said:

"Get you to a good posture of defence, or we are both dead men. See behind you!"

At this he turned and looked, and the sight seemed wonderfully to steady him. He seemed to come to himself with a kind of joy. I heard him sigh as one that casts off a heavy back-burden. For blows were ever mightily refreshing to Wat Gordon's spirits, even as water of Cologne is to a mim-mouthed, spoiled beauty of the court.

As for me, I had no joy in blows, and little skill in them, so that my delight was small. Indeed, I felt the lump rise in my throat, and my mouth dried with fear. So that I could hardly keep the tears from running, being heartily sorry for myself because I should never see bonny Earlstoun and my mother again, or any one else in the pleasant south country — and all on a business that I had no concern with, being only some night-hawk trokings of Wat Gordon's.

But even as he glanced about him, Lochinvar saw where we could best engage them; for in such things he had the captain's eye, swift and inevitable. It was at the angle of the wall, in which is a wide archway that leads into the enclosure of the Palace. The snow had drifted round this arch a great sweep of rounded wreaths, and glistened smoothly white in the moonbeams, but the paved gateway itself was blown clear. Wat thrust me behind him, and, throwing down his cloak, cleared his sword arm with a long sobbing intake of breath, which, having a certain great content in it, was curious to hear.

I stood behind him in the dark of the archway, and there I first laid down my ghastly burden in the corner, wrapping it in my cloak. I made my pistols ready, and also loosened in my belt a broad Italian dagger, shaped like a leaf, wherewith I meant to stick and thrust if any should attempt to run in while I was standing on guard. Between me and the light I could see Walter Gordon, armed in the German fashion, with his rapier in one hand and his dagger in the other. Suddenly, through the hush of waiting, came running footsteps; and men's figures darkened the moonlight on the snow before the arch.

"Clash!" went the rapiers, and I could catch the glitter of the fire as it flew from their first onset. Walter poised himself on his feet with a quick alternate balancing movement, keeping his head low between his shoulders, and his rapier point far out. He was in the dark, and those about the mouth of the arch could not well see at what they were striking, whereas he had them clear against the grey of the moonlit sky.

Steel had not stricken on steel three times when, swift as the flash of the lightning when it shines from east to west, I saw Wat's long rapier dart out, and a man fell forward towards him, clinking on the stones with the jingle of concealed armour. Yet, armour or no, our Wat's rapier had found its way within. Wat spurned the fellow with his foot, lest in falling he should grip to pull him down, which was a common trick of the time, and indeed sometimes resorted to without a wound. But the dark wet stain his body left on the cobble-stones as it turned, told us that he was sped surely enough.

In a moment the others had come up, and the whole archway seemed full of the flicker of flashing swords. Wat's long arm wavered here and there, keeping them all at bay. I could have cried the slogan for pride in him. This was the incomparable sworder indeed, and John Varlet, that misbegotten rogue, had not taught him in vain.

"Let off!" he cried to me, never taking his eyes from his foes. "Ease me a little to the right. They are over heavy for my iron on that hand."

So with that, even as I was bidden, and because there was nothing else I could do, I struck with my broad Italian dagger at a surly visage that came cornerwise between me and the sky, and tumbled a tall fellow out of an angle of the gateway on the top of the first, kicking like a rabbit. The rest were a little dashed by the fall of these two. Still there were four of them, and one great loon determinedly set his head down, and wrapping his cloak on his arm, he rushed at my cousin, almost overbearing him for the moment. He broke within Wat's guard, and the swords of the rogue's companions had been in his heart, but just then Lochinvar gave them another taste of his quality. Lightly leaping to the side just out of the measure of the varlet's thrust, and reaching sideways, he struck the man heavily on the shoulder with the dagger in his left hand, panting with the force of the blow, so that he fell down like the dead. At the same moment Wat leaned far forward, engaging all the points of the other swords with his rapier.

They gave back at the quick unexpected attack, and the points of their swords rose, as it seemed, for no more than a second. But in that pulse-beat Wat's rapier shot out straight and low, and yet another clapped his hand upon his body and cried an oath, ere he too fell forward upon his dead companions. At this the little man, who had stood all the while in the background, took heart of grace and came forward, and I could see the hilt of the steel-pistol in his hand. He crouched low upon his hams, trying to get a sighting shot at us. But I had him clear in the moonbeam, like a pullet on a dyke; and just when I saw his forefinger twitch on the hammer-pull, I dropped him with a bullet fair in the shoulder, which effectually spoilt his aim, and tumbled him beside the others.

Then the remaining two threw down their tools and ran, whatever they were fit, in the direction of the town.

Whereat Walter Gordon with much philosophy straiked his sword on the lapel of one of the dead men's coats, bent its point to the pavement to try its soundness, and returned it to its velvet sheath. Then he solemnly turned and took me by the hand.

"You are a man, Cousin William," he said.

CHAPTER XVI.

THE GREY MOWDIEWORT.

BUT by this time I was shaking like a leaf for fear, together with the thought of what I had done in the taking of life, and the sending of my fellow-creatures to their account. Also the tears came hopping down my cheek, which is ever the effect that fighting has on me. Yet in spite of this weakness Wat shook me again by the hand, and said only:
"You are a man!"

Notwithstanding, I was not cheered, but continued to greet like a bairn, only quietly, though I was grateful for his words, and took them not ill.

Then Walter Gordon went forward to the dead men, and turned them over, looking at each but saying no word. Lastly he went to the little stout man whom I had shot in the shoulder. As he looked in his face, from which the mask had fallen aside, he started so greatly that he almost leaped bodily in the air.

"William, William," he cried, "by the King's head, we must run for it. This is not a 'horning' but a hanging job. *'Tis the Duke of Wellwood himself.*"

Greatly startled at the name of the great Privy Councillor and favourite of the King, I went and looked. The man's face had fallen clear of the velvet mask with which it had been hidden, and looked livid and grey against the snow in the moon's uncertain light. But it was indeed the Duke, for I had often seen him going to the Parliament in his state and dignity, but there in the snow he looked inconceivably mean, dirty and small.

"It's a' by wi' the estate noo, Walter," I said. "You and me maun tak' the heather like the lave."

So saying, I snatched up the head wrapped in the plaid, which I had almost forgotten, and called him to come on. For we were on the outskirts of the waste ground called the King's hunting parks, and could get directly away without passing a house.

But Walter was determined to return and see his mother, lest otherwise the horror of the news might take her unawares. Walter was ever his mother's boy, and I think his undutiful conduct that night now went hard with him, seeing how the affair had turned out.

I argued with him that it was the maddest ploy thus to go back. His lodgings would certainly be searched as soon as the Duke was found, and the two who had escaped should return to assist the watch. But I could not overcome his determination. He had another plan to set against mine.

"There is a vault hereabout that I used to hide in as a boy. Silly folks say that it is haunted. But indeed there be few that know of it. You can bide there and wait till I come."

So we went thither, and found the place commodious enough indeed, but damp and unkindly. It was situate by the chapel wall, but of late years it has been much filled up with rubbish since the pulling down of the Chapel Royal by the mob in the riots of the Revolution year.

Yet even at that time it was not a place I had any stomach for. I had liefer have been going decently to my bed in my lodgings in the West Bow — as indeed at that moment I should, but for that daft heathercat of a cousin of mine, with whose gallantries, for my sins, I thus found myself saddled.

So he went off upon his errand, leaving me alone; and I

hardly looked to see him again, for I made sure that the guard would arrest him or ever he had gone a hundred yards. It was little that I could do in that sorrowful place. But I unwrapped the poor head I had brought with me, and put it with reverence in the farthest corner of the dismal den. Then I retired to an angle to wait, wrapping my plaid about me for warmth; for the night had fallen colder, as it ever does after the ceasing of a storm.

I had time and to spare then for thinking upon my folly, and how I had damaged the cause that I had so nearly gained by my unlucky interference in Walter's vanities. It came to me that now of a certainty both Earlstoun and Lochinvar must pass wholly away from the Gordons, and we become attainted and landless like the red Gregors. And indeed Kenmuir's case was not much better.

So I wore the weary night away, black dismal thoughts eating like canker worms at my heart. How I repented and prayed, no man knows. For that is the young man's repentance — after he has eaten the sour fruit, to pray that he may not have the stomach-ache.

Yet being Galloway-born, I had also in me the fear of the unseen, which folks call superstition. And it irked me more than all other fears to have to bide all the night (and I knew not how much longer) in that horrible vault.

It seems little enough to some, only to abide all night in a place where there is nothing but quiet bones of dead men. But, I warrant you, it is the burgher folk, who have never lain anywhere but bien and cosy in their own beds at home that are the boldest in saying this.

So the night sped slowly in that horrid tomb. I watched the white moonbeams spray over the floor and fade out, as the clouds swept clear or covered the moon's face. I listened to every sough of the wind, with a fear lest the clanking halberts of the watch should be in it. The sound of a man walking far away made me hear in fantasy the grounding of their axe-shafts as they surrounded my place of concealment. It is bad enough to have one's conscience against one, but when conscience is reinforced by a well-grounded fear of the hangman's rope, then the case grows uncouth indeed.

Yet in spite of all I think I slept a little. For once I waked and saw the moon, red and near the setting, shining through a great round hole in the end of the vault, and that so brightly that I seemed to see motes dancing in its light as in a hay-loft in the summer season.

But that was not the worst of it. In my dream my eyes followed the direction of the broad beam, and lo! they fell directly on the poor blackened head of him that had once been John Gordon of Lochinvar. The suns and rains had not dealt kindly with him, and now the face looked like nothing earthly, as I saw it in the moonlight of the ugsome vault. I could have screamed aloud, for there seemed to be a frown on the brow and a writhed grin on the mouth that boded me irksome evils to come.

Now half a dozen times I have resolved to leave out of my tale, that which I then saw happen in my dream of the night. For what I am about to relate may not meet with belief in these times, when the power of Satan is mercifully restrained ; and when he can no longer cast his glamourie over whom he will, but only over those who, like witch-wives and others, yield themselves up to him as his willing subjects.

But I shall tell plainly what, in the moonlight, seemed to me to befal in my dream-sleep.

It appeared then to me that I was staring at the blackened head, with something rising and falling in my throat like water in a sobbing well, when the ground slowly stirred in the corner where the head lay, and even as I looked, a beast came forth — a grey beast with four legs, but blind of eye like a grey mowdiewort, which took the head between its forepaws and rocked it to and fro as a mother rocks a fretful bairn, sorrowing over it and pitying it. It was a prodigy to see the eyes looking forth from the bone-sockets of the head. Then the beast left it again lying by its lone and went and digged in the corner. As the moonlight swept across, broad and slow, through the loud beating of my heart, I heard the grey mowdiewort dig the hole deeper and yet deeper. Now the thing that made me fullest of terror was not the digging of the beast, but the manner of its throwing out the earth, which was not behind it as a dog does, but in front, out of the pit, as a sexton that digs a grave.

Then, ere the moonbeams quite left it and began to climb the wall, I seemed to see the beast roll the black Thing to the edge and cover it up, drawing the earth over it silently. After that, in my fantasy, it seemed to look at me. I heard the quick patter of its feet, and with a cry of fear I started up to flee, lest the beast should come towards me — and with that I knew no more.

CHAPTER XVII.

OVER THE MUIR AMANG THE HEATHER.

WHEN I came to myself my cousin Walter Gordon was standing over me. He was dressed in countryman's apparel, and seemed most like a chapman, with a small pack of goods upon his back for sale in the farm-towns and cottars' houses. It was grey day.

"Where is the beast?" I asked, for I was greatly bewildered by my swound.

"What beast? There is no beast," he replied, thinking that I dreamed.

Then I told him of what I had seen; but as I might have expected he took little heed, thinking that I did but dream in that uncouth place. And in the grey light he went forward with a fair white cloth in his hand wherewith to wrap his father's head for the burial. But when he came to the corner of the vault, lo! there was naught there, even as I had said. And saving that the earth seemed newly stirred, no trace of the horror I had seen, which staggered him no little. Yet me it did not surprise, for I knew what I had seen.

But in a little he said, "That is all folly, William — you and your beasts. Ye buried it yourself in your sleep. How many times have ye walked the ramparts of Earlstoun in your sark!"

This indeed seemed likely, but I still maintain that I saw the mowdiewort.

Nevertheless, when we came to consider the matter, it was

in sooth no time to think of freits or portents. It was no question of our fathers' heads. Our own were in danger whether the Duke of Wellwood lived or died; and we behoved to look limber if we were to save them at all. It is a strange feeling that comes and stays about the roots of the neck, when one first realises that the headsman may have to do therewith or many weeks pass by. And it is a feeling that I have taken to bed with me for years at a time.

Wat Gordon had warned my men as well as his own. So at the outside of the town toward the back of the Boroughmuir, Hugh Kerr met us with the beasts. Here we took horse and rode, having happily seen nothing of the city guard. It was judged best that my cousin and I should ride alone. This we wished, because we knew not whom to trust in the strange case in which we found ourselves. Besides we could the better talk over our chances during the long night marches in the wilderness, and in our weary hidings among the heather in the daytime.

So we steadily rode southward toward Galloway, our own country, for there alone could we look for some ease from the long arm of the Privy Council. Not that Galloway was safe. The dragoons paraded up and down it from end to end, and searched every nook and crevice for intercommuned fugitives. But Galloway is a wide, wild place where the raw edges of creation have not been rubbed down. And on one hillside in the Dungeon of Buchan, there are as many lurking places as Robert Grier of Lag has sins on his soul — which is saying no light thing, the Lord knows.

Once, as we went stealthily by night, we came upon a company of muirland men who kept their conventicle in the hollows of the hills, and when they heard us coming they scattered and ran like hares. I cried out to them that we were of their own folk. Yet they answered not but only ran all the faster, for we might have been informers, and it was a common custom of such-like to claim to be of the hill-people. Even dragoons did so, and had been received among them to the hurt of many.

Our own converse was the strangest thing. Often a kind of wicked perverse delight came over me, and I took speech to mock and stir up my cousin of Lochinvar,' who was moody and distraught, which was very far from his wont.

"Cousin Wat," I said to him, "'tis a strange sight to see your mother's son so soon of the strict opinions. To be converted at the instance of her Grace of Wellwood is no common thing. Wat, I tell thee, thou shalt lead the psalm-singing at a conventicle yet!"

Whereat he would break out on me, calling me "crop-ear" and other names. But at this word play I had, I think, as much the mastery as he at the play of sword-blades.

"Rather it is you shall be the 'crop-head' — of the same sort as his late Majesty!" I said. For it is a strange thing that so soon as men are at peril of their lives, if they be together, they will begin to jest about it — young men at least.

To get out of the country was now our aim. It pleased Wat not at all to have himself numbered among the hill-folk and be charged with religion. For me I had often a sore heart and a bad conscience, that I had made so little of all my home opportunities. My misspent Sabbaths stuck in my throat, although I had no stomach for running and hiding with the intercommuned. Perhaps, if I had loved my brother Sandy better, it had not been so hard a matter. But that, God forgive me, I never did, though I knew that he was a good Covenant man and true to his principles. Yet there is no mistake but that he gave us all a distaste at his way of thinking.

So we wandered by night and hid by day till we reached the hills of our own south country.

At last we came to the white house of Gordonstoun, which

stands on the hill above the clachan of Saint John. It was a lodge of my cousin's, and the keeper of it was a true man, Matthew of the Dub by name. From him we learned that there were soldiers both at Lochinvar and Earlstoun. Moreover, the news had come that very day, with the riding post from Edinburgh, of the wounding of the Duke of Wellwood, and how both of us were put to the horn and declared outlaw.

I do not think that this affected us much, for almost every man in Galloway, even those that trooped with Graham and Lag, half a dozen in all, had been time and again at the horn. One might be at the horn — that is, outlawed, for forgetting to pay a cess or tax, or for a private little tulzie that concerned nobody, or for getting one's lum on fire almost. It was told that once Lauderdale himself was put to the horn in the matter of a reckoning he had been slack in paying, for Seekin' Johnnie was ever better at drawing in than paying out.

But to think of my mother being harassed with a garrison, and to know that rough blades clattered in and out of our bien house of Earlstoun, pleased me not at all. Yet it was far out of my hap to help it. And I comforted me with the thought, that it had been as bad as it could be with us, even before our affray with the Wellwood.

So there was nothing for it, but to turn out our horses to grass at Gordonstoun and take to the hills like the rest. Matthew of the Dub gave us to understand that he could put us into a safe hold if we would trust ourselves to him.

"But it is among the hill-folk o' Balmaghie!" he said, looking doubtfully at his laird.

"Ah, Gordieston," said Lochinvar, making a wry face, and speaking reproachfully, "needs must when the devil drives! But what for did you sign all the papers and take all the oaths against intercommuning, and yet all the time be having to do with rebels?" For Matthew was a cunning man, and had taken all the King's oaths as they came along, holding the parritch and feather beds of Gordieston on the Hill worth any form of words whatsoever — which indeed could be swallowed down like an apothecary's bolus, and no more ado about it.

"'Deed, your honour," said Matthew of the Dub, slyly, "it's a wersh breakfast to streek your neck in a tow, an' I hae sma' stammach for the Whig's ride to the Grassmarket. But a man canna juist turn informer an' gie the gang-by to a' his auld acquaintances. Wha in Gallowa' wants to ride an' mell wi' Clavers an' the lads on the Grey Horses, save siccan loons as red-wud Lag, roaring Baldoun, and Lidderdale, the Hullion o' the Isle?"

"I would have you remember, Matthew," said my cousin, speaking in Scots, "that I rode wi' them no lang syne mysel'."

"Ou, ay, I ken," said independent Matthew, dourly, "there was my leddy to thank for that. The women fowk are a' great gomerils when they meddle wi' the affairs o' the State. But a' the Glen jaloosed that ye wad come oot richt, like the daddy o' ye, when ye tired o' leading-strings, an' gang to the horn like an honest man, e'en as ye hae dune the day."

CHAPTER XVIII.

AULD ANTON OF THE DUCHRAE.

IT was a wintry-like morning in the later spring when at last we got out of hiding in the house of Gordonstoun. During our stay there I had often gone to see my mother just over the hill at Earlstoun, to give her what comfort I could, and in especial to advise about Sandy, who was then on his travels in the Low Countries. That morning Matthew of the Dub came with us, and we took our legs to it, despising horses in our new quality of hill-folk. The wind blew bitter and snell from the east. And May — the bleakest of spring months, that ought to be the bonniest — was doing her worst to strengthen the cold, in proportion as she lengthened her unkindly days.

Matthew told us not whither we were going, and as for me, I had no thought or suspicion. Yet the tear was in my eye as we saw the bonny woods of Earlstoun lying behind us, with the grey head of the old tower setting its chin over the tree-tops and looking wistfully after us.

But we marched south along the Ken, by New Galloway, and the seat of my Lord Kenmuir, where there was now a garrison with Clavers himself in hold. We saw the loch far beneath us, for we had to keep high on the side of Bennan. It ruffled its breast as a dove's feathers are blown awry by a sudden gusty wind. It was a cheerless day, and the gloom on our faces was of the deepest. For we were in the weird case of suffering for conscience' sake, and with no great raft either of conscience or of religion to comfort us.

Not that our case was uncommon. For all were not saints who hated tyranny.

"Wat," I said, arguing the matter, "the thing gangs in the husk o' a hazel. I wear a particular make of glove chevron. It likes me well, but I am not deadly set on it. Comes the Baron-bailie or my Lord Provost, and saith he: 'Ye shall not henceforth wear that glove of thine, but one of my colour and of the fashion official!' Then says I to the Baron-bailie, 'To the Ill Thief wi' you and your pattern gauntlet!' And I take him naturally across the cheek with it, and out with my whinger——"

"Even so," said my cousin, who saw not whither I was leading him, "let no man drive you as to the fashion of your gloves. Out with your whinger, and see what might be the colour of his blood!"

"And what else are the Covenant men doing?" cried I, quick to take advantage. "We were none so fond o' the Kirk that I ken of—we that are of the lairds o' Galloway, when we could please ourselves when and where we would go. Was there one of us, say maybe your father and mine, that had not been sessioned time and again? Many an ill word did we speak o' the Kirk, and many a glint did we cast at the sandglass in the pulpit as the precentor gied her another turn. But after a' the Kirk was oor ain mither, and what for should the King misca' or upturn her? Gin she whummelt us, and peyed us soondly till we clawed where we werena yeuky, wha's business was that but oor ain? But comes King Charlie, and says he, 'Pit awa' your old mither, that's overly sore on you, an' tak' this braw easy step-minnie, that will never steer ye a hair or gar ye claw your hinderlands!' What wad ye say, Wat? What say ye, Wat? Wad ye gie your mither up for the King's word?"

"No," said Wat, sullenly, for now he saw where he was being taken, and liked it little, "I wadna."

I thought I had him, and so, logically, I had. But he was nothing but a dour, donnert soldier, and valued good logic not a docken.

"Hear me," he said, after a moment's silence; "this is my way of it. I am no preacher, and but poor at the practice. But I learned, no matter where, to be true to the King — and, mind you, even now I stand by Charles Stuart, though at the horn I be. Even now I have no quarrel with him, though for the dirty sake of the Duke of Wellwood, he has one with me."

"That's as may be," I returned; "but mind where you are going. Ye will be eating the bread of them that think differently, and surely ye'll hae the sense and the mense to keep a calm sough, an' your tongue far ben within your teeth."

We were passing the ford of the Black Water as I was speaking, and soon we came to the steading of the Little Duchrae in the light of the morning. It was a long, low house, well thatched, like all the houses in the neighbourhood. And it was sending up a heartsome pew of reek into the air, that told of the stir of breakfast. The tangle of the wood grew right up to the windows of the back, and immediately behind the house there was a little morass with great willow trees growing and many hiding-places about it — as well I knew, for there Maisie Lennox and I had often played the day by the length.

Now "Auld Anton" of the Duchrae was a kenned man all over the country-side. The name of Anthony Lennox of Duchrae was often on my father's lips, and not seldom he would ride off to the south in the high days of Presbytery, to have fellowship with him whenever he was low in the spirit, and also before our stated seasons of communion. Thither also I had often ridden in later years on other errands, as has already been said.

Never had I been able to understand, by what extraordinary favour Anthony Lennox had not only been able to escape so far himself, but could afford a house of refuge to others in even more perilous plight. Upon the cause of this immunity there is no need at present to condescend, but certain it is that the house of the Duchrae had been favoured above most, owing to an influence at that time hidden from me. For Auld Anton was never the man to hide his thoughts or to set a curb upon his actions.

With a light hand Matthew of the Dub knocked at the door, which was carefully and immediately opened. A woman of a watchful and rather severe countenance presented herself there — a serving woman, but evidently one accustomed to privilege and equality, as was common in Galloway at that day.

"Matthew Welsh," she said, "what brings you so far from hame so early in the morning?"

"I come wi' thae twa callants — young Gordon o' Earlstoun, and a young man that is near kin to him. It may be better to gie the particulars the go-by till I see you more privately. Is the good man about the doors?"

For answer the woman went to the window at the back and cried thrice. Instantly we saw a little cloud of men disengage themselves irregularly from the bushes and come towards the door. Then began a curious scene. The woman ran to various hiding-places under the eaves, behind dressers, in aumries and presses, and set a large number of bowls of porridge on the deal table. Soon the house was filled with the stir of men and the voices of folk in earnest conversation.

Among them all I was chiefly aware of one young man of very striking appearance, whose dark hair flowed back from a broad brow, white as a lady's, and who looked like one born to command. On the faces of many of the men who entered and overflowed the little kitchen of the Duchrae, was the hunted look of them that oftentimes glance this way and that for a path of escape. But on the face of this man was only a free soldierly indifference to danger, as of one who had passed through many perils and come forth scatheless.

Last of all the Master of the House entered with the familiarity of the well-accustomed. He was alert and active, a man of great height, yet holding himself like a soldier. Three counties knew him by his long grey beard and bushy eyebrows for Anthony Lennox, one of the most famous leaders of the original United Societies. To me he was but Maisie Lennox's father, and indeed he had never wared many words on a boy such as I seemed to him.

But now he came and took us both by the hand in token of welcome, and to me in especial he was full of warm feeling.

"You are welcome, young sir," he said. "Many an hour at the dyke-back have we had, your father and I, praying for our bairns and for poor Scotland. Alack that I left him on the way to Bothwell last year and rode forward to tulzie wi' Robin Hamilton — and now he lies in his quiet resting grave, an' Auld Anton is still here fighting away among the contenders."

With Walter also he shook hands, and gave him the welcome that one true man gives to another. Lochinvar sat silent and watchful in the strange scene. For me I seemed to be in a familiar place, for Earlstoun was on every tongue. And it was not for a little that I came to know that they meant my brother Sandy, who was a great man among them — greater than ever my father had been, though he had "sealed his testimony with his blood," as their phrase ran.

I thought it best not to give my cousin's name, excusing myself in the meantime by vouching that his father had suffered to the death, even as mine had done, for the cause and honour of Scotland's Covenant.

CHAPTER XIX.

THE SWEET SINGERS OF THE DEER-SLUNK.

Now my father had drilled it into me that Anton Lennox, called the Covenanter, was a good and sound-hearted man, even as he was doubtless a manifest and notable Christian. But the tale concerning him that most impressed me and touched my spirit nearest, was the tale of how he served Muckle John Gib and his crew, after godly Mr. Cargill had delivered them over to Satan.

It was Sandy, my brother, that was the eye-witness of the affair. He was ever of the extreme opinion — as my mother used often to say, "Our Sandy was either in the moon or the midden" — but in my judgment oftenest in the latter.

Yet I will never deny that he has had a great deal of experience, though I would rather want than have some of it. Now at this time, Sandy, perhaps by means of his wife, Jean Hamilton (who, like her brother Robert, was just inordinate for preachings and prophesyings), was much inclined to kick over the traces, and betake himself to the wilder extremes that were much handled by our enemies for the purpose of bringing discredit on the good name of the Covenants.

There was one great hulking sailor of Borrowstounness that was specially afflicted with these visions and maunderings. Nothing but his own crazy will in all things could satisfy him. He withdrew himself into the waste with two or three men and a great company of feeble-minded women, and there renounced all authority and issued proclamations of the wildest and maddest kinds.

The godly and devout Mr. Donald Cargill (as he was called, for his real name was Duncan) was much exercised about the matter. And finding himself in the neighbourhood to which these people had betaken themselves, he spared no pains, but with much and sore foot-travel he found them out, and entered into conference with them. But John Gib, who could be upon occasion a most faceable and plausible person, persuaded him to abide with them for a night. Which accordingly he did, but having wrestled with them in prayer and communing half the night, and making nothing of them, presently he rose and went out into the fields most unhappy. So after long wandering he came homeward, having failed in his mission. Then it was that he told the matter to old Anton Lennox, who had come from Galloway to attend the great Society's Meeting at Howmuir. With him at the time was my brother Sandy, and here it is that Sandy's story was used to commence.

And of all Sandy's stories it was the one I liked best, because there was the least chance of his having anything about himself to tell.

"I mind the day" — so he began — "a fine heartsome harvest day in mid-September. We had our crop in early that year, and Anton, my father and I, had gotten awa' betimes to the Societies' meeting at Lesmahagow. It was in the earliest days of them — for ye maun mind that I am one o' the few surviving original members. We were a' sitting at our duty, when in there came into the farm kitchen where we abode, Mr. Donald Cargill himself. He was leaning upon his staff, and his head was hanging down. We desisted from our worship and looked at him steadfastly, for we saw that the hand of the Lord had been upon him and that for grief. So we waited for the delivery of his testimony.

"'My heart is heavy,' he said at long and last, 'for the people of the wilderness are delivered over to the gainsayer, and that by reason of John Gib, called Muckle John, sailor in Borrowstounness, and presently leading the silly folks astray.' Then he told them how he had wrestled with the Gibbites mightily in the Spirit, and had been overthrown. Whereat he was notified that the hearts of all those that hated the Way would be lifted up.

"He also brought a copy of the foolish sheet called the 'Proclamation of the Sweet Singers,' which was much handed about among all the persecutors at this time, and made to bring terrible discredit on the sober and God-fearing folk of the South and West, who had nothing whatever to do with the matter.

"'Let me see it,' said Anton Lennox, holding out his hand for it.

"Mr. Cargill gave it to him, saying sadly, 'The Spirit will not always strive with them!'

"'Na,' said Auld Anton, 'but I'll e'en strive wi' them mysel'! Reek me doon Clickie!'

"He spoke of his great herd's stave that had a shank of a yard and a half long and was as thick as my wrist.

"'Come you, Sandy,' he cried over his shoulder as he strode out, 'and ye will get your bellyful of Sweet Singing this day!'

"Now I did not want to move for the exercise was exceeding pleasant. But my father also bade me go with Auld Anton, and as you know, it was not easy to say nay to my father.

"It was over a moor that we took our way — silent because all the wild birds had by with their nesting, and where Mr. Cargill had left the company of John Gib was in a very desert place where two counties met. But Auld Anton went stegging* over the hills, till I was fair driven

* Walking rapidly with long steps.

out of my breath. And ever as he went he drove his staff deeper and dourer into the sod.

"It was a long season before we arrived at the place, but at last we came to the top of a little brow-face, and stood looking at the strange company gathered beneath us.

"There was a kind of moss-hag of dry peat, wide and deep, yet level along the bottom. Down upon the black coom was a large company of women all standing close together and joining their hands. A little way apart on a mound of peat in the midst, stood a great hulk of a fellow, with a gown upon him, like a woman's smock, of white linen felled with purple at the edges. But whenever it blew aside with the wind, one saw underneath the sailor's jerkin of rough cloth with the bare tanned skin of the neck showing through.

"'Certes, Master Anton,' said I, 'but yon is a braw chiel, him wi' the broad hat and the white cock ontill the bob o't!'

"And indeed a brave, braw, blythesome-like man he was, for all the trashery of his attire. He kept good order among the men and women that companied with him in the Deer-Slunk. There were thirty of them — twenty-six being women — many of them very respectable of family, that had been led away from their duty by the dangerous, persuading tongue of John Gib. But Auld Anton looked very grim as he stood a moment on the knowe-top and watched them, and he took a shorter grip of the cudgel he carried in his hand. It was of black crab-tree, knotted and grievous.

"'John Gib!' cried Anton Lennox from the hill-top suddenly in a loud voice:

"The great sea slug of a man in the white petticoat turned slowly round, and looked at us standing on the parched brae-face with no friendly eye.

"'Begone — ye are the children of the devil — begone to your father!' he cried back.

"'Belike — John Gib — belike, but bide a wee — I am coming down to have a word or two with you as to that!' replied Auld Anton, and his look had a smile in it, that was sour as the crab-apples which his cudgel would have borne had it bidden in the hedge-root.

"'I have come,' he said slowly and tartly, 'that I might converse seriously with you, John Gib, and that concerning the way that you have treated Mr. Donald Cargill, an honoured servant of the Lord!'

"'Poof!' cried John Gib, standing up to look at us, while the women drew themselves together angrily to whisper, 'speak not to us of ministers. We deny them every one. We have had more comfort to our souls since we had done with ministers and elders, with week-days and fast-days, and Bibles and Sabbaths, and came our ways out here by ourselves to the deeps of the Deer-Slunk!'

"'Nay,' said Old Anton, 'ministers indeed are not all they might be. But without them, ye have proved yourself but a blind guide leading the blind, John Gib! Ye shall not long continue sound in the faith or straight in the way if ye want faithful guides! But chiefly for the fashion in which ye have used Mr. Cargill, am I come to wrestle with you,' cried Anton.

"'He is but an hireling,' shouted Muckle John Gib, making his white gown flutter.

"'Yea, Yea, and Amen!' cried the women that were at his back. But Davie Jamie, Walter Ker, and John Young, the other three men who were with him, looked very greatly ashamed and turned away their faces — as indeed they had great need.

"'Stand up like men! David Jamie, Walter Ker, and John Young!' cried Anton to them, 'Do ye bide to take part with these silly women and this hulker from the bilboes, or will ye return with me to good doctrine and wholesome correction?'

"But the three men answered not a word, looking like men surprised in a shameful thing and without their needful garments.

"'Cargill me no Cargills!' said John Gib; 'he is a traitor, a led captain and an hireling. He deserted the poor and went to another land. He came hither to us, yet neither preached to us nor prayed with us.'

"John Young looked about him as John Gib said this, as though he would have contradicted him had he dared. But he was silent again and looked at the ground.

"'Nay,' said Auld Anton, 'that is a lie, John Gib; for I know that he offered to preach to you, standing with his Bible open between his hands as is his ordinary. But ye wanted him to promise to confine his preaching to you — which when he would not consent to do, ye were for thrusting him out. And he came home, wet and weary, with the cold easterly wet fog all night upon the muir, very melancholy, and with great grief for you all upon his spirit!'

"Then at this John Gib became suddenly very furious and drew a pistol upon us. This made Anton Lennox laugh.

"'I shall come down and wrestle with your pistols in a wee, John Gib. But I have a word to say to you all first.'

"He stood awhile and looked at them with contempt as if they were the meanest wretches under heaven, as indeed they were.

"'You, John Gib, that lay claim to being a wizard, I have little to say to you. Ye have drawn away these silly folk with your blasphemous devices. Your name is legion, for there are many devils within you. You are the herd of swine after the devils had entered into them. Hath your master given you any word to speak before I come down to you?'

"'Ay,' said John Gib, leaping up in the air and clapping his hands together as if he would again begin the dance, which, accompanied by a horrid yowling like that of a beaten dog, they called Sweet Singing.

"'Ay, that I have! Out upon you, Anton Lennox, that set up for a man of God and a reprover of others. I alone am pure, and God dwells in me. I lift up my testimony against all the months of the year, for their names are heathen. I alone testify against January and February; against Sunday, Monday, and Tuesday; against Martinmas and holidays, against Lammas-day, Whitsun-day, Candlemas, Beltan, stone crosses, saints' images, Kelton Hill Fair and Stonykirk Sacrament. Against Yule and Christmas, old wife's fables, Palm Sunday, Carlin Sunday, Pasch, Hallow, and Hogmanay; against the cracking of nits and the singing of sangs; again all romances and story-buiks; against Handsel Monday, kirks, kirkyairds and ministers, and specially against cock-ups in the front o' the Sabbath bonnets o' ministers' wives; against registers, lawyers and all lawbooks——'

"He cried out this rigmarole at the top of his voice, speaking trippingly by rote as one that says his lesson in school and has learned it often and well. He rolled his eyes as he recited, and all the women clapped their hands and made a kind of moaning howl like a dog when it bays the moon.

"'Yea, Yea, and Amen!' they cried after him, like children singing in chorus.

"'Peace, devil's brats all!' cried Anton Lennox, like a tower above them.

"And they hushed at his word, for he stood over them all, like one greater than man, till even Muckle John Gib seemed puny beside the old man.

"'David Jamie, hearken to me, you that has your hand on your bit shable.* Better put up your feckless iron spit.

* Short sword.

It will do you no good. You are a good scholar lost, and a decent minister spoiled. I wonder at you — a lad of some lear — companying with this hairy-throated, tarry-fisted deceiver.'

"This David Jamie was a young limber lad, who looked paler and more delicate than the others. What brought him into the company of mad men and misguided women, it is perhaps better only guessing.

"He looked sufficiently ashamed now at all events.

"'Walter Ker and John Young, hearken ye to me; I have more hope of you. You are but thoughtless, ignorant, land-ward men, and the Lord may be pleased to reclaim you from this dangerous and horrible delusion.'

"Anton Lennox looked about him. There was a fire smouldering at no great distance from him. Something black and square lay upon it. He took three great strides to the place. Lifting the dark smouldering object up from off the fire, he cried aloud in horror, and began rubbing with his hands. It was a fine large-print Bible, with more than half of it burned away. There were also several little ones upon the fire underneath. I never saw a man's anger fire up more quickly. For me, I was both amazed and afraid at the awful and unthinkable blasphemy.

"'John Gib,' cried Anton Lennox, 'stand up before the Lord, and answer — who has done this?'

"'I, that am the head of the Sweet Singers, and the Lord's anointed!' said he. 'I have done it!'

"'Then, by the Lord's great name, I will make you sing right sweetly for this!' cried Anton, taking a vow.

"Then one of the women took up the parable.

"'We heard a voice in the Frost Moss,' she said, 'and a light shone about us there; and John Gib bade us burn our Bibles, for that the Psalms in Metre, the chapter headings, and the Table of Contents were but human inventions.'

"'And I did it out of despite against God!' cried John Gib.

"Then Anton Lennox said not a word more, but cast away his plaid, spat upon his cudgel-palm, and called over his shoulder to me:

"'Come, Sandy, and help me to wrestle in the Spirit with these Sweet Singers.'

"As he ran down the brae, David Jamie, the student youth, came at him with a little spit-stick of a sword, and cried that if he came nearer he would run him through.

"'The Lord forgie ye for leein', callant,' cried Anton, catching the poor thin blade on his great oak cudgel, for Anton was a great player with the single-sticks, and as a lad had been the cock of the country-side. The steel, being spindle-thin, shivered into twenty pieces, and the poor lad stood gaping at the sword-hilt left in his hand, which had grown suddenly light.

"'Bide you there and wrestle with him, Sandy!' Auld Anton cried again over his shoulder.

"So I took my knee and tripped David up. And so sat up upon him very comfortable, till his nose was pressed into the moss, and all his members sprawled and waggled beneath me like a puddock under a stone.

"Then Auld Anton made straight for John Gib himself, who stood back among his circle of women, conspicuous in his white sark and with a pistol in his hand. When he saw Auld Anton coming so fiercely at him across the peat-hags, he shot off his pistol, and turned to run. But his women caught hold of him by the flying white robe, thinking that he was about to soar upward out of their sight.

"'Let me be,' he cried, with a great sailor oath; and tearing away from them, he left half the linen cloth in their hands, and betook him to his heels.

"Anton Lennox went after him hot foot, and there they

had it, like coursing dogs, upon the level moor. It was noble sport. I laughed till David Jamie was nearly choked in the moss with me rocking to and fro upon him. Anton Lennox was twice the age of John Gib, but Muckle John being a sailor man, accustomed only to the short deck, and also having his running gear out of order by his manner of life, did exceedingly pant and blow. Yet for a time he managed to keep ahead of his pursuer. But there was no ultimate city of refuge for him.

"Anton Lennox followed after him a little stiffly, with a grim determined countenance; and as he ran I saw him shorten his cudgel of crabtree in his hand. Presently he came up with the muckle man of Borrowstounness. The great stick whistled through the air, soughing like a willow-wand. Once, twice, thrice — it rose and fell.

"And the sound that ensued was like the beating of a sack of meal.

"'I'll learn you to burn the Bible!' cried Anton, as he still followed. His arm rose and fell steadily while John Gib continued to run as if the dogs were after him. The great hulk cried out with the intolerable pain of the blows.

"'I'll mak' ye Sweet Singers a', by my faith! I'll score ilka point o' your paper screed on your back, my man — Sunday, Monday, Tuesday, Pasch, Beltan, and Yule!'

"At the Yule stroke John Gib fell into a moss-hole. We could not easily see what followed then. But the grievous cudgel steadfastly rose and fell like the flail of a man that threshes corn in a barn, and a howling and roaring that was aught but sweet singing came to us over the moor.

"Presently Anton returned, striding back to where I sat upon David Jamie his back.

"'Rise!' he said. And that was all he said.

"But he took his foot and turned the bit clerk over,

pulling him out of the moss with a *cloop* like the cork being drawn out of a brisk bottle of small ale.

"'David, lad, do ye renounce John Gib and all his ways?'

"The limber-limbed student looked doubtful, but the sight of the cudgel and the distant sound of the sweet singing of Muckle John decided him.

"'Ay,' he said. 'I am content to renounce them and him.'

"'See ye and stick to it then!' said Anton, and went after Walter Ker and John Young, who stood together as though they had gotten a dead stroke.

"'Ye saw visions, did ye?' he said. 'See ye if this be a vision?'

"And he gave them certain dour strokes on their bodies, for they were strong carles and could bide the like — not like the poor feckless loon of a colleger.

"'Did ye see a light shining in the moss late yestreen?' he asked them.

"'It was but glow-worms!' said Walter Ker.

"'It was, aiblins, Wull-o'-the-Wisp?' said John Young.

"'Ay, that's mair like the thing, noo!' said Auld Anton, with something like a smile on his face.

"So saying he drove all the women (save two or three that had scattered over the moss) before him, till we came to the place of the ordinary Societies' Meeting at Howmuir, from which we set out.

"Here were assembled sundry of the husbands of the women — for the black shame of it was, that the most part of them were wives and mothers of families, of an age when the faults of youth were no longer either temptation or excuse.

"To them he delivered up the women; each to her own husband, with certain advice.

"'I have wrestled with the men,' he said, 'and overcome

them. Wrestle ye with the women, that are your own according to the flesh. And if ye think that my oaken stave is too sore, discharge your duty with a birch rod, of the thickness of your little finger — for it is the law of the realm of Scotland that every husband is allowed to give his wife reasonable correction therewith. But gin ye need my staff or gin your wives prefer it, it is e'en at your service.'

"So saying, he threw his plaid over his shoulder, and made for the door.

"'Learn them a' the sweet singin',' he said. 'John Gib was grand at it. He sang like a mavis oot by there, on the moor at the Deer-Slunk.'"

This was the matter of Sandy's cheerful tale about John Gib and Auld Anton Lennox.

And this cured Sandy of some part of his extremes, though to my thinking at times, he had been none the worse of Auld Anton at his elbow to give him a lesson or two in sweet singing. I might not in that case have had to buy all over again the bonny house of Earlstoun, and so had more to spend upon Afton, which is now mine own desirable residence.

CHAPTER XX.

THE HOME OF MY LOVE.

ANTHONY LENNOX presently took me by the hand, and led me over to where in the Duchrae kitchen the dark young man sat, whose noble head and carriage I had remarked.

"Mr. Cameron," he said gravely, and with respect, "this is the son of a brave man and princely contender with his Master—William Gordon of Earlstoun, lately gone from us."

And for the first time I gave my hand to Richard Cameron, whom men called the Lion of the Covenant—a great hill-preacher, who, strangely enough, like some others of the prominent disaffected to the Government, had been bred of the party of Prelacy.

As I looked upon him I saw that he was girt with a sword, and that he had a habit of gripping the hilt when he spoke, as though at the pinch he had yet another argument which all might understand. And being a soldier's son I own that I liked him the better for it. Then I remembered what (it was reported) he had said on the Holms of Kirkmahoe when he preached there.

"I am no reed to be shaken with the wind, as Charles Stuart shall one day know."

And it was here that I got my first waft of the new tongue which these hill-folk spake among themselves. I heard of "singular Christians," and concerning the evils of paying the "cess" or King's tax—things of which I had never heard in my father's house, the necessity not having arisen before Bothwell to discuss these questions.

When all the men were gathered into the wide houseplace, some sitting, some standing, the grave-faced woman knocked with her knuckles gently on a door which opened into an inner room. Instantly Maisie Lennox and other two maids came out bearing refreshments, which they handed round to all that were in the house. The carriage of one of these three surprised me much, and I observed that my cousin Wat did not take his eyes from her.

"Who may these maids be?" he whispered in my ear.

"Nay, but I ken not them all," I answered. "Bide, and we shall hear." For, indeed, I knew only one of them, but her very well.

And when they came to us in our turn, Maisie Lennox nodded to me as to a friend of familiar discourse, to whom nothing needs to be explained. And she that was the tallest of the maids handed Wat the well-curled oaten cake on a trencher. Then he rose and bowed courteously to her, whereat there was first a silence and then a wonder among the men in the house, for the manner of the reverence was strange to the stiff backs of the hill-folk. But Anthony Lennox stilled them, telling of the introduction he had gotten concerning Walter, and that both our fathers had made a good end for the faith, so that we were presently considered wholly free of the meeting.

We heard that there was to be a field conventicle near by, at which Mr. Cameron was to preach. This was the reason of so great a gathering, many having come out of Ayrshire, and even as far as Lesmahagow in the Upper Ward of Lanark, where there are many very zealous for the truth.

Then they fell again to the talking, while I noted how the maids comported themselves. The eldest of them and the tallest, was a lass of mettle, with dark, bent brows. She held her head high, and seemed, by her attiring and dignity, accustomed to other places than this moorland farm-town. Yet here she was, handing victual like a servitor, before a field-preaching. And this I was soon to learn was a common thing in Galloway, where nearly the whole of the gentry, and still more of their wives and daughters, were on the side of the Covenant. It was no uncommon thing for a King's man, when he was disturbing a conventicle — "skailing a bees' byke" as it was called — to come on his own wife's or, it might be, his daughter's palfrey, tethered in waiting to the root of some birk-tree.

"Keep your black-tail coats closer in by!" said Duke Rothes once to his lady, who notoriously harboured outed preachers, "or I shall have to do some of them a hurt! Ca' your messans to your foot, else I'll hae to kennel them for ye!"

There was however no such safe hiding as in some of the great houses of the strict persecutors.

So in a little while, the most part of the company going out, this tall, dark-browed maid was made known to us by Matthew of the Dub, as Mistress Kate McGhie, daughter of the Laird of Balmaghie, within which parish we were.

Then Maisie Lennox beckoned to the third maid, and she came forward with shyness and grace. She was younger than the other two, and seemed to be a well-grown lass of thirteen or fourteen.

"This," said Maisie Lennox, "is my cousin Margaret of Glen Vernock."

The maid whom she so named blushed, and spoke to us in the broader accent of the Shire, yet pleasantly and frankly as one well reared.

Presently there came to us the taller maid — she who was called Kate, the Laird's daughter.

She held out her hand to me.

"Ah, Will of Earlstoun, I have heard of you!"

I answered that I hoped it was for good.

"It was from Maisie there that I heard it," she said, which indeed told me nothing. But Kate McGhie shook her head at us, which tempted me to think her a flighty maid. However, I remembered her words often afterwards when I was in hiding.

Thereupon I presented my cousin Wat to her, and they bowed to one another with a very courtly grace. I declare it was pretty to see them, and also most strange in a house where the hill-folk were gathered together. But for the sake of my father and brother we were never so much as questioned.

Presently there was one came to the door, and cried that the preaching was called and about to begin. So we took our bonnets and the maids their shawls about them, and set forth. It was a grey, unkindly day, and the clouds hung upon the heights. There are many woods of pine and oak about the Duchrae; and we went through one of them to an ancient moat-hill or place of defence on a hillside, with a ditch about it of three or four yards wideness, which overlooked the narrow pack road by the water's edge.

As we went Kate McGhie walked by my side, and we talked together. She told me that she came against her parents' will, though not without her father's knowledge; and that it was her great love for Maisie Lennox, who was her friend and gossip, which had first drawn her to a belief in the faith of the hill-folk.

"But there is one thing," said she, "that I cannot hold with them in. I am no rebel, and I care not to disown the authority of the King!"

"Yet you look not like a sufferer in silence!" I said, smiling at her. "Are you a maid of the Quaker folk?"

At which she was fain to laugh and deny it.

"But," I said, "if you are a King's woman, you will

surely find yourself in a strange company to-day. Yet there is one here of the same mind as yourself."

Then she entreated me to tell her who that might be.

"Oh, not I," I replied, "I have had enough of Charles Stuart. I could eat with ease all I like of him, or his brother either! It is my cousin of Lochinvar, who has been lately put to the horn and outlawed."

At the name she seemed much surprised.

"It were well not to name him here," she said, "for the chief men know of his past companying with Claverhouse and other malignants, and they might distrust his honesty and yours."

We had other pleasant talk by the way, and she told me of all her house, of her uncle that was at Kirkcudbright with Captain Winram and the garrison there, and of her father that had forbidden her to go to the field-meetings.

"Which is perhaps why I am here!" she said, glancing at me with her bold black eyes.

As I went I could hear behind us the soft words and low speech of Maisie Lennox, who came with my cousin Wat and Margaret of Glen Vernock. What was the matter of their speech I could not discover, though I own I was eager to learn. But they seemed to agree well together, which seemed strange to me, for I was a much older acquaintance than he.

Now, especially when in the wilder places, we came to walk all four together, it seemed a very pleasant thing to me to go thus to the worship of God in company. And I began from that hour to think kindlier of the field-folks' way of hearing a preacher in the open country. This, as I well know, says but little for me; yet I will be plain and conceal nothing of the way by which I was led from being a careless and formal home-keeper, to cast in my lot with the remnant who abode in the fields and were persecuted.

K

CHAPTER XXI.

THE GREAT CONVENTICLE BY THE DEE WATER.

A Note to the Reader.
  I am warned that there are many folk who care not to hear what things were truly said and done at a conventicle of the hill-folk. I have told the tale so that such may omit the reading of these two chapters. Nevertheless, if they will take a friend's word, it might be for their advantage to read the whole.   *W. G.*

On our way to the conventicle we came to the place that is called the Moat of the Duchrae Bank, and found much people already gathered there. It is a very lonely place on the edge of a beautiful and still water, called the Lane of Grenoch. In the midst of the water, and immediately opposite to the moat, there is an island, called the Hollan Isle, full of coverts and hiding-places among hazel bushes, which grow there in thick matted copses. Beyond that again there are only the moors and the mountains for thirty miles. The country all about is lairy and boggy, impossible for horses to ride; while over to the eastward a little, the main road passes to Kells and Carsphairn, but out of sight behind the shoulder of the hill.

There was a preaching-tent erected on a little eminence in the middle of the round bare top of the moat. The people sat all about, and those who arrived late clustered on the farther bank, across the ditch.

I observed that every man came fully armed. For the oppressions of Lauderdale in Scotland, and especially the severities of John Graham and Robert Grier in Galloway, were bearing their own proper fruit. The three maids sat together, and Wat Gordon and I sat down near them — I as close to Maisie Lennox as I dared, because, for old acquaintance' sake, my liking was chiefly towards her. Also, I perceived that Kate McGhie was more interested to talk to me of my cousin than to hear concerning myself, a thing I never could abide in talking to a woman.

But Maisie kept her head bent, and her face hidden by the fold of her shawl. For she had, even at that time, what I so sadly lacked, a living interest in religion.

From where I sat I could see the watchers on the craigs above the Hollan Isle, and those also over on the hill by the Folds. So many were they, that I felt that not a muirfowl would cry, nor a crow carry a stick to its nest, without a true man taking note of it. I heard afterwards, that over by the Fords of Crae they had come on a certain informer lying couched in the heather to watch what should happen. Him they chased for three miles over the heather by Slogarie, clodding him with divots of peat and sod, yet not so as to do the ill-set rascal overmuch harm. But a sound clouring does such-like good.

Then there arose the pleasant sound of singing. For Mr. Cameron had gone up into the preaching-tent and given out the psalm. We all stood up to sing, and as I noted my cousin standing apart, looking uncertainly about, I went over to him and brought him to my side, where one gave us a book to look upon together. As they sang, I watched to see the sentinel on the craigs turn him about to listen to us, and noted the light glance on his sword, and on the barrel of the musket on which he leaned. For these little tricks of observation were ever much to me, though the true Whig folk minded them not a hair, but stuck to their singing, as indeed it was their duty to do.

But even to me, the sound of the psalm was unspeakably solemn and touching out there in the open fields. It seemed, as we sang of the God who was our refuge and our strength, that as we looked on Grenoch, we were indeed in a defenced city, in a prophesied place of broad rivers and streams, wherein should go no galley with oars, neither should gallant ship pass thereby.

I had never before felt so near God, nor had so sweet an income of gladness upon my spirit; though I had often wondered what it all meant when I heard my father and mother speak together. There seemed, indeed, a gale of the Spirit upon the meeting, and I think that from that moment I understood more of the mind of them that suffered for their faith; which, indeed, I think a man cannot do, till he himself is ready to undergo his share of the suffering.

But when Richard Cameron began to speak, I easily forgat everything else. He had a dominating voice, the voice of a strong man crying in the wilderness. "We are here in a kenned place," he said, "and there be many witnesses about us. To-day the bitter is taken out of our cup, if it be only for a moment. Yea, and a sweet cup we have of it now. We who have been much on the wild mountains, know what it is to be made glad by Thy works — the works of the Lord's hands. When we look up to the moon or stars, lo! the hand of the Lord is in them, and we are glad. See ye the corn-rigs up ayont us there, on the Duchrae Hill — the hand of God is in the sweet springing of them, when the sun shines upon them after rain. And it is He who sendeth forth every pile of the grass that springs so sweetly in the meadows by the water-side."

I own it was very pleasant to me to listen to him, for I

had not thought there was such tenderness in the man. He went on :

"We are hirsled over moss and moor, over crags and rocks, and headlong after us the devil drives. Be not crabbit with us, O Lord ! It is true we have gotten many calls, and have not answered. We in the West and South have been like David, cockered and pampered overmuch. Not even the wild Highlands have sitten through so many calls as we have done here in Galloway and the South.

"For I bear testimony that it is not easy to bring folk to Christ. I, that am a man weak as other men, bear testimony that it is not easy — no easy even to come to Him for oneself!"

And here I saw the people begin to yearn towards the preacher, and in the grey light I saw the tears running silently down his cheeks. And it seemed as if both the minister and also the most part of the people fell into a rapture of calm weeping, which, strangely enough, forced Mr. Cameron often to break off short. Folks' hearts were easily touched in those days of peril.

"Are there none such here?" he asked. And I confess my heart went out to him and all my sins stood black and threatening before me as I listened. I vow that at the time I feared his words far more than ever I did Lag and his riders — this being my first living experience of religion, and the day from which I and many another ground our hope.

Then ere he sufficiently commanded himself to speak again, I took a glance at the maid Maisie Lennox beside me, and the look on her face was that on the face of a martyr who has come through the torture and won the victory. But the little lass that was called Margaret of Glen Vernock clung to her hand and wept as she listened. As for Kate McGhie, she only looked away over the water of the Hollan Isle to the blue barn rigging of the Orchar Hill and seemed neither to see nor to hear anything. Or at least, I was not the man to whom was given the art to see what were her inner thoughts.

Richard Cameron went on.

"Are there any here that find a difficulty to close with Christ? But before we speak to that, I think we shall pray a short word."

So all the people stood up on the hillside and the sough of their uprising was like the wind among the cedar trees. And even as he prayed for the Spirit to come on these poor folk, that were soon to be scattered again over the moors and hags as sheep that wanted a shepherd, the Wind of the Lord (for so I think it was) came breathing upon us. The grey of the clouds broke up, and for an hour the sun shone through so kindly and warm that many let their plaids fall to the ground. But the mists still clung about the mountain tops of the Bennan and Cairn Edward.

Then after he had prayed not long but fervently, he went on again to speak to us of the love and sufferings of Christ, for the sake of whose cause and kingdom we were that day in this wild place. Much he pleaded with us to make sure of our interest, and not think that because we were here in some danger at a field preaching, therefore all was well. O but he was faithful with us that day, and there were many who felt that the gate of heaven was very near to them at the great conventicle by the Water of Dee.

And even after many years, I that have been weak and niddering, and that have taken so many sins on my soul, since I sat there on the bank by Maisie Lennox, and trembled under Mr. Cameron's words, give God thank and service that I was present to hear the Lion of the Covenant roar that day upon the mountains of Scotland.

Yet when he spoke thus to us at this part of his pleading,

it was most like the voice of a tender nursing mother that would wile her wayward bairns home. But when he had done with offering to us the cross, and commending Him that erewhile hung thereon, I saw him pause and look about him. He was silent for a space, his eyes gleamed with an inner fire, and the wind that had arisen drave among his black locks. I could see, as it had been, the storm gather to break.

"There ayont us are the Bennan and Cairn Edward, and the Muckle Craig o' Dee — look over at them — I take them to witness this day that I have preached to you the whole counsel of God. There be some great professors among you this day who have no living grace — of whom I only name Black MacMichael and Muckle John, for their sins are open and patent, going before them into judgment. There are also some here that will betray our plans to the enemy, and carry their report of this meeting to the Malignants. To them I say: 'Carry this word to your masters, the word of a wiser than I, "Ye may blaw your bag-pipes till you burst, we will not bow down and worship your glaiks — no, not though ye gar every heid here weigh its tail, and the wind whistle through our bones as we hang on the gallows-tree."'"

Here he held up his hand and there was a great silence.

"Hush! I hear the sound of a great host — I see the gate of heaven beset. The throng of them that are to be saved through suffering, are about it. And One like unto the Son of Man stands there to welcome them. What though they set your heads, as they shall mine, high on the Netherbow Port; or cast your body on the Gallows' dunghill as they will Sandy's here? Know ye that there waiteth for you at the door One with face more marred than that of any man — One with His garments red coming up from Bozrah, One that hath trodden the winepress alone. And He shall say, as

He sees you come through the swellings of Jordan, 'These are they that have come out of great tribulation, and have washed their robes, and made them white in the blood of the Lamb.' 'Lift up your heads, O ye gates, and be ye lift up, ye everlasting doors, for the redeemed of the Lord shall also enter in!'"

So he made an end, and all the people were astonished at him, because they looked even then for the chariot which it had been foretold should come and snatch him out of mortal sight.

CHAPTER XXII.

PEDEN THE PROPHET.

(Being the concluding of the conventicle by the Dee Water.)

YET the chariot of fire came not, for the time was not yet, though the grinding of its wheels was even then to be heard at the door. But the Lord had yet a great day's darg to do in Scotland with Richard Cameron.

Then after silence had endured for a time, another minister rose up to speak to us. At sight of him a murmur went about, and wonder and joy sat on every face. He was an old man, tall and gaunt. His hair, lyart and long, fell upon his shoulders. His beard descended upon his breast.

"Peden the Prophet!" was the whisper that went about. And all bent eagerly forward to look at the famous wanderer, whom all held to have gifts of utterance and prophecy beyond those of mortal. He it was that had been a thousand times hunted like a partridge upon the mountains, a hundred times taken in the net, yet had ever escaped. He it was for the love of whom men had laid down their lives like water, only that Alexander Peden might go scatheless and speak his Master's will.

Bowed he was and broken; yet when he spoke his natural strength was in no wise abated, and at his first word the fear of the Lord came upon us. I looked at Lochinvar, who in his time had ridden so hard on his track. He sat open-mouthed, and there was a daze of awe in his look.

Alexander Peden had hardly spoken a sentence to us when the spirit of prophecy brake upon him, and he cried out for Scotland as was his wont in those days. His voice rose and rang — not like a war-trumpet as did Cameron's, but rather like the wild wind that goes about the house and about the house, and cries fearful words in at the chinks and crevices.

"A bloody sword, a bloody sword for thee, O puir Scotland! Many a mile shall they travel in thee and see naught but waste places, nor so much as a house reeking pleasantly on the brae. Many a conventicle has been wared on thee, my Scotland. And Welsh and Semple, Cameron and Cargill have cried to thee. But ere long they shall all be put to silence and God shall preach to thee only with the bloody sword. Have ye never witnessed for the cause and Covenants? Or have ye been dumb dogs that would not bark? If that be so, as sayeth godly Mr. Guthrie of Fenwick, God will make the tongues that owned Him not to fry and flutter upon the hot coals of hell. He will gar them blatter and bleeze upon the burning coals of hell!

"Speak, sirs, or He will gar these tongues that He hath put into your mouths to popple and play in the pow-pot of hell!"

As he said these words his eyes shone upon us like to burn us through, and his action was most terrifying as he took his great oaken staff and shook it over us. And we fairly trembled beneath him like silly bairns taken in a wrong.

But he went on his way as one that cries for vengeance over an open grave in which a slain man lies.

"Ye think that there hath been bloodshed in Scotland, and so there hath — dear and precious — but I tell you that that which hath been, is but as the dropping of the morning cloud ere the sun rises in his strength, to the mid-noon thunder plump that is yet to come.

"Not since the black day of Bothwell have I slept in a bed! I have been Nazarite for the vow that was upon me.

Have any of you that are here seen me in New Luce? Not even Ritchie here could have overcrowed me then, for strength and stature. I stood as a young tree by the river of waters. Look upon me now — so crooked by the caves and the moss-hags that I could not go upright to the scaffold. The sword handle is fit for your hands, and the Lord of Battles give you long arms when you measure swords with Charles Stuart. But old Sandy is good for nothing now but the praying. He can only bide in his hole like a toothless tyke, lame and blind; and girn his gums at the robbers that spoil his master's house.

"' Crook-back, crab-heart, sayeth the proverb," Peden cried, " but I think not so, for my heart is warm this day toward you that sit here, for but few of you shall win through the day of wrath that is to come in Scotland."

He turned towards the place where we sat together, the maids, my cousin and I. A great fear in my heart chilled me like ice. Was he to denounce us as traitors? But he only said slowly these words in a soft and moving voice, as one that hath the tears close behind.

"And there are some of you, young maids and weak, here present, that shall make a name in Scotland, a name that shall never die!"

With that he made an end and sat down.

Then came one, white-face and panting from the hill on the east.

"The riders are upon us — flee quickly!" he cried.

Then, indeed, there was great confusion and deray. Some rose up in act to flee. But Anton Lennox, who had the heart of a soldier in him and the wit of a general, commanded the men to stand to their arms, putting the women behind them. And through the confusion I could see stern-faced men moving to the front with guns and swords in their hands. These, as I learned, were the disciplined members of the Praying Societies, whom Cameron and afterwards Renwick, drew together into one military bond of defence and fellowship.

For me I stood where I was, the maids only being with me; and I felt that, come what might, it was my duty to protect them. Kate McGhie clasped her hands and stood as one that is gripped with fear, yet can master it. But Maisie Lennox, who was nearest to me, looked over to where her father stood at the corner ot his company. Then, because she was distressed for him and knew not what she did, she drew a half-knitted stocking out of the pocket that swung beneath her kirtle, calmly set the stitches in order, and went on knitting as is the Galloway custom among the hill-folk when they wait for anything.

There was a great silence — a stillness in which one heard his neighbour breathing. Through it the voice oi Peden rose.

"Lord," he prayed, "it is Thine enemies' day. Hour and power are allowed to them. They may not be idle. But hast Thou no other work for them to do in their master's service? Send them after those to whom Thou hast given strength to flee, for ur strength's gone, and there are many weak women among us this day. Twine them about the hill, O Lord, and cast the lap of Thy cloak over puir Sandy and thir puir things, and save us this one time."

So saying he went to the top of a little hill near by, from which there is a wide prospect. It is called Mount Pleasant. From thence he looked all round and waved his hands three times. And in a minute there befel a wonderful thing. For even as his hands beckoned, from behind the ridges of the Duchrae and Drumglass, arose the level tops of a great sea of mist. It came upon the land suddenly as the "haar" that in the autumn drives up the eastern valleys from the sea. Like a river that rises behind a dam, it rose, till of a sudden it overflowed and came towards us over the moorland, moving with a sound like running water very far away.

Then Peden the Prophet came hastening back to us.

"Move not one of you out of your places!" he cried, "for the Lord is about to send upon us His pillar of cloud." Then the mist came, and made by little and little a very thick darkness, and Peden said:

"Lads, the bitterest of the blast is over. We shall no more be troubled with them this day." And through the darkness I felt a hand placed in mine — whose I could not tell, but I hoped plainly that it might be Maisie Lennox's hand, for, as I have said, she was my gossip and my friend. At least I heard no more the click of the knitting-needles.

The mist came yet thicker, and through it there shone, now and then, the flickering leme of pale lightning, that flashed about us all. Then quite suddenly we heard strangely near us the jangling of the accoutrements of the troopers and the sound of voices.

"Curse the Whig's mist, it has come on again! We canna steer for it!" cried a voice so near that the hill-men stood closer in their ranks, and my own heart leaped till I heard it beat irregularly within me.

We marked the sharp *clip clip* as the shod horses struck the stones with their feet. Now and then a man would clatter over his steed's head as the poor beast bogged or stumbled.

Looking over between the hazel trees, I could faintly discern the steel caps of the troopers through the gloom, as they wound in single file between us and the water-side. It was but a scouting party, for in a moment we heard the trumpet blow from the main body, which had kept the road that winds down to the old ford, over the Black Water on the way from Kirkcudbright to New Galloway and Kenmuir.

In a little the sounds came fainter on our ears, and the swing and trample of the hoofs grew so far away that we could not hear them any more.

But the great cloud of people stood for long time still, no man daring to move. It struck me as strange that in that concourse of shepherds not so much as a dog barked. In a moment I saw the reason. Each herd was sitting on the grass with his dog's head in his lap, wrapped in his plaid. Then came the scattering of the great meeting. Such were the chances of our life at that dark time, when brother might part from brother and meet no more. And when a father might go out to look the lambs, and be found by his daughter fallen on his face on the heather by the sheep ree, with that on his breast that was not bonny to see when they turned him over. As for me I went home with Maisie Lennox and her friend the young lass of Glen Vernock, as was indeed my plain duty. We walked side by side in silence, for we had great thoughts within us of Cameron and Peden, and of the Blue Banner of the Covenant that was not yet wholly put down.

CHAPTER XXIII.

BIRSAY THE COBBLER.

So many of the wanderers abode at the Duchrae that Maisie Lennox was much cumbered with serving; yet in her quiet sedate way she would often take a word with me in the bygoing, as if to let me feel that I was not lonely or forgotten. And it cheered me much to find that I was not despised, because I was (as yet) no great fighting man of many inches or noble make like my brother Sandy. Also I loved women's converse, having been much with my mother — indeed never long away from her side, till my vain adventuring forth to Edinburgh in the matter of the sequestering of the estate.

As for Earlstoun, we heard it was to be forfaulted very soon, and given to Robert Grier of Lag, who was a very grab-all among them. Indeed no one was better than another, for even Claverhouse got Freuch, "in consideration," it was quaintly said, "of his good service and sufferings." His brother David likewise got another estate in the Shire, and Rothes and Lauderdale were as "free coups" for the wealth of the fined and persecuted gentry. Whenever there was a man well-to-do and of good repute, these men thought it no shame to strive to take him in a snare, or to get him caught harbouring on his estate some intercommuned persons. They rubbed hands and nudged one another in Council when they heard of a rising in arms. They even cried out and shook hands for joy, because it gave them colour for more exactions, and also for keeping an army in the field, whose providing and accoutring was also very profitable for them.

But at the Duchrae we abode fairly secure. At night we withdrew to the barn, where behind the corn-mow a very safe and quaint hiding-place had been devised. In the barn-wall, as in most of the barns in that country-side, there were no windows of any size — in fact nothing save a number of three-cornered wickets. These were far too small to admit the body of a man; but by some exercise of ingenious contrivance in keeping with the spirit of an evil time, the bottom stone of one of these wickets had been so constructed that it turned outwards upon a hinge, which so enlarged the opening that one man at a time had no difficulty in passing through. This right cunning trap-door was in the gable-end of the barn, and conducted the fugitive behind the corn-mow in which the harvest sheaves were piled to the ceiling. Here we lay many a time while the troopers raged about the house itself, stabbing every suspected crevice of the corn and hay with their blades, but leaving us quite safe behind the great pleasant-smelling mass of the mow.

Yet for all it was a not unquiet time with us, and I do not deny that I had much pleasant fellowship with Maisie Lennox.

But I have now to tell what befel at the Duchrae one Sabbath evening, when the pursuit had waxed dull after Bothwell, and before the Sanquhar affair had kindled a new flame.

At that time in Galloway, all the tailors, shoemakers, and artificers, did their work by going from house to house according as the several families had need of them. Now there was one man, who sat near us at the conventicle, whose actions that day it was impossible to mistake. When the troopers were jingling past beneath us, he flung himself on the ground, and thrust his plaid into his mouth, to prevent his crying out for fear. So pitiful did he look that, when all was past, my cousin Wat went over and asked of him:

"What craven manner of hill-man art thou?"

For indeed the men of the broad bonnet were neither cowards nor nidderlings. But this fellow was shaking with fear like the aspen in an unequal wind.

"I am but poor Birsay the cobbler," the man answered, "an it please your honour, I like not to come so near thae ill loons of soldiers."

"What sent you to the conventicle, then, when you fear the red-coats so greatly?" asked my cousin.

The little man glanced up at my cousin with a humoursome gleam in his eyes. He was all bent together with crouching over his lap-stone, and as he walked he threw himself into all kinds of ridiculous postures.

"Weel," he said, "ye see it's no easy kennin' what may happen. I hae seen a conventicle scale in a hurry, and leave as mony as ten guid plaids on the grund—forbye Bibles and neckerchiefs."

"But surely," I said to the cobbler, "you would not steal what the poor honest folk leave behind them in their haste?"

The word seemed to startle him greatly.

"Na, na; Birsay steals nane, stealin's no canny!" he cried. "Them that steals hings in a tow—an' forbye, burns in muckle hell—bleezin' up in fuffin lowes juist as the beardie auld man Sandy Peden said."

And the cobbler illustrated the nature of the conflagration with his hand.

"Na, na," he cried, in the strange yammering speech of the creature, "there's nae stealin' in gatherin' thegether what ither folks hae strawed, surely. That's i' the guid Buik itsel'. An' then after the bizz is bye, and the sough calmed doon, Birsay can gang frae auld wife to auld wife, and say to ilka yin, 'Ye wadna loss ocht lately, did ye, guid wife?' 'Aye,' says she. 'I lost my Bible, my plaid, or my kercher at the field preachin'!' 'Ay, woman, did ye?' says I. 'They're terrible loons the sodgers for grippin' and haudin'. Noo I mak' shoon for a sergeant that has mony a dizzen o' thae things.'

"Wi' that the auld wife begins to cock her lugs. 'Maybes he has my Bible!' 'I wadna wunner,' says I. 'O man, Birsay,' she says, 'I hae aye been a freen' o' yours, ye micht e'en see gin he has it, an' seek it aff him? There's the texts an' heads an' particulars o' mony sermons o' guid Maister Welsh and precious Maister Guthrie in the hinner end o' the Buik!'

"'So,' says I, aff-hand like, 'supposin' noo, just supposin' that Sergeant Mulfeather has gotten your bit buik, an' that for freendship to me he was wullin' to pairt wi't, what wad the bit buik be worth to ye. Ye see it's treason to hae sic a thing, and rank conspiracy to thig and barter to get it back — but what wull freends no do to obleege yin anither?'"

"Ay, man Birsay," I said, to encourage him, for I saw that the little man loved to talk. "An' what wull the auld body do then?"

"Faith, she'll gie me siller to tak' to Sergeant Mulfeather and get back her bit buikie. An' that's just what Birsay wull do wi' richt guid wull," he concluded cantily.

"And hae ye ony mair to tell me, Birsay?" I asked him. For his talk cheered the long and doleful day, and as for belief, there was no reason why one should believe more than seemed good of Birsay's conversation.

"Ay, there's yan thing mair that Birsay has to say to ye. You an' that braw lad wi' the e'en like a lassie's are no richt Whigs, I'm jaloosin'. Ye'll aiblins be o' the same way o' thinkin' as mysel'!"

At this I pretended to be much disconcerted, and said:

"Wheest, wheest, Birsay! Be canny wi' your tongue! Mind whaur ye are. What mean you?"

"Trust Birsay," he returned cunningly, cocking his frowsy head like a year-old sparrow. "Gin the King, honest man, never comes to mair harm than you an' me wusses him, he'll come gey weel oot o' some o' the ploys that they blame him for."

"How kenned ye, Birsay," I said, to humour him, "that we werna Whigs?"

"O, I kenned brawly by the fashion o' your shoon. Thae shoon were never made for Whigs, but for honest King's folk. Na, na, they dinna gree well wi' the moss-broo ava — thae sort wi' the narrow nebs and single soles. Only decent, sweering, regairdless folk, that wuss the King weel, tryst shoon like them!"

It was clear that Birsay thought us as great traitors and spies in the camp as he was himself. So he opened his heart to us. It was not a flattering distinction, but as the confidence of the little man might be an element in our own safety and that of our friends on some future occasion, I felt that we would assuredly not undeceive him.

But we had to pay for the distinction, for from that moment he favoured us with a prodigious deal of his conversation, which, to tell the truth, savoured but seldom of wit and often of rank sculduddery.

Birsay had no sense of his personal dishonour, and would tell the most alarming story to his own discredit, without wincing in the least. He held it proof of his superior caution that he had always managed to keep his skin safe, and so there was no more to be said.

"Ay, ay," said Birsay, "these are no canny times to be amang the wild hill-folk. Yin wad need to be weel payed for it a'. There's the twa black MacMichaels — they wad think nae mair o' splatterin' your harns again the dyke than o' killing a whutterick. Deil a hair! An' then, on the ither hand, there's ill-contrived turncoats like Westerha' that wad aye be pluff-pluffin' poother and shot at puir men as if they were muirfowl. An' he's no parteecler eneuch ava wha he catches, an' never will listen to a word.

"Then, waur than a', there's the awesome nichts whan the ghaists and warlocks are aboot. I canna bide the nicht ava. God's daylicht is guid eneuch for Birsay, an' as lang as the sun shines, there's nae fear o' deil or witch-wife gettin' haud o' the puir cobbler chiel! But when the gloamin' cuddles doon intil the lap o' the nicht, and the corp-cannles lowe i' the bogs, an' ye hear the deils lauchin' and chunnerin' to themselves in a' the busses at the road-sides, I declare every stound o' manhood flees awa' clean oot o' Birsay's heart, an' he wad like to dee but for thocht o' the After come. An' deed, in the mirk-eerie midnicht, whether he's fearder to dee or to leeve, puir Birsay disna ken!"

"But, Birsay," I said, "ill-doers are aye ill-dreaders. Gin ye were to drap a' this thievery an' clash-carryin' wark, ye wadna be feared o' man or deil!"

"Weel do I ken," Birsay said, "that siccan ploys are no for the like o' me; but man, ye see, like ither folk, I'm terrible fond o' the siller. An' there's nocht so comfortin', when a' thae things are yammerin' to get haud o' ye, as the thocht that ye hae a weel-filled stockin'-fit whaur nane but yersel' can get haud o't!"

And the creature writhed himself in glee and slapped his thigh.

"Yae stockin' fu', man," he said, "an' tied wi' a string, an' the ither begun, an' as far up as the instep. O man, it's blythe to think on!

"But heard ye o' the whummel I gat aff this verra Duchrae kitchen laft?" said Birsay. He often came over in the gloaming on a news-gathering expedition. For it was a pleasure to give him news of a kind; and my cousin, who had not a great many occupations since Kate McGhie had gone back to the great House of Balmaghie, took a special delight in making up stories of so ridiculous a nature that Birsay, retailing them at headquarters, would without doubt soon find his credit gone.

"The way o't was this," Birsay continued. "As I telled ye, I gan frae hoose to hoose in the exercise o' my trade, for there's no sic a suitor i' the country-side as Birsay, though he says it himsel', an' no siccan water-ticht shoon as his ever gaed on the fit o' man. Weel, it was ae nicht last winter, i' the short days, Birsay was to begin wark at the Duchrae at sax by the clock on Monday morn. An' whan it comes to coontin' hours wi' Auld Anton Lennox o' the Duchrae, ye maun begin or the clock has dune the strikin'. Faith an' a' the Lennoxes are the same, they'll haud the nose o' ye to the grundstane — an' the weemen o' them are every hair as bad as the men. There's auld Lucky Lennox o' Lennox Plunton — what said ye? — aweel, I'll gang on wi' my story gin ye like, but what's a' the steer so sudden, the nicht's afore us?

"As I was sayin', I had to start at Auld Anton's on the Monday mornin', gey an' early. So I thocht I wad do my travellin' in time o' day, an' get to the Duchrae afore the gloamin'. An' in that way I wad get the better o' the bogles, the deils o' the bogs, the black horse o' the Hollan Lane, an' a' sic uncanny cattle.

"But I minded that the auld tod, Anton Lennox, was a terrible man for examinin' in the Carritches, an' aye speerspeerin' at ye what is the Reason Annexed to some perfectly unreasonable command — an' that kind o' talk disna suit Birsay ava. So what did I do but started ower in the afternoon, an' gat there juist aboot the time when the kye are milkit, an' a' the folk eyther at the byre or in the stable.

"So I watched my chance frae the end o' the hoose, an'

when no a leevin' soul was to be seen, I slippit up the stairs, speelin' on the rungs o' the ladder wi' my stockin' soles as quiet as pussy.

"Then whan I got to the middle o' the laft, whaur the big hole o' the lum is, wi' the reek hingin' thick afore it gangs oot at the riggin' o' the hoose, I keekit doon. An' there at the table, wi' his elbows on the wood, sat Auld Anton takin' his lesson oot o' the big Bible — like the bauld auld Whig that he is, his whinger in a leather tashe swingin' ahint him. It's a queerie thing that for a' sae often as I hae telled the curate aboot him, he has never steered him. There maun be something no very thorough aboot the curate, an' he none so great a hero wi' the pint stoup either, man!

"Aweel, as the forenicht slippit on, an' the lassies cam' in frae the byre, an' the lads frae the stable, it was just as I expected. They drew up their stools aboot the hearth, got oot their Bibles an' warmed their taes. Lord preserve me, to see them sittin' sae croose an' canty ower Effectual Callin' an' Reason Annexed, as gin they had been crackin' an' singin' in a change-hoose! They're a queer fowk thae Whigs. It wad hae scunnered a soo! An' twa-three neebours cam' in by to get the benefit o' the exerceeses! Faith! if Clavers had chanced to come by the road, he wad hae landed a right bonny flaucht o' them, for there wasna yin o' the rive but had grippit sword at either o' the twa risin's. For a' the auld carles had been at Pentland an' a' the young plants o' grace had been at Bothwell — ay, an' Auld Anton an' twa-three mair warriors had been at them baith. An' gin there had been a third he wad hae been there too, for he's a grim auld carle, baith gash an' steeve, wi' his Bible an' his brass-muntit pistols an' his Effectual Callin'!

"Then bywhiles, atween the spells o' the questions, some o' the young yins fell a-talkin', for even Auld Anton canna haud the tongues o' the young birkies. An' amang ither things what did the loons do but start to lay their ill-scrapit tongues on me, an' begood to misca' puir Birsay for a' that was ill!"

"'Listeners hear nae guid o' themselves,' is an auld-farrant say, Birsay," I said.

"Aweel," the suitor went on, "that's as may be. At ony rate, it was 'Birsay this' an' 'Birsay that,' till every porridge-fed speldron an' ill-gabbit mim-moo'ed hizzie had a lick at puir Birsay.

"But at the lang an' last the auld man catched them at it, an' he was juist the man to let them hear aboot it on the deafest side o' their heids. He was aye a don at reprovin', was Auld Anton. No mony o' the preachers could haud a can'le to him on the job.

"Is it no a gey queer thing," said Birsay, breaking off his story, "that when we set to an' curse a' an' sundry, they ca' it profane sweerin', and misca' us for awesome sinners; but when they lay their tongues to their enemies an' curse them, it's ca'ed a Testimony an' printed in a buik?"

The thing did indeed strike me as strange, but I desired to keep Birsay to his story, so I only said:

"But, Birsay, what did the auld man say to them when he heard them misca'in' you?"

"Oh, he e'en telled them that it wad fit them better to look to their ain life an' conversation. An' that it wad be tellin' them yae day, gin they had made as guid a job o' their life wark as Birsay made o' his bits o' shoon — a maist sensible an' just observe! Faith, the auld tog is nane sae ill an auld carle, though siccan a dour an' maisterfu' Whig. He kens guid leather wark when he sees it!

"So when they were a' sittin' gey an' shame-faced under this reproof — *whang!* Doon on the hearthstane fell my suitor's elshin — the cankersome thing had slippit oot o' my pooch an' drappit ower the edge o' the hole in the laft aboon the fireplace.

"'Preserve us,' I thought to mysel', 'it's a' by wi' Birsay noo. They'll be up the stair swarmin' like a bee's byke.' But when I keeked it ower, they were a' sittin' gapin' at the elshin that had stottit on to the floor. An' what wi' me steerin' an' lookin' ower the edge, *clash* fell my braid knife, that I cut the leather wi', oot o' my pooch!

"It fell on the clean stane, an' then lap to the side, nearly on to the knees o' a great fat gussie o' a loon they ca' Jock Wabster. An' Jock was in siccan a hurry to get oot o' the road o' the thing — for he thocht it wasna canny — that he owerbalanced himsel', and, certes! ower he gaed amang the lassies, stool an' a', wi' an awesome clatter. An' a' the lassies cried oot wi' fricht an' gruppit the lad they likit best — for there's a deal o' human nature even amang the Whigs, that the Covenants canna fettle, nor yet Effectual Callin' keep in bounds, and nae doot there's Reason Annexed for that too!

"My sang, but whan Auld Anton got him straucht on his chair again, whatna tongue-threshin' did he no gie the lassies, an' indeed a' the lave o' them. He caa'ed them for a'thing that was bad, an' telled them what kin' o' black ill consciences they bood hae, to be feared o' a wee bit thing that was but wood an' airn. But when they showed him the knife whaur it lay glintin' on the hearth (for nae man o' them daured to touch it), Anton was a wee bit staggered himsel', an' said it was a sign sent to reprove them for speakin' aboot puir Birsay on a Sabbath nicht. 'It was a deil's portent,' he said, 'an' nae mortal man ever forged that steel, an' gin onybody touched it he wadna wunner but it wad burn him to the bane, comin' direc' frae sic a place as it had dootless loupit frae.'

"This tickled me so terribly that I creepit a wee nearer to see the auld tod's face, as he laid it aff to them aboot the deil's elshin an' his leather knife — that had baith been bocht frae Rab Tamson, the hardware man in the Vennel o' Dumfries, an' wasna payed for yet! When what d'ye think happened?

"Na, ye couldna guess—weel, I creepit maybe a hair ower near the edge. The auld rotten board gied way wi' me, an' doon Birsay fell amang the peats on the hearthstane, landin' on my hinderlands wi' a *brange* that nearly brocht the hoose doon. I gaed yae skelloch as I fell, but, gracious me," said Birsay, waving his hands, "that was as naething to the scraich that the fowk aboot the fire gied. They scattered like a flock o' wild deuks when a chairge o' shot splairges amang them. They thocht the ill auld boy was comed into the midst o' them, an' wi' yae consent they made for the door. Jock Wabster took the hill baa-haain' like a calf as he ran, and even bauld Auld Anton stood by the door cheek wi' his sword point atween him an' the deil whummelt on his hearthstane!

"But I didna bide lang amang the reed peats, as ye may guess. I was scramblin' oot, whan the auld man gruppit me by the cuff o' the neck, an', maybes because he had been a kennin' frichtit himsel', he gied puir Birsay an awesome warm pair o' lugs. He near dang me stupit. Gin I had gane to the laft to escape Effectual Callin', he didna scruple to gie me Effectual Daudin', an' that without ony speerin' or as muckle's a single reason annexed!"

"And what," I said, "came o' Jock Wabster?"

"'Deed as for Jock," said Birsay, "thereupon he got great experience o' religion and gaed to join John Gib and his company on the Flowe o' the Deer-Slunk, where Maister Lennox vanquished them. But he didna catch Jock, for Jock said gin he had beat the deil flat-fit in a race, he wasna feared for any Lennox o' the squad. But Jock was aye ower great wi' the weemen folk, an' sae John Gib's notions just suited him."

Here Birsay made an end of his story, for Anton Lennox himself came in, and of him Birsay stood in great and wholesome awe.

CHAPTER XXIV.

THE SANQUHAR DECLARATION.

I THINK it was during the week I lay thus in the barn at the Duchrae, often with Richard Cameron or his young brother Michael at my back in the quiet of the corn mow, that first I got within me the true spirit of the Covenant. Then it was that I heard all the troubles and the sins of Scotland redd* up and made plain; for in the night watches Cameron and his brother had great communings together. Richard was all for being done with the authority of the King, and making but one cast for it. Michael thought that the time was not ripe nor the men ready.

Now these two youths were they who chiefly set Scotland in a lowe at this time, when Lauderdale had so nearly trampled out the red cinders of the fire of Presbytery. It was strange to think, that he who should blow them again into a flame had once been a Prelatist, and that from the wicked shire of Fife. When one cast it up to him, Richard Cameron said:

"Ay, it humbles us all to remember the pit from which we were digged!"

Then one night in the barn we gave in very solemnly our adhesions to the disowning of Charles Stuart and his brother James — all save my cousin Wat, who said:

"I canna bide to cast off the blood of Bruce. I had rather kiss the Red Maiden."

And with that, early in the morning he left us, which was

* Cleared up.

a surprising grief to me, for he and I had been brothers in peril during many months. Whither he went I knew not then, but it shall be related in its proper place and all that befel him in his lonely wanderings, after he parted from me.

"We must not do this thing lightly or gladly," said Richard Cameron to us that abode with him in the barn. "We have laid our accounts with the worst that the Government may do to us. We count not our lives dear. We see plainly that naught is to be gained save by defiance, any more. The Indulgence is but a dish of sowens with a muzzle thereafter, to make us for ever dumb dogs that will not bark. Who shall hinder or blame, if we choose to lay down our lives in the high places of the field, that the old faith be not forgotten, neither the old Covenant engagements to our Lord Christ for ever abrogated?"

Yet I think there was not one of us that was not heart-sorry to break with the House of Stuart. For after all we were of Scotland, and we or our fathers had stood for the Scots House and the Scots King against Cromwell and the supplanters. At any rate, let it not be said of us that we did this thing lightly; but rather with heavy hearts, because the King had been so far left to himself as to forswear and abandon the solemn engagements which he had undertaken.

So it came to pass in the mid days of the year, that one afternoon we rode away through the lonely hills by Minnyhive, and turned north up the fair valley of the water of Nith. Here and there we gathered one to whom the word had been passed, finding them waiting for us at some green loaning foot or at the mouth of some glen. Little we said when a friend joined us; for our work was sad and solemn, and to be done once and for all. We rode as it were under the shadow of the scaffold. Yet I think we thought not so much of ourselves, as of the women folk that abode at home. I know that I was wae for my mother, who was now like to lose her two sons as she had aforetime lost her husband, and sometimes also I thought of the lass Maisie Lennox, and what she would do wanting her father.

But this I put from me, for after all Covenanting was man's business. And as Richard Cameron said:

"They that are trysted to the Bridegroom's work, must taigle themselves with no other marriage engagements!"

At the Menick foot, where that long stey pass begins, there met us ten men of the Upper Ward, all douce and stalwart men, armed and horsed as well as any of our men out of Galloway. I was the youngest of them all there, and indeed the only one that was not a mighty man of his arms. There had been indeed some talk of leaving me at the Duchrae to keep the place — which I knew to be but an excuse. But one James Gray of Chryston, a laird's son and a strong man, cried out, "Let the lad come, for his brother Sandy's sake!"

A saying which nettled me, and I replied instantly:

"Let any man stand out against me with the pistol and small sword, and I will show him cause why I should come for mine own!"

At this Cameron rebuked me:

"Ah, William, I see well that thou hast the old Adam in thee yet. But was there ever a Gordon that would not go ram-stam at the boar, whatever his religion?"

Then I, who knew that I had spoken as a carnal man, was somewhat shamed. Yet was I glad also that no man took my challenge, for indeed I had small skill of the sword. And with the shearing sword especially, my blows were as rat-tail licks to the dead strikes of Richard Cameron or even those of my brother Sandy. But nevertheless only to say the thing, did me good like medicine.

So into the town of Sanquhar we rode two and two, very slow and quiet, for Cameron had forbidden us to ride with a tight rein and the horses champing, as indeed I longed to do for pride and the lust of the eye.

"For thus," said he, " do the King's troopers, when they enter a town, to take the eyes of the unthinking. But contrariwise, we are come to do a deed in Scotland that shall not be forgotten while Nith water runs, and to tie a band which shall not be broken through. We ourselves shall fall and that speedily — that know we well — but, nevertheless, that which we do this day shall one day bring the tyrant's downfall!"

And so indeed it proved to be.

Sanquhar is ever a still place, as though there were no other day there but the Sabbath only. Also the inhabitants are douce and grave, and so remain to this day — buying and selling, eating and drinking, as though they were alone on God's universe. But that day as we came riding up the street, there was a head at every window and I heard the wives cry:

"'The hill-folk have risen and come riding into Sanquhar!"

And this pleased me in the heart, though I know well I should have had my mind set on other matters.

At the cross we formed up, setting our horses ten on either side and Richard Cameron in the midst, he alone dismounted and standing on the steps of the cross. We sat still and quiet, all being bareheaded. For show I had plucked my brand out of its scabbard. But Cameron sternly bade me put it back again, and gave me his horse to hold instead. Which thing grieved and shamed me at the time sadly enough, though now I am both proud and glad of it.

"The time for drawn steel is yet to come, William. Be sure that thou art then as ready as now," he said.

We sang our psalm of Covenant-keeping, and the hills

gave it back to us, as though the angels were echoing the singing of it softly in heaven. After that, Cameron stood up very straight, and on his face, which was as the face of a lion, there was a great tenderness, albeit of the sterner sort.

The townsfolk stood about, but not too near, being careful and cautious lest they should be called in question for compliance with the deed, and the strange work done by us that day; for the King's scoop-net gathered wide. Also the innocent were often called to judgment, especially if they had something to lose in goods or gear, as was the case with many of the well-doing burghers of Sanquhar.

"This day," cried Cameron, loudly and solemnly, after he had prayed, "do we come to this town of Sanquhar to cast off our allegiance to Charles Stuart and his brother James. Not hastily, neither to make ourselves to be spoken about, but with solemnity as men that enter well-knowing into the ante-chamber of death. An we desired our own lives, we should receive Tests and Indulgences thankfully; and go sit in our kennels, like douce tykes that are ready to run at the platter and whistle.

"But for all that, we are loyal men and no rebels, though to-day we cast off Charles Stuart — ay, and will do our best to make an end of his rule, so that he shall no more reign over this realm. This we shall do, not by private assassination, which we abhor and abominate; but by the levying of open war. We declare ourselves loyal to any covenanted king — ay, and had Charles Stuart kept his engagements, plighted and sworn, there is no man here that would not right gladly have laid down his life for him.

"All ye that stand by, hear this word of Richard Cameron! There are those behind me, who heard with their ears the oath that the King sware at Perth, when before the Solemn Convocation he spake these words: 'I Charles, King of Great Britain and Ireland, do assure and declare by my solemn oath in the presence of Almighty God, the Searcher of hearts, my allowance and approbation of the National Covenant and of the Solemn League and Covenant above written, and faithfully oblige myself to prosecute the ends thereof in my station and calling.'

"The King," cried Cameron, "who sware these oaths hath cast us off. We have not cast off the King! There is one waiting in the Low Countries whence I came, and looking towards the hills of Scotland, to see if there be any faithful. Shall the fortress be utterly broken down with none to build her up? Are there no watchmen to tell the towers thereof — none to cry from rampart to rampart, 'What of the night?' Ay, there be here in Sanquhar town this day at the least twenty men that have not bowed the knee to Baal. This day we come to lay down our lives, as happily as children that have spent their play-day in the fields, and being tired, would lay them down to sleep. But ere we go, because the time cannot be long, we come to give the banner of the Lord once more to the winds — the banner of that other Kingdom in Scotland that is Christ's. Behold!"

And with that he lifted up the banner-staff which he held in his hand, and there floated out upon the equal-blowing wind the blue banner of Christ's Covenant. And as the golden scroll of it took the air, there came that into the hearts of most of us, which filled them to the overflow. The tears ran down and fell upon our horses' necks. "FOR CHRIST'S CROWN AND COVENANT," ran the legend. Then we gathered ourselves closer about the battle-flag, for which we had come out to die. As one man we drew our swords, nor did Cameron now gainsay us — and lifting them high up, till the sun glinted bonnily upon them, we sang our solemn banding song. I never felt my heart so high or heaven so near, not even at the great field-preaching by the water of Dee, when I sat by the side of Maisie Lennox. Even thus we sang,

> " God is our refuge and our strength,
> In straits a present aid ;
> Therefore, although the earth remove,
> We will not be afraid."

Then we rode out of Sanquhar town, for once gallantly enough, having solemnly set ourselves to face the King in open field — we that were but twenty men against three kingdoms. Well we knew that we should be put down, but we knew also that so long as there were a score of men in Scotland, to do as we had done that day, the cause and the flag would never be wholly put down.

So the douce burghers of Sanquhar watched us ride away, our swords gleaming naked because we had appealed to the sword, and were prepared to perish by the sword, as the word is. Also our blue banner of the Covenant waved bravely over our heads, in token of our dependence on Jehovah, the God of battles.

And as we rode was it not I, William Gordon of Earlstoun, who carried the banner-staff, for Richard Cameron had given it into my hands. So I had not lived in vain, and Sandy would never again bid me sew bairn-clouts, and bide at home among the women. I wished my father had been alive to see me.

CHAPTER XXV.

THE LAST CHARGE AT AYRSMOSS.

THE morning of the twenty-second of July dawned solemnly clear. It promised to be a day of slumberous heat, for the haze lay long in the hollows, hesitating to disappear, and there was the brooding of thunder in the air. We that were of Cameron's little company found ourselves in a wild place on the moors. Most of our Galloway men had betaken themselves home, and they that had come out of Lanarkshire and Ayr were the greater part of the scanty company. The name of the place where we sojourned was Ayrsmoss. We had lain sleepless and anxious all night, with watchers posted about among the moss-hags. Richard Cameron spoke often to us, and told us that the matter had at last come to the narrow and bitter pass.

"It is the day of the Lord's anger," he said, "and it is expedient that some men should die for the people!"

We told him that we were ready, and that from the beginning we had counted on nothing else. But within me I felt desperately ill-prepared: yet, for the sake of the banner I carried, I tholed and said nothing.

It was about ten of the day, and because we heard not from our folk who had been posted to give warning, we sent out other two to find them. Then having taken a meal of meat for the better sustaining of our bodies, we lay down to sleep for an hour on a pleasant green place, which is all surrounded by morasses, for we had gotten no rest the night before.

Now I think we were all fey at this time, for we laid us down on the edge of the moss in a place that is open to all. And this when we might have withdrawn ourselves deep into the bog, and so darned ourselves among the "quakking quas"—dangerous and impassable flowes, so that no dragoons in the world could have come at us. But this we did not, for the word and doom were written. It was our enemies' day. As Cameron said that morning as we passed the house of William Mitchell in Meadowhead, and when they brought him out a basin and water to wash his hands, also a towel wherewith to dry them:

"This is their last washing. My head and hands are now cleansed for the offering!"

So we laid us down among a great swirling of whaups and crying of peesweeps. For the season of their nesting was hardly over, and all the moorland was astir with their plaintive notes.

After a long time I awoke, dreaming that Maisie Lennox stood by my bedside and took my hand, saying, "The kye are in the corn!" I sat up, and, lo, there within half a mile, and beating the moor in search of us, were two companies of dragoons, of the number of about one hundred and twenty, as near as at a glance I could reckon. My heart gave a stound, and I said to myself, "This is surely thy death-day, William Gordon!" And the word sounded strangely in my heart, for I had begun to think my life worth living in these latter days, and was none so keen upon the dying as were some others of our company.

But on the instant I awakened Cameron and his brother Michael, and also David Hackstoun of Rathillet, that was a soldier most stern, but yet a just man according to his lights. And they sat up and saw the soldiers sweeping the moor. But, as I say, we were all fey. For even then it was within our power to have escaped the violence of the men of

THE LAST CHARGE AT AYRSMOSS. 163

war. Very easily could we have left our horses, and betaken us into the deepest parts of the bottomless shaking bogs, where no man could have followed us. But the thought came not to us at the time. For God had so ordered it, that Scotland was best to be served that day by the death of many of His servants.

There were in our company twenty-three that had horses and forty that had none. But we were all armed in some sort of fashion.

Now, this Richard Cameron had in him both the heart of a fighter and the fearlessness of a man assured of his interest. He cried out to inquire of us if we were firmly set in our minds to fight, and with one voice we answered him, "Ay!" We were of one heart and one mind. Our company and converse had been sweet in the darkness, and now we were set to die together in the noonday, gladly as men that have made them ready for the entering in of the bride-chamber.

So in that sullen morning, with the birds crying and the mist drawing down into thunder-clouds, we rose to make our last stand. I had given up all thought of escape, and was putting in hard steeks at the praying. For the sins that were on my soul were many, and I had too recently taken to that way of thinking to have the comfort and assurance of my elders.

Now, the soldiers that came against us were the finest companies of Airly's and Strachan's dragoons — gallant lads all — newly brought to that country-side and not yet inured to the cruel riding and shooting, as other companies were. I have not a word to say against the way they fought, though as their duty was, they came against us with haste and fury. Our quarrel was not with them, but with their master.

They rode gallantly enough this way and that through the morasses, and came on bravely. Bruce of Earlshall was over them, but John Crichton was their best fighter. A stark and cruel man he was, that would have hunted us all down if he could. He fought that day with his blade swinging all the time, damning and cursing between every blow. But, for all that, he was sick and sorry ere he left this field. For if ever man did, he met his match when he crossed swords with the Lion of the Covenant. It was Rathillet who chose the place of strength for us to make our stand, and as it seemed and mostly proved, to take our deaths upon. There was little time for the Word and the Prayer. But, as was our custom, we sang a cheerful psalm, and lifted up our bonnets while Cameron prayed:

"Lord, spare the green, and take the ripe!" That was the whole matter of his supplication. "We may never be in better case to die. I see the gates of heaven cast wide open to receive us."

And I noted that all the time of our singing, David Hackstoun of Rathillet was looking to the priming of his pistols, and drawing the edge of his sword-blade along the back of his hand, as one that tries a razor ere he sets it to his chin. Then the companies of the enemy halted on the edge of the moss where the ground was yet firm. They seemed not disinclined for a parley.

"Do you own the King's authority?" cried one among them. It was Bruce of Earlshall, a buirdly* chiel and one not greatly cruel; but rather like Monmouth, anxious to let the poor remnant have its due.

"Ay!" cried Cameron, "we own the King's authority."

"Wherefore, then, stand ye there in arms against his forces?" came the answer back. "Yield, and ye shall have quarter and fair conduct to Edinburgh!"

The man spake none so evilly for a persecutor, and in my heart I liked him.

* Sturdy.

"I thank you, Captain Bruce, for your fair speech," said Cameron, "but I wot well you mean fair passage to the Grassmarket. The King we own is not King Charles Stuart, and it liketh us to go to our King's court through the crash of battle, rather than through the hank of the hangman's twine."

"This preacher is no man of straw — fight he will," I heard them say one to the other, for they were near to us, even at the foot of the opposite knoll.

Then our horsemen, of whom I was one, closed in order without further word, and our foot drew out over the moss in readiness to fire. David Hackstoun was with us on the left, and Captain Fowler on the right. But Richard Cameron was always a little ahead of us all, with his brother Michael with him on one side, and I, riding my Galloway nag, close upon his right flank — which was an honourable post for one so young as I, and served withal to keep my spirits up.

Just before he gave the word to charge, he cried out to us, pointing to the enemy with his sword:

"Yonder is the way to the good soldier's crown!"

The day had been clouding over, the heat growing almost intolerable. It was now about two in the afternoon. It was easy to see, had we had the eyes to observe it, that a thunderstorm was brewing, and even as Richard Cameron stretched out his sword over his horse's head, and cried on to us to charge in the name of the Lord, the first levin-bolt shot down, glittering into the moor like a forked silver arrow. And over our head the whole firmament raired and crashed.

"The Captain of our Salvation calls for us!" cried Cameron. "Who follows after, when the Son of God rides forth to war!"

So with that we lowered our sword-points and drave at

them. I think I must have ridden with my eyes shut, down that little green knowe with the short grass underfoot. I know that, even as we rode, the thunder began to roar about us, girding us in a continuous ring of lightning-flashes.

Yet, at the time, I seemed to ride through a world of empty silence, even when I struck the red broil of battle. I could see Cameron crying out and waving his sword before us as our horses gathered way, but I remember no more till the shock came and we found ourselves threshing headlong among them. I fired my pistols right and left, and set them in my belt again, though the habit was to throw them away. I had my sword dangling by a lingel or tag at my right wrist, for I had learned from Wat Gordon how to fight it upon horseback when it came to the charge. The first man that I came against was a great dragoon on a grey horse. He shouted an oath of contempt, seeing me so slender and puny. Yet, for all his bulk, I had him on the wrong side, so that he could not use his sword-arm with advantage. And as I passed on my stout little nag, I got my sword well home under his armpit and tumbled him off into the mire.

The stoutness of our charge took the enemy entirely by surprise. Indeed, afterwards they gave us all the testimony of being brave, resolute men; and, like soldiers and gentlemen as they were, they used them that were taken very civilly. I could see Cameron before me smiting and slaying, slaying and smiting, rising in his stirrup at every blow and calling on his men. It was a wild, fierce time, all too short — a happy turmoil of blows wherein I drank for the first time the heady delight of battle. All over the wild moss of Ayr that great day the swords flickered like lightning-flashes, and the lightnings darted like sword-blades. Oh, how many quiet times would I not give for such another glorious wager of battle!

Overhead all the universe roared as we fought, and I had

no thought save of the need to keep my point up — thrusting, parrying, and striking as God gave me ability.

Right in the midst of the press there came two at me from opposite sides; and I saw very well that, if I got no help, there was no more of life for me. "Richard!" I cried, and the shout must have gone to our leader's ear, though I myself could not hear it, so great was the clangour and the din.

Cameron had been smiting with the strength of ten immediately on my front. In a moment more he cleared his point, pierced his man, and turned. The man on my left swerved his horse out of his way, for Cameron came with a surge. But the other, whom I took to be Crichton, met him fair, blade to blade. The first clash of the swords was mighty. These two lowering black men met and knew each other, soon as they looked one another in the eyes.

But I could see that Cameron was ever the stronger and swifter, though Crichton had somewhat the more skill. Crichton tried to pass him a little, that he might get arm-play for his famous back-strokes, wherewith he was renowned to have cut off a man's head at a blow; but Cameron measured his guard and the blow whistled harmless past his ear. Then came the return. The preacher's sword streaked it out straight and level, and for a moment seemed to stand full mid-blade in the dragoon's side.

The next moment we too found ourselves outside their first line. We had broken our way through, and the enemy were in confusion behind us. I saw many single combats going forward, and in especial a most noble fight between David Hackstoun of Rathillet and one of his own acquaintances, by name David Ramsay, a gentleman of his country. As they fought I could hear Hackstoun, whom nothing could daunt or disturb, asking Ramsay all the news of the countryside, and how such a one did, what wife had gotten another child and whether it were a lad or a lass. Which is a thing I should never have believed if any man had told me. And when I set it down here I expect not to be believed of any, save by those who have been in the thick of a civil war themselves. But all that knew David Hackstoun of Rathillet will believe that this thing is true of him.

So he fought, clashing swords and talking at his ease, without change of countenance, till he was stricken down with three coming on him at once from behind.

Then, seeing our horsemen scattered, Cameron cried them to him, and we galloped towards their second line that came riding unbroken towards us. Now it was our misfortune that the dragoons were stark fellows and had seen service, so that they gave not back as others might have done, seeing us come on so determinedly. Rather they reserved their powder till we were almost at the sword's length. Then they fired, and I saw our men falling over in twos and threes. But Richard Cameron still rode steadily with Michael and myself behind him. His horse had once been white, but now was mostly dripping red — a fearsome sight to see. I heard afterwards from old soldiers that had been in the fights of the ancient days, that no such terrifying figure had they ever seen in the wars, since Noll led on the Ironsides at Marston Moor.

But Cameron's case was far more desperate than had ever been that of Oliver.

"Smite! Smite!" he cried, "The sword of the Lord and of Gideon!"

Over all the field there was only the whinnying of swords as they whistled through the air, and at the edges of the fray the dropping rattle of the musketry. As we touched their second line we seemed to ride in upon a breast-high wave of flame, which might have been Earlshall's flashing muskets or God's own level lightnings. I rode as best I could behind

THE LAST CHARGE AT AYRSMOSS. 169

Cameron, striking when I had opportunity and warding as I had need. But, though I was here in the forefront of the battle, I was in the safest place. For Richard Cameron ploughed a lane through their company, sending them to right and left before him as the foam is ploughed by a swift vessel.

But our desperate riders were now wearing few. I looked behind us, and only two seemed to be in the saddle — James Gray of Chryston and Michael Cameron, who had both promised to ding the stoor that day out of his Majesty's red-clouts. I could see Chryston striking, and grunting as he struck, exactly like a man hagging hard wood with a blunt axe.

So I found myself out at the side of the fight. But, just when I thought myself clear, there came a blow on my steel cap that nearly dang me out of the saddle, and I drew out further again. Cameron also had won clear; but, seeing his brother Michael hard beset, he turned rein and drave in among the smother again, raging like the lion he was. How his horse kept his feet on the moss I know not, for Cameron seemed constantly to be standing up in his stirrups, leaning forward to give his blade more play. So he rode into the midst of them, till he was brought to a stand in what seemed a ring of foes. Even there I could see his arm rise and fall, as steadily as a man that flails corn in a barn. And wherever he struck was a gap, for there a man went down. But more and more of them gathered about, threshing at him with their swords, some on horse and some on foot, like boys killing wasps at the taking of a byke.

Then when Richard Cameron saw that he could do no more, and that all the men were down that had followed him, his brother Michael also dying at his feet, he swept his sword every way about him to clear a space for a moment. Then he swung the brand over his head high in the air, casting it from him into the sky, till it seemed to enter into the dark cloud where the thunder brooded and the smoke of powder hung.

"God of battles, receive my sinful soul!" he cried.

And with that he joined his hands like a man that dives for swimming; and, unwounded, unhurt, yet fighting to the last, Richard Cameron sprang upon a hundred sword-points. Thus died the bravest man in broad Scotland, whom men called, and called well, the Lion of the Covenant.

And, even as he passed, the heavens opened, and the whole firmament seemed but one lightning-flash, so that all stood aghast at the marvellous brightness. Which occasioned the saying that God sent a chariot of fire with horses of whiteness to bring home to Him the soul of Richard Cameron. Whereof some men bear testimony that they saw; but indeed I saw nothing but a wondrous lightning-flash over the whole heaven. Then, a moment after, the thunder crashed like the breaking up of the world, and there was an end.

CHAPTER XXVI.

HIDING WITH THE HEATHER-CAT.

As for me, when I had seen this, thinking it to be enough, I put spurs to my little Galloway, and we were soon at speed over the moss-hags. My beast was well acquainted with moss running, for it had not carried me so often over the moor to Lochinvar for nothing. I heard tempestuous crying, as of men that pursued, and, strangely and suddenly, behind me the roar of battle sank into silence. Once I glanced back and saw many footmen running and horsemen rising and falling in their saddles. But, all being lost, I left the field of Ayrsmoss behind me as fast as I might, and set my horse's head over the roughest and boggiest country, keeping toward Dalmellington, for the wilderness was now to be my home. For the time I had had enough of rebellion under arms. I was not unfaithful to the cause, nor did I regret what I had done. But I judged that, for some time to come, it were better for me not to see company, for I had no pleasure in it.

Now, in further telling my tale I must put together all the incidents of my fleeing to the heather — for that being a thing at the time very frequently resorted to, it became at last a word in Scotland that "to take to the heather was to be in the way of getting grace."

Now, when I sped away to the south-east from Ayrsmoss, the folk I loved were all killed, and I had no hope or hold of any present resistance to the King. But my Galloway sheltie, being nimble on its feet, took me bravely over the moss-hags, carrying me lightly and willingly as if I had been hare-coursing on the green holms of the Ken.

As I fled I kept glancing behind me and seeing the soldiers in red clothes and flashing arms still pursuing after. I saw also our foot (that had stood off when we charged, and only fired as they saw need) scattering through the moss, and the enemy riding about the borders wherever their horses could go, firing at them. Yet I think that not many of them were hurt in the pursuit, for the moss at that place was very boss, and full of bottomless bogs, like that from which Patrick Laing drew the redoubtable persecutor Captain Crichton. This incident, indeed, bred in the breasts of the dragoons a wholesome fear of the soft boggish places, which made greatly in many instances for the preservation of the wanderers, and in especial favoured me in my present enterprise.

In a little after, two of the four dragoons that followed me, seeing another man running like to burst through the moss, turned aside and spurred their horses after him, leaving but two to follow me.

Yet after this I was harder put to it than ever, for the sun was exceedingly hot above and the moss as difficult beneath. But I kept to it, thinking that, after all, by comparison I was in none such an evil case. For, though my head ached with the steel cap upon it and my horse sweated, yet it must have been much more doleful for the heavy beasts and completely accoutred dragoons toiling in the rear. So over the broken places of the moor I went faster than they, though on the level turf they would doubtless soon have ridden me down. But then, after all, they were but riding to kill one Whig the more, while I to save my neck — which made a mighty difference in the earnestness of our intents on that day of swithering heat.

Many a time it came to me to cast myself from my beast

and run to the side, trusting to find a moss-hag where I might lie hidden up to my neck among the water with my head among the rushes. I saw many good and safe places indeed, but I remembered that my sheltie would be an advertisement to the pursuers, so I held on my way. Besides, Donald had been a good friend to me, and was the only one of our company that had ever been on the bonny holms of Earlstoun. So that I was kindly affectioned to the beast, and kept him to his work though the country was very moorish and the sun hot on my head.

Once I was very nearly taken. For as I went, not knowing the way, I came to a morass where in the midst there was a secure place, as it seemed to me. I put Donald at it, and when I reached the knoll — lo, it was only some nine or ten yards square — the bottomless swelter of shaking bogs girding it in on the further side. Donald went to the girth at the first stride on the other side, so that there was nothing for it but to dismount and pull him out.

Then up came the dragoons, riding heavily and cursing the sun and me. They rode round skirting the moss; for, seeing the evil case I was in, they dared not come nearer for fear of the same or worse. They kept, therefore, wide about me, crying, "Come out, dog, and be shot!"

Which, being but poor encouragement, I was in no wise eager to obey their summons.

But by holding on to the heather of the moss — by the kind providence of God, it was very long and tough — I managed to get Donald out of his peril. He was a biddable enough beast, and, being a little deaf, he knew not fear. For reesting and terror among horses are mostly but over-sharpness in hearing, and an imagination that they were better without. But Donald had no good hearing and no bad forebodings. So when I pulled him among the long heather, and put his head down, he lay like a scent-dog, cowered along by the side of the moss-hags. Then the pair by the edge of the morass began to shoot at me, for the distance was within reach of a pistol-ball. The first bullet that came clipped so close to my left ear that it took away a lock of my hair, which, contrary to my custom, had now grown longish.

All this time they ceased not for a moment to cry, "Come out, dog, and be shot!" They were ill-mannered rampaging lowns with little sense, and I desired no comings and goings with them. So in no long time I tired of this, and also of lying still to be shot at. I bethought me that I might show them a better of it, and afford some sport. So very carefully I charged both my pistols, and the next time they came near, riding the bog-edge to fire at me, I took careful aim and shot at the first of them. The ball went through the calf of his leg, which caused him to light off the far-side of his horse with a great roar.

"You have killed me," he cried over to me complainingly, as if he had been a good friend come to pay me a visit, to whom I had done a treachery. Then he cursed me very resentfully, because forsooth (as he said) he was about to be made a sergeant in the company, and, what with lying up with his wounded leg, some other (whom he mentioned) would get the post by favour of the captain.

"See what you have done!" said he, holding up his leg.

But I took aim with the other pistol and sent a ball singing over his head, very close.

"Trip it, my bonny lad," I cried, "or there will be a hole of the same size in your thick head — which will be as good as a cornet's commission to you in the place to which it will send you!"

Then I charged my pistols again and ordered them away. The trooper's companion made bold to leave his horse and come towards me crawling upon the moss. But I turned my pistols so straightly upon him, that he was convinced that I must be a marksman by trade and so desisted from the attempt.

All this made me proud past reasoning, and I mounted in their sight, and made a work of fastening my accoutrements and tightening Donald's girths.

"So good-day to you!" I cried to them, "and give my compliments to your captain and tell him from me that he hath a couple of varlets in his company very careful of their skins in this world — which is, maybe, as well — seeing that in the next they are secure of getting them well paid."

Now this was but the word of a silly boy, and I was sorry for taunting the men before ever I rode away. But I set it down as it happened, that all may come in its due place, nothing in this history being either altered or extenuated.

So all that night I fled and the next day also, till I came into my own country of the Glenkens, where near to Carsphairn I left Donald with a decent man that would keep him safe for my mother's sake. For the little beast was tired and done, having come so far and been ridden so hard. Yet when I left him out in the grass-park, there was not so much as the mark of a spur upon him, so willingly had he come over all the leagues of heather-lands.

While life lasts shall I not forget Donald.

My father used often to tell us what Maxwell of Monreith said when he lit off his grey horse at the stable-door and turned him out after riding him home from Rullion Green: "'Thou hast done thy day's work, Pentland. There is a park for thee to fill thy belly in for the rest of thy days. No leg shall ever cross thy back again!'"

So when I came to my own in the better days, I made it my care that Donald was not forgotten; and all his labour in the future, till death laid him low, was no more than a gentle exercise to keep him from over-eating himself on the meadow-lands of Afton.

After the great day of dule, when Cameron was put down at Ayrsmoss and I escaped in the manner I have told of, I made my way by the little ferry-port of Cree, which is a sweet and still little town, to Maryport, on the other side of the Solway, and thence in another ship for the Low Countries.

When we came within sight of the land we found that it was dismally grey, wearisome looking, and flat. The shipmen called it the Hook of Holland. But this was not thought right for the port of our destination, so we put to sea again, where we were too much tossed about for the comfort of my stomach. Indeed, every one on board of the ship felt the inconvenience; and two exceedingly pious women informed me that it interfered with their religious duties. It was upon a Thursday night, at six o'clock, that we arrived at an outlandish place called, as I think, Zurichsee, where we met with much inhumanity and uncourteousness. Indeed, unless a Scots merchant, accustomed to adventuring to the Low Countries, had been of our company, it might have gone hardly with us, for the barbarous folk had some custom of ill-treating strangers who arrive upon a day of carnival. They entered our bark and began to ill-treat us even with blows and by taking from us what of money we had. But mercifully they were restrained before I had put my sword into them, which, in their own country and engaged in ungodliness, it had been no little folly to do.

Then also it grieved us very sore that we had five soldiers who had come from Scotland with us — the very scum of the land. They called themselves Captain Somerville's band; but if, indeed, they were any soldiers of his

Majesty's, then God help their captain in his command, for such a pack of unwashed ruffians it never was my hap to see.

Specially did these men disquiet us upon the Sabbath-day. So dreadful were their oaths and curses that we feared the boat would sink because of their iniquities. They carried themselves so exceeding wickedly — but more, as I think, that we, who desired not their company, might take note of them. For at least three of them were but sullen, loutish boys, yet the others led them on, and praised them when they imitated their blasphemies and sculduddery.

At last about eight o'clock in the evening we came to Rotterdam, where we quartered with a good merchant, Mr. Donaldson, and in the morning we went to a Mr. Hay's, where from that good man (whom may God preserve) we met with inexpressible kindness.

Thence we went to Groningen, where many of the Covenant already were. To be brief — that part of my life for the present not coming into the history — I spent four years there, the most of it with a young man named James Renwick, a good student, and one very full of great intents which were to make Scotland strong against the House of Stuart. He came from Minnyhive, a village on the borders of Galloway and Dumfries, and was a very decent lad — though apt, before he learned modesty on the moors, to take too much upon him. We were finally summoned home by a letter from the United Societies, for they had made me a covenanted member of standing because of Ayrsmoss, and the carrying of the banner at Sanquhar.

While at Groningen I got a great deal of civility because of Sandy, my brother, whose name took me everywhere. But I think that, in time, I also wan some love and liking on my own account. And while I was away, I got many letters from Maisie Lennox, chiefly in the name of my

N

mother, who was not good at writing; for her father, though a lord of session, would not have his daughters taught overly much, lest it made them vain and neglectful of those things which are a woman's work, and ought to be her pleasure so long as the world lasts.

But though I went to the University, I could not bring myself to think that I had any call to the ministry. I went, therefore, for the name of it, to the study of the law, but read instead many and divers books. For the study of the law is in itself so dreary, that all other literature is but entertainment by comparison. So that, one book being easy to substitute for another, I got through a vast deal of excellent literature while I studied law at the University of Groningen. So did also, even as I, all the students of law whom I knew in Holland and elsewhere, for that is their custom.

But when at last I was called home, I received a letter from the United Societies, written in their name, from a place called Panbreck, where their meeting was held. First it told me of the sadness that was on Scotland, for the many headings, hangings, hidings, chasings, outcastings, and weary wanderings. Then the letter called me, as the branch of a worthy family, to come over and take my part, which, indeed, I was somewhat loath to do. But with the letter there came a line from Maisie Lennox, which said that they were in sore trouble at the Earlstoun, sometimes altogether dispossessed, and again for a time permitted to abide in safety. Yet for my mother's sake she asked me to think of returning, for she thought that for me the shower was surely slacked and the on-ding overpast. So I took my way to shipboard with some desire to set my foot again on the heather, and see the hills of Kells run blue against the lift of heaven, from the links of the Ken to the headend of Carsphairn.

It was the high time of the killing when I came again to

Scotland, and landed at Newcastle. I made for Galloway on foot by the tops of the Cheviots and the Border hills. Nor did I bide more than a night anywhere, and that only in herds' huts. Till I saw, from the moors above Lochinkit, the round top of the Millyea, which some ill-set people call an ugly mountain, but which is to me the fairest hill that the sun shines on. So at least it appeared, now returning from the Lowlands of Holland, where one can make the highest hill with a spade in an afternoon. Ay, for I knew that it looked on Earlstoun, where my mother was — whom I greatly desired to see, as was most natural.

Yet it was not right that I should recklessly go near Earlstoun to bring trouble on my mother without knowing how the land lay. So I came down the west side of the water of Ken, by the doachs, or roaring linn, where the salmon sulk and leap. And I looked at the house from afar till my heart filled, thinking that I should never more dwell there, nor look any more from my mother's window in the quiet hour of even, when the maids were out milking the kye.

Even as I looked I could see the glint of scarlet cloth, and the sun sparkling on shining arms, as the sentry paced from the wall-gate to the corner of the wall and back again. Once I saw him go within the well-house for a drink, and a great access of desire took me in my stomach. I remembered the coolness that was there. For the day was exceedingly hot, and I weary and weak with travel.

CHAPTER XXVII.

THE WATER OF THE WELL OF BETHLEHEM THAT IS BESIDE THE GATE.

WITH that a kind of madness came over me and took possession of my mind and body. I cannot account for or excuse it, save that the sun had stricken me unawares and moidered my head.

I remember saying over and over to myself these words, which I had often heard my father read as he took the Book, "O that one would give me to drink of the water of the Well of Bethlehem that is beside the Gate." So I rose out of the lair where I was, took off my shoes and stockings, and went down to the river-side. Ken Water is very low at that season, and looking over I could see the fish lying in the black pools with their noses up stream, waiting for a spate to run into the shallows of the burns. I declare that had my mind not been set on the well-house, I should have stripped there and then for a plunge after them. But in a trice I had crossed the river, wading to my middle in the clear warm pool. I think it was surely the only time that man ever waded Ken to get a drink of spring water.

When I reached the farther side — the nearer to my mother — I lay for a long time on the bank overcome with the water and the sun. Now I was plainly to be seen from the house, and had the sentinel so much as looked my way, I could not have escaped his notice. But no one came near me or stirred me in any way. Then at last, after a long time, I roused myself, and betook me through the thick woods which lie on the side towards the Clachan of St. John. The wood here is composed of great oaks — the finest, as all allow, in Galloway — of which that wherein my brother Sandy was afterwards often concealed, is but one. Underneath was a thick growth of hazel and birch. The whole makes cover of the densest, through which no trooper could ride, and no seeing eye pierce.

So I was here upon well-kenned ground. Every tree-stem I knew by touch of hand, and in my youth I had creeped into every hidie hole that would hold a squirrel. Times without number had Sandy and I played at hide-and-seek in the woods. And there, at the back of one of the great trees, was where we had fought because he had called me "puny crowl." Whereat I bit him in the thumb till it bled grievously, to teach him not to call names, and also (more generally) for the health of his soul.

Now lying here in the Earlstoun wood, all this came back to me, and it seemed that Sandy and I were again playing at hiding. Nearly had I cried out the seeking signal; aye, and would have done it, too, but for the little rattle of arms when the sentry turned sharp at the corner of the house, with a click of his heels and a jingle of his spurs. The house of Earlstoun stands very near the water edge, with nothing about it save the green hawthorn-studded croft on the one hand, and the thick wood on the other.

I lay a long while watching the house to see if I could discover any one at the windows. But not even a lounging soldier could I discern anywhere, except the single clinking loon who kept the guard. Once Jean Hamilton, Sandy's wife, came to the window; and once her little daughter, Alison, shook a tablecloth over the sash — a sight which cheered me greatly, for by it I knew that there was still folk could eat a meal of meat within the towers of Earlstoun.

But more and more the desire for the sweet well water of

the gateway tower, came to me as I lay parched with thirst, and more than the former yearning for home things. It seemed that no wine of sunny France, no golden juice of Zeres could ever be one-half so sweet as the water of that Earlstoun well, "that is beside the Gate."

Aye, and I declare I would have grappled with the sentry for it, save that I had the remnants of some sense left about me, which told me that so I should not only bring destruction upon myself, but on others that were even more dear to me.

Presently I heard the voice of a serving lass calling from within the courtyard, and at the sound the sentry listened and waited. He looked furtively this way and that round the corners. He stood a moment in the shade of the archways and wiped his brow. Then he leaned his musket against the wall and went within. I thought to myself, "It is now or never, for he is gone to the kitchen for a bite-and-sup, and will be out again in a moment, lest his captain should return and find him gone from his post."

So with that I made a rush swiftly round the corner, and entered the well-house. For a moment only, as I ran fleet-foot, was I bathed in the hot sunshine, then drenched again in the damp, cool darkness of the tower. Within there is an iron handle and chain, which are used to wrap up the great dipper over the windlass. There is also a little dipper which one may let down by a rope, when only a drink or a little household water is needed, and there is no servitor at hand to turn the crank. This last I let down, and in a moment after I was draining icy nectar from the cup, for which I had risked so much. Yet all I could do when I got it, was only to sip a little, and let the rest run back again into the well. While like the refrain of a weary song, over and over the words ran in his mind, "O that one would give me — of the water of the Well of Bethlehem — that is beside the Gate."

Then, like a far-away voice calling one out of a dream, I heard the sound of the sentry returning to his post. Quite clearly I discerned him lifting his musket, shifting it from one side to the other, and so resuming his equal tramp. I heard everything, indeed, with a kind of acuteness beyond the natural. Yet all the while I was strangely without sense of danger. I thought how excellent a jest it would be, to shout out suddenly when the soldier came near, to see him jump; and but for the remembrance of my mother, I protest I had done it.

So there I lay on the margin of the well, just as at the first I had flung myself down, without so much as troubling thoroughly to shut the door. I am sure that from the corner where the sentry turned, he might have seen my boot-heel every time, had he but troubled to peep round the door. But he had been so often within the well-house during his time on guard, that he never once glanced my way. Also he was evidently elevated by what he had gotten within the house from the serving maid, whatever that might have been.

It was strange to hear his step alternately faint and loud as he came and went. He paced from the well-house to the great gate, and from thence to the corner of the tower. Back again he came, to-and-fro like the pendulum of a clock. Once he took the butt of his musket and gave the door, within which I lay, a sharp fling to. Luckily it opened from without, so that the hasp caught as it came and I was shut within.

So there I lay without power to move all that day, and no one came near me till late in the gloaming. For it was the custom at the Earlstoun to draw the water for the day in the early morning, and that for the night uses when the horses were suppered at bed-time. Sometimes my head seemed to swell to so great a size, that it filled the well-house and was pressed against the roof. Anon, to my thinking, it grew wizzened and small, waxing and waning as I sickened and the shoots of pain ran round my brows.

At last I heard feet patter slowly down the turret stair and out at the door. Through the courtyard I heard them come towards me, and of a sudden something sang in my heart, though I could have given no great reason therefor.

Softly the door of the well-house opened, and one came in, giving a little cry at so nearly stumbling over me. But no power had I to move or speak, even though it had been Clavers himself who entered. My visitor gently and lightly shut to the door, and knelt at my head.

"William!" said a voice, and I seemed in my phantasy to be running about among the flowers as a child again.

I opened my eyes, and lo! it was Maisie of the Duchrae —she that had been so kind to me. And the wonder of seeing her in my own house of Earlstoun, where the garrison was abiding, was a better incitement to renewed vigour than a double tasse of the brandy of France.

But there was no time for speech, so pulling me farther within, she bent and whispered:

"William, I will go and bring your mother. The soldiers may not be long away!"

So she rose to go out with her pail full of the water, for which she had come.

Yet ere she went, she laid her hand upon my brow, and murmured very low, lest the sentry should hear,

"My poor lad!"

Only that; but it was a thing which was mightily sweet to me.

Nor was she long gone before she returned with my mother. They had called the sentry in to his evening meal, and supplied him with something to drink. For they had had the garrison long enough with them to learn that all soldiers are great trenchermen, and can right nobly " claw a bicker " and " toom a stoup " with any man.

CHAPTER XXVIII.

THE WELL-HOUSE OF EARLSTOUN.

So as soon as the soldier was snugly housed with the servant lass, the two women came to me, where I sat at the back of the door of the well-house. Chiefly I wanted to hear what had brought Maisie of the Duchrae so far from home as the house of Earlstoun. It seemed to betoken some ill befallen my good friends by the Grenoch water-side. But my mother stooped down and put her arms about me. She declared that she would have me taken up to the west garret under the rigging, where, she said, none of the soldiers had ever been. But there I would in no wise go, for well I knew that so soon as she had me there, and a dozen soldiers between me and a dash for liberty, she would forthwith never rest until she had me out again.

Then the next idea was that I should go to the wattled platform on the oak, to which Sandy resorted; but I had fallen into a violent horror of shaking and hot flushes alternating with deadly cold, so that to bide night and day in the sole covert of a tree looked like my death.

At last Maisie Lennox, who had a fine discernment for places of concealment in the old days when we two used to play at "Bogle-about-the-Stacks" at the Duchrae, cast an eye up at the roof of the well-house.

"I declare, I think there is a chamber up there," she said, and stood a moment considering.

"Give me an ease up!" she said quietly to my mother. She did everything quietly.

"How can there be such a place and I not know it?" said my mother. "Have I not been about the tower these thirty years?"

But Maisie thought otherwise of the matter, and without more ado she set her little feet in the nicks of the stones, which were rough-set like the inside of a chimney.

Then putting her palm flat above her, she pushed an iron-ringed trap-door open, lifted herself level with it, and so disappeared from our view. We could hear her groping above us, and sometimes little stones and lime pellets fell tinkling into the well. So we remained beneath waiting for her report, and I hoped that it might not be long, for I felt that soon I must lay me down and die, so terrible was the tightness about my head.

"There is a chamber here," she cried at last. "It is low in the rigging and part of the roof is broken towards the trees, but the ivy hides it and the hole cannot be seen from the house."

"The very place! Well done, young lass!" said my mother — much pleased, even though she had not found it herself. For she was a remarkable woman.

Maisie looked over the edge.

"Give me your hand?" she said.

Now there is this curious thing about this lass ever since she was in short coats, that she not only knew her own mind in every emergency, but also compelled the minds of every one else. At that moment it seemed as natural that I should obey her, and also for my mother to assist her, as if she had been a queen commanding obedience. Yet she hardly ever spoke above her breath, and always rather as though she were venturing a suggestion. This is not what any one can ever learn. It is a natural gift. Now there is my brother Sandy. He has a commanding way with him certainly. He gets himself obeyed. But at what an expenditure of breath. You can hear him at the Mains of Barskeoch telling the lass to put on the porridge pot. And he cannot get his feet wet and be needing a change of stockings, without the Ardoch folk over the hill hearing all about it.

But I am telling of the well-house.

"Give me your hand," said the lass Maisie down from the trap-door. It is a strange thing that I never dreamed of disobeying. So I put out my hand, and in a trice I was up beside her.

My mother followed us and we looked about. It was a little room and had long been given over to the birds. I marvelled much that in our adventurous youth, Sandy and I had never lighted upon it. But I knew the reason to be that we had a wholesome dread of the well, having been told a story about a little boy who tumbled into it in the act of disobedience and so was drowned. We heard also what had become of him afterwards, which discouraged us from the forbidden task of exploration.

I think no one had been in the place since the joiners left it, for the shavings yet lay in the corner, among all that the birds and the wild bees had brought to it since.

My mother stayed beside me while Maisie went to bring me a hot drink, for the shuddering grew upon me, and I began to have fierce pains in my back and legs. My mother told me how that the main guard of the soldiers had been a week away over in the direction of Minnyhive, all but a sergeant's file that were left to keep the castle. To-day all these men, except the sentry, were down drinking at the change-house in the clachan, and not till about midnight would they come roaring home.

She also told me (which I much yearned to know), that the Duchrae had at last been turned out, and that old Anton had betaken himself to the hills. Maisie, his daughter,

THE WELL-HOUSE OF EARLSTOUN. 189

had come to the neighbourhood with Margaret Wilson of Glen Vernock, the bright little lass from the Shireside whom I had first seen during my sojourn in Balmaghie. Margaret Wilson had friends over at the farm of Bogue on the Garpelside. Very kind to the hill-folk they were, though in good enough repute with the Government up till this present time. From there Maisie Lennox had come up to Earlstoun, to tell my mother all that she knew of myself and my cousin Wat. Then, because the two women loved to talk the one to the other, at Earlstoun she abode ever since, and there I found her.

So in the well-house I remained day by day in safety all through my sickness.

The chamber over the well was a fine place for prayer and meditation. At first I thought that each turn of the sentry would surely bring him up the trap-door with sword and musket pointed at me, and I had little comfort in my lodging. But gradually, by my falling to the praying and by the action of time and use, I minded the comings and goings of the soldiers no more than those of the doves that came in to see me at the broken part of the roof, and went out again with a wild flutter of their wings, leaving a little woolly feather or two floating behind them.

And often as I lay I minded me how I had heard Mr. Peden say at the Conventicle that "the prayers of the saints are like to a fire which at first gives off only smoke and heat, but or all be done breaketh out into a clear light and comfortable flame."

These were times of great peace for us, when the soldiers and the young lairds that rode with them for the horsemanship part of it, went off on their excursions, and came not back till late at eventide, with many of the Glenkens wives' chuckies swinging head down at their saddle bows.

CHAPTER XXIX.

CUPBOARD LOVE.

The well-house was indeed a strait place, but my mother had gotten one of our retainers to put therein a little truckle bedstead and bedding, so that I was none so evilly bestowed. This man, whom she had perforce to trust, was not one of our ancients, but only a stranger that had recently come into the country and taken service with us. He had been a soldier and had even served in His Majesty's Guards. But, being a Covenanter at heart, he had left the service at the peril of his life and come again to the north. His name was Patrick Laing, and he came of decent folk over about Nithsdale. He was in high favour with the garrison because of his feats of strength; but he had to keep carefully out of the sight of Tam Dalzyell, Grier of Lag, and the old officers who remembered him in the days when he had been a sergeant with the King's colours. Also he was the only man that could keep steeks with John Scarlet at the sword play, and I longed rarely to see him try a bout with Wat of Lochinvar himself.

Often at night I had converse with him, when the soldiers were not returned and it was safe for him to come to see me. Here I lay long prostrate with the low fever or ague that had taken me after Ayrsmoss. But because I was in my own country and within cry of my mother and Maisie Lennox, I minded my imprisonment not so much as one might think.

My mother came not often, for she was closely watched in her incomings and outgoings. But every eventide Maisie

Lennox brought me what she could lay hands upon for my support.

As I grew whole we had much merriment, when she told me of the straits she was often in to get slipping away, without betraying the object of her solicitude.

The two eldest of my brother Sandy's bairns were a boy of seven and a girl of eight, and in a house where the soldiers took the most and the best, there was sometimes but scant fare for the younger folk.

Now none of the serving folk or even of the family knew that I was in the neighbourhood, saving only my mother, Maisie of the Duchrae, and Patrick Laing. To tell more people was to risk a discovery, which meant not less than a stretched tow rope for my neck, and that speedily.

Of all Sandy's bairns little Jock was the merriest and the worst, and of him Maisie had many stories to tell me, making merry when she brought me my piece in the twilight.

"You are getting me a terrible name for a great eater," she said. "It was but this day at dinner time that Jock cried out, 'Whatna daft-like chuckie hen! It's gotten twa wings but only ae leg!' For I had hidden the other on my lap for you. That caused much merriment, for we all laughed to think of a chuckie hopping and standing upon but one leg. Yet because Cornet Graham was there, we had all to laugh somewhat carefully, and pass the matter off with a jest."

"On another occasion," said Maisie, "when half a dozen eggs could not be found, little Jock cried out, 'The ae-legged chuckie wull be clockin' them!' And this caused more merriment."

Such tales as these Maisie Lennox told me in the quiet of the gloaming, when I abode still in the well-house chamber, and only the drip, drip of the water at the bottom came to us. It was strange and pleasant for me to lie there and hear her kind low voice telling me humoursome tales of what had befallen during the day.

Jean Hamilton, Sandy's wife, came but once to see me, and gave me much religious advice. She was ever a great woman for experiences, being by nature one of those who insist that all shall be exactly of her pattern, a thing which I saw no hope of — nor yet greatly desired.

"My life is all sin," she would say, "if it were but to peel the bark off a kail castock and eat, I sin in the doing of it!"

"That would show a great want of sense, at any gate, gin ye could get better meat to eat!" I replied, for the woman's *yatter, yatter* easily vexed me, being still weak. Also, I wished greatly for her to be gone, and for Maisie or my mother to come to me.

And again I remember that she said (for she was a good woman, but of the troublesome kind that ofttimes do more ill than good — at least when one is tired and cannot escape them), "William, I fear you never have had the grip o' the fundamentals that Sandy hath. Take care that you suffer not with the saints, and yet come to your end as a man of wrath!"

Now this I thought to be an ill-timed saying, considering that I had ridden at Ayrsmoss while Sandy was braw and snug in the Lowlands of Holland, disputing in Master Brackel's chamber at Leeuwarden with Rob Hamilton, her brother, concerning declarations and protests.

"As for me," she went on, liking methinks the sound of her own voice, "that is, for my corps, I care not gin it were cast up to the heaven, and keppit upon iron graips, so that my soul had peace!"

"I think that I would even be content to lie at the

bottom of this well if I might have peace!" said I, for the spirit within me was jangled and easily set on edge with her corncrake crying.

"William, William," she said, "I fear greatly you are yet in the bond of iniquity! I do but waste my time with you!"

Saying which, she let herself down on the well-edge, lifted her pails and was gone.

In a little came Maisie Lennox with other two buckets. The sentinel, if he thought at all, must have set us down for wondrous clean folk about Earlstoun during these days; but all passed off easily and no notice taken.

Then when Maisie came, it was a joy to greet her, for she was as a friend — yes, as David to Jonathan — exceeding pleasant to me. As I have often said, I am not a man to take the eyes of women, and never looked to be loved by woman other than my mother. But for all that, I liked to think about love, and to picture what manner of man he should be to whom Maisie Lennox would let all her heart go out.

Every night she came in briskly, laughing at having to pull herself up into the well-chamber, and ever with some new story of cheer to tell me.

"Ken ye what little Jock said this day?" she asked ere her head was well above the trap-door.

I told her that I knew not, but was eager to hear, for that I ever counted Jock the best bairn in all the coupe.

"It was at dinner," she said, taking a dish from under her apron, "and I minded that when you were with us at the Duchrae, you kept a continual crying for burn-trout. These being served for a first course, I watched for a time when the servants were taken up at the chamber-end with their serving, and when the bairns were busy with their noses at their plates.

o

"Then, when none observed, I whipped the most part of the dainty platterful of fish underneath my apron and sat very still and innocent, picking at the bones on my plate.

"Soon little Jock looked up. 'O mither, mither!' he cried, 'wull ye please to look at Aunty Maisie, she has eaten the hale kane o' trootses, banes, plate an' a', while we were suppin' our broth.'

"At this there was great wonderment, and all the children came about, expecting to see me come to some hurt by so mighty a meal.

"'Tell me,' cried Jock, being ever the foremost, 'how far doon the platter has gotten. Are ye sure it is not sticking somewhere by the road?'

"All the time I sat with the half score of burn-trout on my lap covered by my apron, and it was only by pretending I had burned myself, that I got them at last safe out of the room."

With such tales she pleased me, winning my heart all the while, causing me to forget my weakness, and to think the nights not long when I lay awake listening to the piets and hoolets crying about me in the ancient woods of Earlstoun.

CHAPTER XXX.

THE BULL OF EARLSTOUN'S HOMECOMING.

It was about this time that Sandy came home. It may seem from some parts of this history that we agreed not over well together. But after all it was as brothers may disagree among themselves; though they are banded stoutly enough against all the world beside. I think it made us love one another more that recently we had been mostly separate; and so when Sandy came home this time and took up his old lodging in the tree, it was certainly much heartsomer at the Earlstoun. For among other things our mother mostly went to carry him his meals of meat, taking with her Jean Hamilton, Sandy's wife, thus leaving only Maisie Lennox to bring me my portion to the well-house.

But often in the gloaming Sandy himself came climbing up by the ivy on the outside of the well-tower, letting his great body down through the narrow broken lattice in the tiles. And in that narrow chamber we cheered one another with talk. This I liked well enough, so long as he spoke of Groningen and the Low Countries. But not so well when he began to deafen me with his bickerings about the United Societies — how there was one, Patrick Laing, a man of fierce and determined nature, that could not company with other than himself; how Mr. Linning wrestled with the other malcontents, and especially how he himself was of so great honour and consideration among them, that they had put off even so grave a matter as a General Meeting that he might have time to come from Edinburgh to attend it. And in what manner, at the peril of his life, he did it.

One night, while he was in the midst of his recital, the mighty voice of him sounding out upon the night brought the sentry from his corner — who listened, but could not understand whence came the sounds. Presently the soldier called his comrade, and the pair of them stole to the door of the well-house, where I had lain so long in safety. Sandy was in the heat of his discourse, and I sitting against the chamber wall in my knee-breeches, and with a plaid about me, listening at my ease. For long immunity had made us both careless.

"At Darmead, that well-kenned place, we had it," Sandy was saying, his long limbs extended half-way across the floor as he lay on the bare boards, and told his story; "it was a day of glorious witnessing and contesting. No two of us thought the same thing. Each had his own say-away and his own reasons, and never a minister to override us. Indeed, since Ritchie lay down at length on Ayrsmoss to rest him, there is no minister that could. But I hear of a young man, Renwick, that is now with Mr. Brackel of Leeuwarden, that will scare some of the ill-conditioned when he comes across the water —— "

Even as he spoke thus, and blattered with the broad of his hand on his knee, the trap-door in the floor slowly lifted up. And through the aperture came the head of a soldier — even that of the sentry of the night, with whose footfalls I had grown so familiar, that I minded them no more than the ticking of the watch in your pocket or the beating of your heart in the daytime.

The man seemed even more surprised than we, and for a long moment he abode still, looking at Sandy reclining on the floor. And Sandy looked back at him with his jaw dropped and his mouth open. I could have laughed at another time, for they were both great red men with beards of that colour, and their faces were very near one another, like those of the yokels that grin at each other emulously out of the horse collars on the turbulent day of the Clachan Fair — which is on the eve of St. John, in the time of midsummer.

Then suddenly Sandy snatched an unlighted lantern, and brought it down on the soldier's head, which went through the trap-door like Jack-out-of-the-box being shut down again.

"Tak' the skylight for it, William," Sandy cried. "I'll e'en gang doon an' see what this loon wants!"

So snatching a sword that lay upon the boards by his side, Sandy went down the trap after his man. I heard him fall mightily upon the two soldiers to whom had been committed the keeping of the house that night. In that narrow place he gripped them both with the first claucht of his great arms, and dadded their heads together, exhorting them all the time to repent and think on their evil ways.

"Wad ye, then, vermin," he cried as one and another tried to get at him with their weapons round the narrow edge of the well-curb; and I heard one after another of their tools clatter down the masonry of the well, and plump into the water at the bottom. The men were in their heavy marching gear, being ready at all times for the coming of Clavers, who was a great man for discipline, and very particular that the soldiers should always be properly equipped whenever it might please him to arrive. And because he loved night marches and sudden surprises, the men took great pains with their accoutrement.

"Can I help ye, Sandy?" I cried down through the hole.

"Bide ye whaur ye are, man. I can manage the hullions

fine! Wad ye, then? Stan' up there back to back, or I'll gie ye anither daud on the kerb that may leave some o' your harns * stickin' to it. Noo, I'll put the rape roon ye, an' ease ye doon to a braw and caller spot!"

I looked down the trap and saw Sandy roving the spare coil of well-rope round and round his two prisoners. He had their hands close to their sides, and whenever one of them opened his mouth, Sandy gave his head a knock with his open hand that drave him silent again, clapping his teeth together like castanets from Spain.

As soon as he had this completed to his satisfaction, he lifted the bucket from the hook, and began to lower the men down the shaft, slinging them to the rope by the bellybands of His Majesty's regimental breeches.

The men cried out to ask if he meant to drown them.

"Na, na, droon nane," said Sandy. "There's but three feet o' water in the well. Ye'll be fine and caller doon there a' nicht, but gin ye as muckle as gie a cry afore the morrow's sunrise — weel, ye hae heard o' Sandy Gordon o' the Earlstoun!"

And this, indeed, feared the men greatly, for he was celebrated for his strength and daring all athwart the country; and especially among soldiers and common people, who, as is well known, are never done talking about feats of strength.

This being completed, he brought me down from my loft and took me into the house to bid the women folk farewell. They cried out with terror when he told them what he had done as a noble jest, and how he had bound the soldiers and put them in the well-bottom. But my mother said sadly, "It is the beginning of the end! O Sandy, why could you not have been content with scaring them?"

"It was our lives or theirs, mither," said Sandy. "Had

* Brains.

they gotten room to put steel into me, your first-born son wad hae been at the well-bottom, wi' his heid doon an' his mooth open, and your second dangling in a hempen collar in the Grass Market. The eggs are all in one basket now, mither!"

"Haste ye away!" cried she, "lest the soldiers break lowse and come and find ye here!"

"They hae somewhat better sense than to break lowse this nicht," said Sandy, grimly smiling. "I'm gaun nane to tak' the heather withoot my supper."

So he sat him down on the settle like a man at ease and well content.

"Jean, fetch the plates," he said to his wife; "it's graund to be hungry an' ken o' meat!"

Maisie Lennox stood quietly by; but I could see that she liked not the turn of affairs, nor the reckless way that Sandy had of driving all things before him.

"Haste ye, young lass," he said to her, and at the word she went quietly to help Jean Hamilton.

"Whither gang ye?" our mother said to us, as we made us ready to flee. "Mind and be canny wi' that laddie, Sandy, for he has been ill and needs care and tendance to this day."

And it pleased me to see that Maisie Lennox looked pale and anxious when she came near me. But no word spoke she.

"Na, mither. I'll no tell ye whaur we gang, for ye micht be put to the question, and now ye can say ye dinna ken wi' a guid conscience."

I got a word with Maisie at the stair foot as she went up to bring some plaid or kerchief down, which our mother insisted I should take with me.

"Maisie," I said, " ye'll no forget me, will ye?"

But she would give me no great present satisfaction.

"There are so many gay things in my life to gar me forget a friend!" was all she said; but she looked down and pulled at her apron.

"Nay, but tell me, my lassie, will ye think every day o' the lad ye nursed in the well-house chamber?"

"Your mother is crying on me," she said; "let me go, William" (though indeed I was not touching her).

I was turning away disappointed with no word more, but very suddenly she snatched my hand which had fallen to my side, pressed it a moment to her breast, and then fled upstairs like a young roe.

So, laden with wrappings, Sandy and I took our way over the moor, making our path through our own oakwood, which is the largest in Galloway, and out by Blawquhairn and Gordiestoun upon the moor of Bogue — a wet and marshy place, save in the height of the dry season. Sandy was for going towards a hold that he had near the lonely, windswept loch of Knockman, which lies near the top of a hill of heather and bent. But as we came to the breast of the Windy Brae, I felt my weakness, and a cold sweat began to drip from me.

"Sandy," I said to my brother, taking him by the hand lest he should go too fast for me, "I fear I shall be but a trouble to you. Leave me, I pray you, at Gordiestoun to take my chance, and hie you to the heather. It'll maybe no be a hanging matter wi' me at ony gate."

"Hear till him," said Sandy, "leave him! I'll leave the laddie nane. The man doesna breathe that Sanquhar and Ayrsmoss are no eneuch to draw the thrapple o', were it my Lord Chancellor himsel'!"

He bent and took me on his back. "There na, is that comfortable?" he said; and away he strode with me as though he had been a giant.

"Man, ye need mony a bow o' meal to your ribs," he

cried, making light of the load. "Ye are no heavier than a lamb in the poke-neuk o' a plaid."

I think he was sorry for stirring me from the well-chamber, and the thought of his kindness made me like him better than I had manned to do for some time.

And indeed my weight seemed no more to him, than that of a motherless suckling to a shepherd on the hill, when he steps homeward at the close of the day. It is a great thing to be strong. If only Sandy had possessed the knack of gentleness with it, he would have been a great man. As it was, he was only the Bull of Earlstoun.

We kept in our flight over the benty fell towards Milnmark, but holding more down to the right towards the Garpel burn where there are many dens and fastnesses, and where the Covenant folk had often companied together.

I was afraid to think what should come to my sickness, when the cold shelves of the rock by the Dass of the Holy Linn would be my bed, instead of the comfortable blankets of the well-house. And, truth to tell, I was not thanking my brother for his heedlessness in compelling the exchange, when I felt him stumble down the steep bank of the Garpel and stride across, the water dashing about his legs as he waded through — taking, as was his wont, no thought of an easy way or of keeping of himself dry, but just going on ram-stam till he had won clear.

CHAPTER XXXI.

JEAN'S WA'S.

THEN on the other side he brushed through a little wood of oak and hazel. I felt the twigs rough in my face. Climbing a steep brae, Sandy set me down at the end of a house with some bits of offices about it, and a pleasant homely smell of cows and pasturage. Saving these, there were none of the other signs of a farm-town, but rather a brisk cleanliness and well-ordered neatness.

Sandy went to the door and knocked, and in a little while one answered at the southmost of the windows. Then a whispered word was given and taken. The door was opened and we went into the dark house. A sweet-faced old lady who stood in the narrow passage, gowned even at that time of night with some precision, took me by the arm. She held a candle aloft in her hand.

"Come awa', laddie," she said. "Ye shallna try the unkindly dasses o' the Linn yet awhile, nor yet lie in 'Duncan's Pantry,' which has small store of victual in it. But ye shall bide this nicht wi' Jean Gordon o' the Shirmers, that has still some spunk in her yet, though folk say that she died o' love thirty years syne. Hoot, silly clavers, Jean Gordon could hae gotten a man ony time, had she been wantin' yin."

We were indeed at Jean Gordon's famous cot by the side of the bonny Garpel burn. And it was not long till she had me cosy in bed, and Sandy, to whom all weathers and lodgings were alike, away to his hiding in the Cleuch beneath, where some of his society men were that night holding a meeting for prayer.

The cottage sat bonnily on the brink of a glen, and almost from my very window began the steep and precipitous descent. So that if the alarm were suddenly given, there was at least a chance of flinging myself out of the window and dropping into the tangled sides of the Linn of Garpel. The thought of the comfort in Jean's cot made me the more willing to take the risk. For I knew well that if I had to venture the damps and chills of the glen without any shelter after my illness, it would fare but poorly with me. So all that night I lay and listened to the murmur of the water beneath, dashing about the great upstanding rocks in the channel.

But other sound there was none, and to this sweet sequestered spot came none to seek us.

Here in the fastnesses of the Garpel, Sandy and I abode many days. And though the glen was searched, and patrol parties more than once came our way, not one of them approached near the fastness of thickets where in the daytime we were hidden. And each night, in all safety, I betook me to the cottage of Jean Gordon.

Jean's story had been a sad one, but she made little of it now, though it was well known to all the country-side.

"The Lord has taken away the stang of pain out of my life," she said. "I was but a lass when I came to the Garpel thinking my heart broken. Yince I loved a braw lad, bonny to look upon — and he loved me, or I was the more deceived. Lindsay was his name. Doubtless ye have heard the common tale. He slighted my love and left me without a word. Waes me, but the very lift turned black when I heard it, and I cried out on the liars that said the like. But belief came slowly to me. The loch is very near to the Shirmers where I dwelt, and the tower window looks down into the black deeps from among the ivy bushes on the wall. My thoughts ofttimes turned on the short and easy road to peace. But praise be to His marvellous name, I saw another way. So I biggit me this bit house on the bonny birk-grown sides o' the Garpel, and e'en came my ways to bide here.

"'Ye'll sune get a man, for ye're bonny! Never fash your thumb for Lindsay!' said my kin."

"'I'll get nae man,' I threepit to them. 'What one slighted shall never be given to another.' So forty year have I bidden here, and heard little but the mavis sing and the cushie complain. Think weel o' yoursel', Willie, lad, for ye are the first man body that has ever bidden the nicht within Jean's Wa's. Sandy, great as he thinks himsel', can tak' the Linn side for it. He is weather-seasoned like the red tod o' the hills; but ye are shilpit and silly, boy William, so ye had best bide wi' auld Jean when ye can. There's few in Gallowa' daur meddle wi' puir Jean, for she is kin to John Graham o' Claverhouse himsel', and even the erne's cousin is no a canny bird to meddle wi'."

So again I had fallen on my feet, as has mostly been my fortune with women. Though, alas, that I should have to confess it, chiefly because of my weakness, and with the elder sort of them.

Here after a day or two, there came to Jean Gordon, my hostess of the night season, a letter from Sandy's wife, Jean Hamilton, with sad news of them at Earlstoun. It was intended for my brother, but according to the custom of these days, it was not so addressed, for the transmission of such letters was too dangerous at that time.

"Dear Mistress" (so it ran), "your letter did yield great satisfaction to me, and now I have good words to tell you. The Lord is doing great things for me. Colvin and

Clavers (Cornel) have put us out of all that we have, so that we know not where to go.

"I am for the present in a cot house. Oh, blessed cottage! As soon as my enemies began to roar against me, so quickly came my kind Lord to me and did take my part. He made the enemies to favour me, and He gave me kindly welcome to this cottage.

"Well may I say that His yoke is easy and His burden light.

"Dear Mistress Jean, praise God on my behalf, and cause all that love Him to praise Him on my behalf. I fear that I miscarry under His kind hand.

"Colvin is reigning here like a prince, getting 'his honour' at every word. But he hath not been rude to me. He gave me leave to take out all that I had. What matters suffering after all! But, oh! the sad fallings away of some! I cannot give a full account of them.

"I have nothing to write on but a stone by the water-side, and know not how soon the enemy may be upon me. I entreat you to send me your advice what to do. The enemy said to me that I should not get to stay in Galloway gif I went not to their kirk.

"They said I should not even stay in Scotland, for they would pursue me to the far end of it, but I should be forced to go to their church. The persecution is great. There are many families that are going to leave their houses and go out of the land. Gif you have not sent my former letter, let it not now go, but send this as quickly as you can. I fear our friends will be much concerned. I have written that Alexander may not venture to come home. I entreat that you will write that to him and close mine within yours. I have not backed his. Send me all your news. Remember me to all friends. I desire to be reminded to them.

"I rest, in haste, your loving friend and servant,

"JEAN HAMILTON."

Now, I declare that this letter made me think better than ever before of Sandy's wife, for I am not gifted with appropriate and religious reflections in the writing of letters myself. But very greatly do I admire the accomplishment. Jean was in time of peace greatly closed up within herself; but in time of extrusion and suffering, her narrow heart expanded. Notwithstanding the strange writing-desk of stone by the water-side, the letter was well written, but the great number of words which had been blurred and corrected as to their spelling, revealed the turmoil and anxiety of the writer. I have kept it before me as I write this history, so that I might give it exactly.

Thus we learned that Sandy's side of the house was safe; but what of our mother and Maisie Lennox?

"Jean says nothing," said Sandy, when I told him. "Good news is no news!"

And truly this is an easy thing for him to say, who has heard news about his own. Jean Gordon sent over to her sister's son at Barscobe for word, but could hear nothing save that the Earlstoun ladies had been put out of their house without insult or injury, and had gone away no man knew whither. So with this in the meantime we were obliged to rest as content as we might.

CHAPTER XXXII.

PLAIN WORDS UPON MEN.

"HEIGHTY-TEIGHTY," said Jean Gordon, of the Shirmers, coming in to me with a breakfast piece one morning as soon as she heard that I was awake. "The silly folks keep on bletherin' that I cam' awa' here to dee for love. Weel, I hae leeved forty year in Jean's cot o' the Garpel and I'm no dead yet. I wat no! I cam' here to be oot o' the men's road. Noo, there's my sister ower by at Barscobe. She was muckle the better o' a man, was she no? Never sure whether he wad come hame sober and weel conditioned frae kirk or market. In the fear o' her life every time that she heard the soond o' his voice roarin' in the yaird, to ken what was crossin' him, and in what fettle the wee barn-door Almichty wad be pleased to come ben-the-hoose in! Wadna the like o' that be a bonny exchange for the peace and quaitness o' the Garpel side?"

And the old lady shook the white trimmings of her cap, which was daintily and fairly goffered at the edges. "Na, na," she said, "yince bitten, twice shy. I hae had eneuch o' men — nesty, saucy, ill-favoured characters. Wi' half a nose on ye, ye can tell as easy gin yin o' them be in the hoose, as gin he hed been a tod!"

"And am I not a man, Aunty Jean?" I asked, for indeed she had been very kind to me.

"Hoot, a laddie like you is no a man. Nae beard like bristles, nae luntin' stinkin' pipes an' a skin like my lady's — that's no a man. By my silk hose and shoe strings, gin I get as muckle as the wind o' a man body atween me and the

Bogue road, I steek baith the inner and the outer doors to keep awa' the waff o' the brock. Foul fa' them every yin!"

This made me laugh, indeed; but after all it did not please me greatly to hear that I was taken for less than a man.

"Now there's Sandy," she went on, for she ever loved to talk, "he's a great senseless sturdy o' a craitur. Yet he could get a' the wives he wants, by just coming doon like a tod aff the hill, and takin' yin below his oxter. An' the puir bit bleatin' hizzie wad think she likit it. Lord! some folk tak' a man as they tak' a farm, by the acre. But no me — no me. Na! Gin I was thinkin' o' men, the bonny ticht lad is the lad for me; the lad wi' the cockade set in his bonnet an' a leg weel shapit; neither bowed out frae the knees like haystack props, nor yet bent in like a cooper ridin' on the riggin' o' a barrel."

"But what for did ye no tak' yin then?" I said, speaking through the door of the spence as she moved about the house, ordering the porridge-making and keeping an eye on the hen's meat as well.

It eased my heavy thought, to hear the heartsome clip of her tongue — for all the world like a tailor's shears, brisker when it comes to the selvage. So when Jean Gordon got in sight of the end of her sentence, she snipped out her words with a glibness beyond any Gordon that ever I heard of. For the Gordons are, according to proverb, slow people with their tongues, save as they say by two and two at the canny hour of e'en.

But never slow at morn or mirk was our Aunt Jean of Wa's by the Garpel burn.

"It's a strange thing," she said, looking through the hall door at me, "that you an' me can crack like twa wives that hae gotten their men out o' the hearin'. My lad, I fear ye will creep into women's hearts because ye make them vexed for ye. Ye hae sic innocent ways. Oh, I doot na but it's the guile o' ye; but it was ever sae.

"Mony a mewlin', peuterin' body has great success wi' the weemen folk. They think it's a peety that he should be so innocent, an' they tak' haud o' the craitur, juist to keep off the ither designin' weeman. Oh, I'm far frae denyin' that we are a pack o' silly craiturs. A'thing that wears willy-coats; no yin muckle to better anither!"

"But aboot yoursel', Aunty Jean?" I ventured, in order to stir her to reckless speech, which was like fox-hunting to me.

"Wha? Me? Certes, no! I gat the stoor oot o' my e'en braw an' early. I took the cure-all betimes, as the lairds tak' their mornin' o' French brandy. When Tam Lindsay gaed aff wi' his fleein' flagarie o' a muckle-tochered Crawford lass, *I* vowed that I wad hae dune wi' men. An' so I had!

"Whenever a loon cam' here in his best breeks, and a hingin' look in the e'e o' the craitur that meant courtin', faith, I juist set the dowgs on the scullion. I keepit a fearsome tyke on purpose, wi' a jaw ontill him like Jonah's whale. Aye, aye, mony's the braw lad that has gane doon that brae, wi' Auld Noll ruggin' an' reevin' at the hinderlands o' him — bonny it was to see!"

"Did ye think, as ye watched them gang, that it was your Lindsay, Aunty Jean?" I asked; for, indeed, her well-going talk eased my heart in the midst of so many troubles. For I declare that during these thirty years in Scotland, and especially in the Glenkens, folk had almost forgotten the way to laugh.

"Na, na, callant," so she would say to me in return, "I ne'er blamed him sair ava'. Tam Lindsay was never sair fashed wi' sense a' the days o' his life — at least no to hurt him, ony mair nor yersel', as yin micht say. It was the Crawford woman and her weel-feathered nest that led him awa', like a bit silly cuddie wi' a carrot afore his nose. But I'll never deny the randy that she was clever; for she took the craitur's size at the first look, as neat as if she had been measurin' him for a suit o' claes. But she did what I never did, or my name had been Jean Lindsay this day. The Lord in His mercy be thankit continually that it is as it is, and that I hae nae auld dotard, grumphin' an' snortin' at the chimley lug. She cuitled Tam Lindsay an' flairdied him an' spak' him fair, till the poor fathom o' pump water thocht himsel' the brawest lad in braid Scotland. Faith, I wadna sae bemean mysel' to get the king oot o' Whitehall — wha they tell me is no that ill to get, gin yin had the chance — and in muckle the same way as Tam Lindsay. Oh, what a set o' blind, brainless, handless, guid-for-naethings are men!"

"It was with that ye began, Aunty Jean," I said.

"Aye, an' I shall end wi' it too," she answered. "I'm no theology learned, but it looks terribly like as if the rib story were gye near the truth. For the poorest o' weemen can mak' a great muckle oot o' a very little, an' the best o' men are sadly troubled wi' a sair want. I misdoot that Aydam maun hae missed mair nor the rib when he waukened."

My pleasant time in the cottage by the Garpel came all too soon to an end. It is, indeed, a rare and heartsome place to bide in on a summer's day. There is the sound of the birds singing, the plash of the water into the pool beneath the Holy Linn, where the ministers held the great baptizing of bairns, when the bonny burn water dropped of its own accord on their brows as their fathers held them up. There are the leaves rubbing against one another with a pleasant soughing noise. These kept my heart stirring and content as long as I abode in the Glen of the Garpel.

There is in particular one little hill with a flat top, from which one may spy both up and down the Glen, yet be hidden under the leaves. Here I often frequented to go, though Sandy warned me that this would be my death. Yet I liked it best of all places in the daytime, and lay there prone on my belly for many hours together, very content, chewing sorrel, clacking my heels together, and letting on that I was meditating. But, indeed, I never could look at water slipping away beneath me, without letting it bear my thoughts with it and leave me to the dreaming. And the Garpel is an especially pleasant burn to watch thus running from you. I have had the same feelings in church when the sermon ran rippleless and even over my head.

The only thing that annoyed me was that on the Sabbath days the Garpel became a great place for lovers to convene. And above all, at one angle behind Jean Gordon's cot, there is a bower planted with wild flowers — pleasant and retired doubtless, for them that are equipped with a lass. But as for me, I pleased myself by thinking that one day I should shape to bring Maisie Lennox there to see my hiding-place, for, as a little maid, she ever loved woods that rustle and waters that flow softly. So chiefly on the Sabbath I kept close in my covert with a book; but whether from motives of safety or envy, it misliketh me to tell.

CHAPTER XXXIII.

THE GARDENER OF BALMAGHIE.

I WAS wakened one morning by Jean coming to the side of my bed. She was fully dressed, as if to receive company, and her tall and straight figure looked imposing enough.

"Rise!" she said. "Rise! there's a chiel here, that wants ye to gang wi' him."

"A chiel, Jean Gordon?" said I, in a sleepy kind of surprise. "What ken ye aboot him?"

"Oh, I ken he's a honest lad," she said, "an' he brings ye a message frae the gardener o' Balmaghie that ye are to accompany him there for greater safety."

"A likely story!" returned I, for I was none too well pleased to be wakened up out of my sleep at that time in the morning to see a regiment of Balmaghie gardeners. "There is great safety in the neighbourhood of the eagle's nest!"

"There is so," said Jean Gordon, dryly — "for sparrows. 'Tis the safest place in the world for the like of them to build, for the eagle will not touch them, an' the lesser gleds dare not come near."

Nor do I think that this saying pleased me over well, because I thought that a Gordon of Earlstoun, of whatever rank, was a city set on a hill that could not be hid.

Then Jean Gordon, the hermit of the Garpel glen, bade me an adieu, giving me an old-fashioned salutation as well, which savoured little of having forgotten all that she had lightlied to me.

"Tak' tent to yoursel'," she said. "Ye are a good lad and none so feckless as ye look. There's stuff and fushion in ye, an' ye micht even tak' the e'e o' woman — gin ye wad pad your legs."

And with this she went in, leaving me in a quandary whether to throw a stone at her, or run back and take her round the neck.

I found the gardener of Balmaghie standing with his back towards me. He walked on a little before me without speaking, as though wishing me to follow him. He was, to the back view, dressed but ordinarily, yet with some of the neatness of a proper gentleman's servant.

And this was a great deal in a country where for common the men wear little that is handsome, save and except the Sabbath cloak — which if it do not, like charity, cover a multitude of sins, of a truth hides a multitude of old duddy clothes.

At the foot of the burn, where by the bridge it runs over some black and rugged rocks, the gardener stopped and turned round. I declare I never gat a greater or more pleasant surprise in my life, save as it may be, once — of what I have yet to tell.

"Wat, dear Wat!" I cried, and ran to him. We clasped one another's hands, and then we stood a little off, gazing each at the other. I had not known that I was so fond of him. But nothing draws the heart like coming through trials together. At least, so it is with men. 'Twixt women and men so many things draw the heart, that it is well-nigh impossible to separate one thing from the other.

"How came Jean Gordon to say that you were the gardener at Balmaghie?" I asked of him, when I was a little satisfied with looking at him.

"Why, because I am the gardener at Balmaghie — second gardener!" answered Wat, smiling in a sly way that he had when he meant to provoke and mystify me. Yet a way that I liked not ill, for he never used it save when he had within him a light and merry heart.

But I knew by this time how to counter his stroke, which was to hold one's peace, as if one cared nothing about the matter. For in this Wat was just like a woman, or a fencer, whom it provokes more to measure a thrust and avoid, than a hundred times to parry and return.

But for all I could not keep the anxiety out of my eyes as we walked along.

"You do not want to hear," said he, provoking me; for because of Maisie Lennox and my mother, he knew that he had the better of me.

"But I do, though!" That was all I could say.

For indeed the matter was a mystery to me, as well it might be. Wat Gordon of Lochinvar, sometime favourite of her Grace the Duchess of Wellwood, now gardener to a latitudinarian and cavalier Galloway laird, that had been a ferlie even on a day of miracles.

Wat continued to smile and smile.

"Well, I will tell you," he said. Yet for a while did not, but only walked on smiling.

At last he pursed his mouth and began to whistle. It was a bar or two of the air "Kate Kennedy is my darling."

Now at that time I own that I was not bright in the uptake about such things. For I had not till lately concerned me much with love and women's favours, but it came across me all in an instant.

"Oh!" I said.

"Ah!" said Wat.

And we looked at one another and nodded — Wat defiantly.

"Kate of the black eyebrows!" I said musingly. "They are joined over her brow," I went on, "and her ear comes straight down to her neck without any rounded lobe. They are two well-considered signs!"

Wat Gordon stopped suddenly, and cried out at me.

"See here, William Gordon, what mean you by that? What if her eyebrows meet under her chin and her ears hang down like band strings? What is that to you?"

"Happily nothing!" said I — for I was patiently paying him out, as it is ever easy to do with a spit-fire like young Lochinvar.

"Speak plain, Will," he cried, "or by the Lord I will immediately run you through!"

"With a spade," said I, mocking. "Mind, Wat, you are a laird's second gardener now."

But when I perceived that he was really angry, I hastened to appease him.

"Joined eyebrows and lobeless ear have been held by learned folk to prefigure some temper, Wat!" I said.

His brow cleared on an instant.

"Pshaw!" he exclaimed, "I like a lass with a sparkle. No mim missie for Wat Gordon of Lochinvar, but a lass that keeps you in doubt till the last moment, whether your best wooing will speed you to a kiss or a bodkin-prick — that's the maid for me!"

"For me, I would e'en take the kiss," I said — "take it plain!"

"Tush, slow-coach!" he said, "your Earlstoun blood always did run like so much moss water!"

Now I had borne the burden of the day on the moss of Ayr, and felt that I need not take his scornful word.

"I have been where other than women's bodkins flashed — aye, ten against a hundred, and this was the only brand that wan through," I said, putting my hand on my side. "There was small time for kisses then! Ye may kiss your lass gin ye like, about the woods of Balmaghie. As for me, I prefer to ride upon Cameron's flank, on a day when the garments are rolled in blood."

This I said dourly, for my gall was working hot within me. So far from our first friendship had the clack of foolish tongues brought us. 'Deed, we were but silly boys that needed skelping, but I far the worst, for my head was by nature cooler and I knew better all the while.

"And so perhaps would I have preferred it," answered he gently.

"Aye," said he again, "I think it is somewhat late in the day for Wat Gordon of Lochinvar, to have to prove his courage upon his cousin William of Earlstoun. So then, take it from me that but for my oath sworn to the King, it had been more pleasure to ride with you in the charge at Ayrsmoss, than to be bridegroom to any maid soever in the world!"

And at the name of the King, he lifted his worn old countryman's bonnet as nobly and loyally as though it had been the plumed hat, whose feather had been so proudly set that night when he defied heaven and hell to keep him from his tryst beyond the Netherbow.

At the word I stretched out my hand to him.

"Forgive me, Wat," I said, and would have taken his arm, but he moved it a little away for a moment.

"Pray remember," he said grandly, "that though I am a jerkined man and handle the mattock in another man's kail yaird,—aye, though I be put to the horn and condemned unheard as a traitor, I am true King's man. Vive le Roi!"

"Well," replied I, "so be it, and much good may it do you. At any rate, there is no need to make such a work about it. After all, gin ye be at the horn, it's Guid's truth that ye gied Duke Wellwood's lads some most unmerciful jags aneath the ribs!"

While thus we snarled and fought between ourselves, the very strife of our tongues made the legs go faster, and we drew southward between the two lochs, Ken and Grenoch, crossing over the Black Water and leaving the Duchrae behind. And this made me very wae, to mind the days that we had there, with that brave company which should meet no more on the earth together.

CHAPTER XXXIV.

THE TESTING OF THE TYKE.

At the head of the high natural wood which fringes about all the mansion house of Balmaghie, we held down to the right through the copses, till we came to the green policies that ring in the great house of McGhies. As we went linking down this green pleasaunce, there met us one who came towards us with his hands behind his back, stooping a little from the shoulders down. He had on him a rich dress of dark stuff a good deal worn, being that of a fashion one or two removes from the present. But this rather, as it seemed, from habit and preference than from need — like one that deigns not to go too fine.

"Where away, Heather Jock?" he cried as we made to go by, and turned toward us.

"Whom have we here?" he asked, so soon as he saw me.

"A cousin o' mine from the hill country, laird," said Wat, with the gruff courtesy of the gardener.

"Hoot, hoot — another! This will never do. Has he taken the Test?" said the laird.

"I doubt he cannot read it even," said Wat, standing sheepishly before him.

"That is all the better," said the tall grey man, shaking his head gently and a little reproachfully. "It is easier gotten over that way."

"Have not you read it, sir?" asked Wat, glancing up at him curiously as he stood and swung his cane.

"Faith no," he answered quickly; "for if I had read it, Heather Jock, I might never have taken it. I could not run the risks."

"My friend will e'en take the Test the way that the Heriot's hospital dog took it," said Wat, again smiling, "with a little butter and liberty to spit it out."

"How now, Heather Jock, thou art a great fellow! Where didst thou get all the stories of the city? The whaups do not tell them about the Glenkens."

"Why, an it please your honour, I was half a year in the town with the Lady Gordon, and gat the chapman's fly sheets that were hawked about the causeways," answered Wat readily enough, making him an awkward bow.

"Tell me the story, rascal," said the tall man, whom I now knew for Roger McGhie of Balmaghie. "I love a story, so that it be not too often told."

Now I wondered to hear Wat Gordon of Lochinvar take the word "rascal" so meekly, standing there on the road. It was, indeed, very far from being his wont.

However, he began obediently enough to tell the story which Roger McGhie asked of him.

For a Kate of the Black Eyebrows in the plot makes many a mighty difference to the delicateness of a man's stomach.

"The story was only a bairn's ploy that I heard tell of, when I was in town with my lady," he said, "nothing worth your honour's attention, yet will I tell it from the printed sheet which for a bodle I bought."

"Let me be the judge of that," said the other.

"Well then, laird, there was in the hospital of George Heriot, late jeweller to the King, a wheen loon scholar lads who had an ill-will at a mastiff tyke, that lived in a barrel in the yard and keeped the outermost gate. They suspected this dog of treason against the person of his Majesty, and especially of treasonable opinions as to the succession of the Duke of York. And, indeed, they had some ground for their suspicion, for the mastiff growled one day at the King's High Commissioner when he passed that way, and even bit a piece out of the calf of one of the Duke of York's servitors that wore his Highness' livery, at the time when his Grace was an indweller in Holyrood House."

The eye of the tall grave man changed. A look of humorous severity came into it.

"Be cautious how you speak of dignities!" he said to Wat.

"Well," said Wat, "at any rate, this evil-minded tyke held an office of trust, patently within the meaning of the act, and these loon lads of Heriot's ordained him duly to take the Test, or be turned out of his place of dignity and profit.

"So they formed a Summary Court, and the tyke was called and interrogated in due form. The silly cur answered all their questions with silence, which was held as a sign of a guilty conscience. And this would have been registered as a direct refusal, but that one of the loons, taking it upon him to be the tyke's advocate, argued that silence commonly gave consent, and that the Test had not been presented to his client in the form most plausible and agreeable to his tender stomach.

"The debate lasted long, but at last it was agreed that a printed copy of the Test should be made into as little bulk as possible, smoothed with butter, tallow, or whatever should be most tempting to his doggish appetite. This being done, Tyke readily took it, and made a shift by rowing it up and down his mouth, to separate what was pleasant to his palate. When all seemed over and the dog appearingly well tested, the loons saw somewhat, as it were one piece after another, drop from the side of his mouth.

Whereupon it was argued, as in the case of my Lord Argyle, that this was much worse than a refusal, because it was a separating of that which was pleasant from what was irksome. And that this therefore, rightly interpreted, was no less than High Treason.

"But the tyke's advocate urged that his enemies had had the rowing up of the paper, and very likely they had put some crooked pin or other foreign object, unpleasant to a honest tyke's palate, within. So he asked for a fair trial before his peers for his client.

"Then the Court being constitute and the assize set, there fell out a great debate concerning this tyke dog. Some said that his chaming and chirking of the paper was very ill-done of him, that he was over malapert and took too much upon him. For his office being a lowly one, it was no business of his to do other than bolt the Test at once.

"But his advocate urged that he had done his best, and that if one part of the oath fell to hindering the other and fighting in his hass, it was not his fault, but the fault of them that framed such-like. Also, that if it had not hindered itself in going down, he would have taken it gladly and willingly, as he had taken down many other untoothsome morsels before, to the certain knowledge of the Court — such as dead cats, old hosen and shoes, and a bit of the leg of one of the masters in the hospital, who was known to be exceedingly unsavoury in his person.

"But all this did not save the poor tyke, for his action in mauling and beslavering his Majesty's printing and paper was held to be, at least, Interpretive Treason. And so he was ordered to close prison till such a time as the Court should call him forth to be hanged like a dog. Which was pronounced for doom."

Roger McGhie laughed at the tale's end with a gentle, inward laughter, and tapped Wat with his cane.

"Thou art indeed a merry wag, and speak over well for a gardener," he said; "but I know not if John Graham would not put a charge of lead into thee, if he heard thy way of talking. But go thy ways. Tell me quickly what befel the poor tyke."

"None so evil was his fate," said Wat, "for in the midst of the great debate that the surprising verdict raised, the tyke drew on a fox's skin, laid hold of the tail of another tyke, and so passed unobserved out of the prison. At which many were glad. For, said they, he was a good tyke that would not sup kail with the Pope nor yet the deil, and so had no need of his long spoon. And others said that it were a pity to hang so logical a tyke, for that he was surely no Aberdeen man, ever ready to cant and recant again.'

Roger McGhie laughed aloud and knocked his cane on the ground, for right well he understood the meaning of all these things, being versed in parties and politics, which I never was.

"It is mighty merry wit," he said, "and these colleginers are blythesome blades. I wonder what John Graham will say to this. But go to the bothies of the bachelor foresters, and get that which may comfort the inner parts of your cousin from the hills—who, from the hang of his head, seems not so ready of tongue as thou."

For, indeed, I had been most discreetly silent.

So the tall, grey-headed gentleman went away from us, tapping gently with his fine cane on the ground, and often stopping to look curiously at some knot on a tree or some chance puddock or grasshopper on the roadside.

Then Wat told me that because of his quaint wit and great loyalty, Roger McGhie of Balmaghie was in high favour with the ruling party, and that none on his estates were ever molested. Also that Claverhouse frequented the house greatly, often riding from Dumfries for a single night only to have the pleasure of his society. He never quartered his men near by the house of Balmaghie, but rode over alone or with but one attendant in the forenights — perhaps to get away from roystering Lidderdale of the Isle, red roaring Baldoon, drinking Winram, and the rest of the boon companions.

"The laird of Claverhouse will come hither," said Wat, "with a proud set face, stern and dark as Lucifer's, in the evening. And in the morning ride away with so fresh a countenance and so pleasing an expression that one might think him a spirit unfallen. For, as he says, Roger McGhie does his heart good like medicine."

CHAPTER XXXV.

KATE OF THE DARK BROWS.

BETIMES we came to a little row of white cottages deep in the wood, with only a green clearing at the door, and the trees swaying broad branches over the roof.

Here we washed ourselves, and Wat set to shaving me and cutting my hair close, in order that if necessary I might wear a wig. Then we went into the gardens, where we found the chief gardener of Balmaghie, whose name was Samuel Irving.

Samuel was a grave man with a very long upper lip, which gave him a sour and discontented expression, but secretly he was a good man and a great favourer of the hill-folk. Also he was very upright and well-doing in the matters of seeds and fruits and perquisites, and greatly in favour with his master, Mr. Roger McGhie.

So we set out much refreshed, and were going by a path through the woods, when suddenly who should come upon us at a turn but Kate McGhie. Wat ran to her to take her hands, but she gave him the go-by with the single frugal favour of a saucy glance. "Strangers first!" she said, and so came forward and greeted me.

"You are welcome to Balmaghie, William Gordon," she said. "I would you came as guest, and not as servitor; but some day I know you shall enter by the front door."

She glanced round with a questioning air. Wat was standing half turned away, very haughty in his demeanour.

Kate McGhie looked towards him. She was in truth a comely maid — for one that is black of favour.

"Now you may come," she said.

He seemed as if he would refuse and turn away. But she looked fixedly at him, defying him with her eyes to do it, and after a moment's battle of regards he came slowly towards us.

"Come nearer!" she commanded imperiously.

He came up with his eyes kindling. I think that no less than kissing was in his mind, and that for a moment he thought that she might permit it.

But suddenly she drew herself proudly away, and her look was disdainful and no doubt hard to be borne.

"Are these fit manners from a servant?" she said. "They that eat the meat and sit below the salt, must keep the distance."

Wat's countenance fell in a moment. I never saw one with so many ups and downs in such short space. The allures and whimsies of this young she-slip made him alternately sulk and brighten like an April day.

"Kate!" he began to say, in the uncertain tone of a petitioner.

"Mistress Katerine McGhie, if you please!" said she, dropping him a courtly courtesy.

"Have you forgotten quite?" Wat said.

"Ah," she said, "it is you who have forgotten. You were not the gardener then. I do not allow gardeners to kiss me — unless my hand on Sundays when their faces are more than ordinarily clean. Would you like to have that, Heather Jock?"

And she held out the back of her hand.

The silly fellow coloured to his brow, and was for turning away with his head very much in the air.

But she ran after him, and took him by the hand.

Then he would have caught her about with his arms, but she escaped out of them lightly as a bird.

"Na, na, Lochinvar," she cried merrily, in the common speech. "That is as muckle as is good for you"—she looked at him with the light of attraction in her eyes—"afore folk," she added, with a glance at him that I could not fathom.

Nevertheless, I saw for the first time all that was between them. So with no more said, Kate fled fleet-foot down the path towards the great house, which we could see standing grey and massive at the end of the avenue of beeches.

"There's a lass by yon burn-side that will do as muckle for you; but dinna bide to speer her leave!" she cried to me over her shoulder, a word which it was hard to understand.

I asked Wat, who stood staring after her in a kind of wrapt adoration, what she could mean.

He gazed at me, as if he did not see what kind of animal was making the noise like talking. I am sure that for the time he knew me not from John Knox.

"What did she mean?" I asked him.

"Mean!" said he, "mean——" speaking vaguely as one in a swither.

"You are heady and moidered with not getting a kiss from a lass," said I, with, I grant, some little spite.

"Did she ever kiss you?" cried he, looking truculently at me.

"Nay!" said I bluntly, for indeed the thing was not in my thought.

"Then you ken naught about it. You had better hold your wheesht!"

He stood so long thinking, sometimes giving his thigh a little slap, like one that has suddenly remembered something pleasant which he had forgotten, that I was near coming away in disgust and leaving the fool, when I remembered that I knew not where to go.

In a while he came to himself somewhat, and I told him what Kate McGhie had said to me over her shoulder.

"Did Kate say that?" he cried. "She could surely not have said all that and I not hear her."

"Out, you fool," I said, for so of custom I spoke to him, being my cousin and playmate. "You had other matter to think of. Say it she did."

He repeated the words which I told him, and I declare even the sound of them seemed to be in danger of throwing him into another rhapsody.

But at last he said, suddenly, "Oh, I ken what she means ——" And he drew a long breath. "I suppose we had better go down to the water-side. She will not come out again, if we wait all night." And he went some way along the avenue and looked long and hard at one heavy-browed window of the old house which seemed to be winking at us.

It is a strange thing how love affects different people. You never can tell beforehand how it will be. I could not have believed that the presence of a forward lass with black eyebrows could have made a moon-struck fool of Wildcat Wat of Lochinvar.

He still stood and looked at the window till my patience was ended.

"Come on, man," I cried. "I declare you are not Heather Jock, as she called you, but Heather Jackass!"

At another time he would have knocked my head off, but now my jesting affected him no more than a sermon. And this I took to be the worst sign of all.

"Well, come on then," he said. "You are surely in an accursed sweat of haste to-night!"

And we took our way down to the water-side, having wasted more than an hour. We had not advanced far down the pillared avenue of the beech trees, when suddenly we came in sight of Maisie Lennox. She was coming slowly towards us along one of the forest roads. At the same time I saw my mother, walking away from me down a path which led along the side of the Dee water. She had her back to me, and was going slowly with her head down. To my shame I ran to meet Maisie Lennox. But first ere I reached her she said quietly to me, " Have you not seen your mother?"

"Aye," answered I. "She has gone down the road to the water-side."

"Then let no greeting come before your mother's," she said, looking very ill-pleased at me as I ran forward to take her hand.

So with a flea in my ear I turned me about and went off, somewhat shamed as you may believe, to find my mother. When I got back to the path on which I had seen her, I left Wat far behind and ran after my mother, calling loudly to her.

At the sound of my voice she turned and held up her hands.

"Willie, boy!" she cried.

And in a moment she had me in her arms, crooning over me and making much of me. She told me also, when she had time to look well at me, that I was much better in health than when I had lain in the well-house of Earlstoun.

"And you came first to see your old mother. That was like my ain Willie!" she said, a word which made me ashamed. So I had no answer to make, though nevertheless I took the credit of the action as much by silence as by speech.

Then Maisie Lennox came through the wood, and demeaning herself right soberly, she held out her hand.

"Did you not see William before?" asked my mother, looking from one to the other of us.

"Only at a distance, on his way to you," said Maisie, speaking in her demure way.

It was in the little holding of Boatcroft by the side of the Dee, and among the water meadows which gird the broad stream, that we found my mother, Maisie Lennox, and little Margaret Wilson snugly settled. Their position here was not one to be despised. They were safe for the time being at least, upon the property of Roger McGhie. Every day the old man passed their loaning-end. And though he knew that by rights only a herd should live at the Boatcroft, yet he made no complaint nor asked any question for conscience' sake, when he saw my mother with Maisie Lennox at her elbow, or little Margaret of Glen Vernock moving about the little steading.

In the evening it fell to me to make my first endeavours at waiting at table, for though women were safe enough anywhere on the estate, Balmaghie was not judged to be secure for me except within the house itself.

So my mother gave me a great many cautions about how I should demean myself, and how to be silent and mannerly when I handed the dishes.

CHAPTER XXXVI.

THE BLACK HORSE COMES TO BALMAGHIE.

As Wat and I went towards the great house in the early gloaming, we became aware of a single horseman riding toward us and gaining on us from behind. At the first sound of the trampling of his horse, Wat dived at once over the turf dyke and vanished.

"Bide you!" he said. "He'll no ken you!"

A slender-like figure in a grey cavalry cloak and a plain hat without a feather, came, slowly riding alongside of me, in an attitude of the deepest thought.

I knew at a glance that it was John Graham of Claverhouse, whom all the land of the South knew as "the Persecutor."

"Are you one of Balmaghie's servants?" he asked.

I took off my bonnet, showing as I did so my shaven poll, and answered him that I was.

No other word he uttered, though he eyed me pretty closely and uncomfortably, as if he had a shrewd thought that he had seen me before elsewhere. But the shaven head and the absence of hair on my face were a complete disguise.

For, indeed, though Maisie Lennox made little of it, the fact was that I had at the time quite a strong crop of hair upon both my chin and upper lip.

Claverhouse waved me behind him with the graceful and haughty gesture, which they say he constantly used even to the Secretary in Council, when he was hot with him in the matter of the house and lands of Dudhobe.

Meekly enough I trudged behind the great commander of

horse, and looked with much curiosity and some awe both upon him and on his famous steed "Boscobel," which was supposed by the more ignorant of the peasantry to be the foul fiend in his proper person.

So in this manner we came to the house. The lights were just beginning to shine, for Alisoun Begbie, the maid of the table, was just arranging the candles. At the doorway the master of the house met his guest, having been drawn from his library by the feet of the charger clattering upon the pavement of the yard.

"Ah, John," he said, "this is right gracious of you, in the midst of your fighting and riding, to journey over to cheer an old hulk like me!"

And he reached him a hand to the saddle, which Claverhouse took without a word. But I saw a look of liking, which was almost tender, in the war-captain's eyes as I passed round by the further door into the kitchen.

Here I was roughly handled by the cook — who, of course, had not been informed of my personality, and who exercised upon me both the length of her tongue and the very considerable agility thereof.

But Alisoun Begbie, who was, as I say, principal waiting-maid, rescued me and in pity took me under her protection; though with no suspicion of my quality, but only from a maidish and natural liking for a young and unmarried man. She offered very kindly to show me all my duties, and, indeed, I had been in a sorry pass that night without her help.

So when it came to the hour of supper, it was with some show of grace that I was enabled to wait at table, and take my part in the management of the dishes thereupon. Alisoun kept me mostly in the back of her serving pantry, and gave me only the dishes which were easy to be served, looking kindly on me with her eyes all the while and shyly touching my hand when occasion served, which I thought it not politic to refuse. For all this I was mightily thankful, because I had very small desire to draw upon me the cold blue eyes of John Graham — to whom, in spite of my crop head and serving-man's attire, there might arrive a memory of the side of green Garryhorn and the interrupted fight which Wat of Lochinvar, my cousin, had fought for my sake with Cornet Peter Inglis.

The two gentlemen sat and supped their kail, in which a pullet had been boiled, with quite remarkable relish. But it was not till the wine had been uncorked and set at their elbows, that they began to have much converse.

Then they sat and gossiped together very pleasantly, like men that are easing their hearts and loosening their belts over trencher and stoup, after a hard day's darg.

It was John Graham who spoke first.

"Have you heard," he said, "the excellent new jest concerning Anne Keith, what she did with these vaguing blasties up at Methven, when the laird was absent in London?"

"Nay," replied Roger McGhie, "that have I not. I am not in the way at Balmaghie to hear other misdeeds than those of John Graham and his horse Boscobel, that is now filling his kyte in my stable, as his master is eke doing in hall."

"Well," said Claverhouse, "we shall have to give Anne the justiciar power and send her lord to the spence and the store chamber. She should have the jack and the riding breeks, and he the keys of the small ale casks. So it were better for his Majesty's service."

"But I thought him a good loyal man," said Roger McGhie.

"One that goes as easy as an old shoe — like yourself, Roger. Not so my lady. Heard ye what our Anne did? The conventiclers came to set up a preaching in a tent on the laird's ground, and they told it to Anne. Whereupon she rose, donned her lord's buff coat and slung his basket hilt at her pretty side. And so to the woodside rode she. There were with her none but Methven's young brother, a lad like a fathom of pump water. Yet with Anne Keith to captain him, he e'en drew sword and bent pistol like a brave one. I had not thought that there was so much good stuff in David."

Roger McGhie sipped at his wine and nodded, drawing up one eyebrow and down the other, as his habit was when he was amused — which indeed was not seldom, for he was merry within him much more often than he told any.

"Then who but Anne was the pretty fighter," Clavers went on lightly, "with a horseman's piece on her left arm, and a drawn tuck in her right hand? Also was she not the fine general? For she kept the enemy's forces sindry, marching her servants to and fro, all armed to the teeth — to and fro all day between them, and threatening the tent in which was the preacher to the rabble. She cried to them that if they did not leave the parish of Methven speedily, it would be a bloody day for them. And that if they did not come to the kirk decently and hear the curate, she would ware her life upon teaching them how to worship God properly, for that they were an ignorant,. wicked pack ! A pirlicue * which pleased them but little, so that some rode off that they might not be known, and some dourly remained, but were impotent for evil.

"I never knew that Anne Keith was such a spirity lass. I would all such lasses were as sound in the faith as she."

This was the word of Roger McGhie, uttered like a meditation. I felt sure he thought of his daughter Kate.

"Then," continued John Graham, "after that, Anne took her warlike folk to the kirk. And lo ! the poor curate was

* In this case, the application of the discourse.

so wandered and feared, that he could make no suitable discourse that day, but only stood and bleated like a calf, till the Lady Anne said to him, 'Sir, if you can neither fight nor preach, ye had better go back to the Hielands and herd kye, for by the Lord, I, Anne Keith, can fight and preach too!'"

"As they do say the Laird of Methven right well knoweth," said Roger McGhie, in the very dry and covert way in which he said many things.

"Ah!" said Clavers, and smiled a little as if he also had his own thoughts. But he went on.

"So on the very next day Anne held a court in the hall, and all the old canting wives of the parish were there. She set the Test to all their throats, and caused them to forswear conventicling at the peril of their lives — all but one old beldame that would in no wise give way, or be answerable for her children, who were well kenned and notour rebels.

"Then Anne took from the hag her apron, that was a fine braw one with pockets, and said to her, 'This I shall retain till you have paid your son's fines. If ye cannot keep your other brats out of the dirt, at least I shall keep this one clean for you.'"

"Ha, very well said, Anne!" cried Roger McGhie, clapping the table. For "brat" is but the Scots word for apron, and such a brisk conceity saying was like that very spirited lady, Anne Keith.

"But with yourself, how goes it?" asked the Laird of Balmaghie.

Claverhouse turned a silver spoon over and over, and looked at the polish upon it thoughtfully.

"Ill, ill, I fear. I ride night and day through all the country of Galloway, and it is like so much pudding in mud. That which you clear out before you, closes up behind. And at headquarters there is the Duke Hamilton, who desires no better than to load me to the chancellor. I have many enemies."

" But surely also many friends," said Balmaghie.

" Not many so true as thou art, Roger," said Claverhouse, stretching out a white hand across the table, which his friend took for a moment.

"And I am plagued on the one side by the Council to make the folk keep to the kirk, and on the other sore vexed with weary-winded preachers like Andrew Symson over on Creeside, who this very day writes me to say that ever since muckle Davie Dunbar of Baldoon hath broken his neck, he gets no congregation at all. And be sure the poor wretch wishes me to gather him one."

He threw a bit of paper across the table to Balmaghie.

" Read ye that," he said. " It is about swearing Baldoon."

The laird looked at it all over and then began to smile.

" This is indeed like Andrew Symson, doddering fool body that he is — aye scribing verses, and sic-like verse. Heaven forfend us ! "

And he began to read.

UPON BALDOON.

> " He was no schismatick. He ne'er withdrew
> Himself from the house of God. He with a few,
> Some two or three, came constantly to pray
> For such as had withdrawn themselves away.
> Nor did he come by fits. Foul day or fair,
> I being in the kirk, was sure to see him there.
> Had he withdrawn, 'tis like, these two or three
> Being thus discouraged, had deserted me :
> So that my muse 'gainst Priscian avers,
> He, he alone, was my parishioners ! "

" Aye," said Balmaghie, " I warrant the puir hill-folk werna muckle the better o' Baldoon's supplications."

Then Claverhouse, receiving back the paper, looked up with great alertness.

"But I have chanced in that very country to fall on a nest of the fanatics."

He looked cautiously about, and I had no more than time to step back into the little pantry where Alisoun Begbie was already washing the dishes. She put her arm about me to keep me within, and before she let me go, she kissed me. Which I suffered without great concern — for, being a lass from Borgue, she was not uncomely, though, like all these shore lassies, a little forritsome.

CHAPTER XXXVII.

A CAVALIER'S WOOING.

JOHN GRAHAM assured himself that none of the servants were in the room, and then he said :

"I have sure informations from one Birsay Smith, a cobbler, by which I have my hand as good as upon the throat of that arch-fanatic, Anthony Lennox of the Duchrae, and also upon Sandy Gordon of Earlstoun, his younger brother William, Maclellan of Barscobe, and some others. It will be a great taking, for there is a long price on every head of them."

"Think you, John," said Balmaghie, shrewdly, "that you will add Earlstoun and Barscobe to your new lands of Freuch?"

"Nay," said Clavers, "that is past hoping. They will give them to their English colonels, Oglethorpe and the like. Aye, even though, at my own request, I had the promise from the Council of the estates of any that I should find cause of forfeiture against, a thing which is only my due. But as by this time you may know, a plain soldier hath small chance among the wiles of the courtiers."

"I question, John, if thou hadst all Galloway and Nidsdale to boot, thou wouldst be happy, even with the fairest maid therein, for one short week. Thou wouldst be longing to have Boscobel out, saddled and bridled, and be off to the Whig-hunting with a 'Ho-Tally-Ho!' For that is thy way, John!"

Claverhouse laughed a little stern laugh like a man that is

forced to laugh at himself, yet is somedeal proud of what he hears.

"It is true," he said. "There is no hunting like this hunting of men, which the King's service sees in these days. It makes it worth living to keep the crown of the moorland with one's company of dragoons, like a man hefting lambs on a sheep farm; and know that no den, no knowe, no moss, no hill has been left unsearched for the King's rebels."

"And how speeds the wooing, John?" I heard Balmaghie say after a little pause, and the opening of another bottle.

For I thought it no shame to listen, since the lives of all that were dear to me, as well as my own, were in this man's power. And, besides, I knew very well that Kate McGhie had put me in this place, that I might gain good intelligence of the intentions of the great captain of the man-hunters.

Clavers sat awhile silent. He looked long and scrupulously at his fine white hand and fingered the lace ruffle upon his sleeve.

"It was of that mainly that I came to speak to you, Roger. Truth to tell, it does not prosper to my mind."

"Hath the fair Jean proved unkind?" said Roger McGhie, looking over at Claverhouse, with a quiet smile in his eye.

John Graham leaned back in his chair with a quick amused look and threw back his clustering love locks.

"No," he said; "there is, I think, little fear of that."

"What then is the difficulty — her mother?"

"Aye," said Claverhouse, "that is more like it. Yet though the Lady Dundonald drills me and flytes me and preaches at me, I care not so much. For like the hardships of life, that will come to an end. Nevertheless, I own that at times I am tempted to take the lady at my saddle-bow, and ride out from Paisley to return no more."

"You will not do that, John!" said Balmaghie quietly, with a certain light of irony in his eye.

Claverhouse looked up quickly.

"How so, Balmaghie?" he said, and I saw through my little slant wicket the pride grow in his eye.

"The forty thousand marks, John."

Claverhouse struck his hand on the table.

"Thank you ―― " he said coldly, and then for a moment was silent.

"There is no man that dare say that to me but yourself, Roger McGhie," he added.

"No," said the Laird of Balmaghie, sipping at his canary, "and that is why you rode over to see me to-night, John — a silly old man in a dull house, instead of guzzling at Kirkcudbright with Winram and the burgesses and bailies thereof. You are a four-square, truth-telling man, and yet hear little of it, save at the house of Balmaghie."

Claverhouse still said nothing, but stared at the table, from which the cloth had been removed.

The elder man reached over and put his hand on the sleeve of the younger.

"Why, John," he said softly, "pluck up heart and do nothing hastily — as I know thou wilt not. Forty thousand marks is not to be despised. It will help thee mightily with Freuch and Dudhope. It is worth having thy ears soundly boxed once or twice for a persecutor, by a covenanting mother-in-law."

"But that is not the worst of it, Roger," said Claverhouse, who had gotten over his pique; "my enemies lay it against me to York and the King, that I frequent a suspected and disloyal house. They will put me down as they put down Aberdeen―― "

At this moment I felt a hand upon my arm. It was that of Kate McGhie. She drew me out of the closet where Alisoun had bestowed me, intending, as she intimated, to come cosily in beside me when she had washed the dishes.

But Kate took me by the hand, and together we passed out into the cool night. Wat met us by the outer gate. He was standing in the shadow. There was then no time for me to tell Kate what I had heard Claverhouse reveal to the laird of his intentions regarding Anton Lennox and my brother Sandy. To which there was added a further great uncertainty, lest Birsay had been able to add to his other informations an account of my mother's hiding-place and our own disguises. Nay, even though he had not already done so, there was no saying how soon this might come about.

However, as we stood conferring a moment together, there was one came running hastily from the house to the stables, carrying a lantern.

Then in a little, out of the stable door came clattering the war-horse of the commander of dragoons.

William McCutcheon, the serving-man and chief groom of the stables, led Boscobel with a certain awe, as if he might actually be leading the Accuser of the Brethren, haltered and accoutred.

He had not been at the door a minute, when Claverhouse come out and went down the steps, drawing on his riding gauntlets as he came. Roger McGhie walked behind him carrying burning candles in a great silver triple candlestick. He held the light aloft in his hand while the cavalier mounted with a free, easy swing into the saddle; and, gathering the reins in his hand, turned to bid his host adieu. "Be a wee canny with the next Whig ye catch, for the sake of your ain bonny Whiggie, Jean Cochrane!" cried Roger McGhie of Balmaghie, holding the cresset high above his head.

"Deil a fear!" laughed Clavers, gaily waving his hand. "'Tis not in the power of love or any other folly to alter my loyalty."

"Pshaw!" said the laird; "then, John, be assured ye ken nothing about the matter."

But Claverhouse was already clattering across the cobble stones of the yard. We drew back into the deep shadow of the bushes and he passed us, a noble figure of a man sitting slenderly erect on his black horse Boscobel, and so riding out into the night, like a prince of darkness going forth to war.

* * * * *

That night, down in the little holding of Waterside, upon the broad meadows of the Dee, we held a council. My mother was for setting out forthwith to look after her son Sandy.

But I gently dissuaded her, telling her that Sandy was far better left to his own resources, than with her safety also to provide for.

"I daresay," said she, a little shortly; "but have you thought how I am like to sleep when you are all away—when in every foot that comes by the door, I hear the messenger who comes to tell me of my sons streeked stiff in their winding sheets?"

But, after all, we managed to persuade her to bide on at the Boatcroft, where little Margaret of Glen Vernock was to stay with her for company. As for the rest of us, we had information brought us by sure hands, of the hiding-places of Anton Lennox and the rest of the wanderers.

The maids were set upon accompanying us—Maisie Lennox to see her father, and Kate McGhie because Maisie Lennox was going. But after a long controversy we also prevailed on them to abide at home and wait for our return. Yet it came to me afterwards that I saw a look pass between them, such as I had seen before, when it is in the heart of the women folk to play some trick upon the duller wits of mankind. It is as though they said, "After all, what gulls these men be!"

So that night I slept with Wat in the gardener's hut, and early in the morning we went down to the great house to bid the maids good-bye. But there we found only Alisoun Begbie. The nest was empty and the birds flown. Only Roger McGhie was walking up and down the beech avenue of the old house, deep in thought. He had his hands behind his back, and sometimes the corners of his mouth seemed to smile through his gloom with a curious pleasantry. Wat and I kept well out of his sight, and I could not help wondering how much, after all, he understood of our ongoings. More than any of us thought at that time, I warrant, for it was the man's humour to know much and say little.

Alisoun Begbie, who seemed not unwilling that we should stop and converse with her, told us that after Clavers had departed, Mistress Kate had gone in to her father to tell him that she was going away for a space of days.

"Mind, ye are not to rise before your ordinary in the morning, father," she said; "I shall be gone by the dawn."

"Very well, Kate," he replied, continuing to draw off his coat and prepare for bed; "I shall sell the Boreland to pay the fine."

This was all he said; and having kissed his daughter good-night, calmly and pleasantly as was his wont, he set a silken skull-cap on his crown and fell asleep.

Truly a remarkable man was Roger McGhie of Balmaghie.

CHAPTER XXXVIII.

IN COVE MACATERICK.

WAT and I took our way immediately towards those wilds where, as we had been advised, Auld Anton Lennox was hidden. He was (so we were informed) stricken with great sickness and needed our ministrations. But in the wild country into which we were going was no provision for the up-putting of young and delicate maids, specially such as were accustomed to the luxuries of the house of Balmaghie.

The days, however, were fine and dry, and a fanning wind from the north blew in our faces as we went. It was near to the road-end of the Duchrae, up which I had so often helped the cars (or sledges of wood with birch twigs for wheels) to drag the hay crop, that we met Roderick MacPherson, a Highland man-servant of the Laird of Balmaghie, riding one pony and leading other two. We knew them at once as those which for common were ridden by Kate McGhie and Maisie Lennox.

"Hey, where away, Roderick?" cried Wat, as soon as he set eyes on the cavalcade.

The fellow looked through his lowering thatch of eyebrows and grunted, but whether with stupidity or cunning it had been hard to say.

"Speak!" said Wat, threateningly; "you can understand well enough, when they cry from the kitchen door that it is porridge time."

"The leddies was tak' a ride," MacPherson answered,

with a cock in his eye that angered Wat, whose temper, indeed, in these days was not of the most enduring.

"Where did you leave them?" cried he of Lochinvar.

"It was on a muir, no far frae a burnside; I was fair forget where!" said Roderick, with a look of the most dense stupidity.

Then I saw the fellow had been commanded not to tell, so I said to Wat,

"Come on, Wat. Kate has ordered him not to tell us."

"This is a bonny like thing," said Wat, angrily, "that I canna truss him up and make him tell, only because I am riding with the hill-folk. Oh, that I were a King's man of any sort for half an hour."

For, indeed, it is the glory of the field-folk, who have been blamed for many extremes and wild opinions, that though tortured and tormented themselves by the King's party, they used not torture upon their enemies — as in later times even the Whigs did, when after the Eighty-eight it came to be their time to govern.

So we permitted the Highland tyke to go on his way. There is no need to go into the place and manner of our journeyings, in such a pleasant and well-kenned country as the strath of the Kells. But, suffice it to say, after a time we betook ourselves to the broad of the moors, and so held directly for the fastnesses of the central hills, where the poor hunted folk kept sanctuary.

We kept wide of the rough and tumbled country about the lochs of Neldricken and Enoch; because, to our cost and detriment, we knew that place was already much frequented by the ill-contriving gipsy people thereabouts — rascals who thought no more of taking the life of a godly person, than of killing one of the long-woolled mountain sheep which are the staple of these parts. So there was no need to run into more danger. We were in plenty already without that.

After a long while we found ourselves under the front of the Dungeon Hill, which is the wildest and most precipitous in all that country. They say that when it thunders there, all the lightnings of heaven join together to play upon the rocks of the Dungeon. And, indeed, it looks like it; for most of the rocks there are rent and shattered, as though a giant had broken them and thrown them about in his play.

Beneath this wild and rocky place we kept our way, till, across the rounded head of the Hill of the Star, we caught a glimpse of the dim country of hag and heather that lay beyond.

Then we held up the brae that is called the Gadlach, where is the best road over the burn of Palscaig, and so up into the great wide valley through which runs the Eglin Lane.

Wat and I had our precise information as to the cave in which lay the Covenanter, Anton Lennox. So that, guiding ourselves by our marks, we held a straight course for the corner of the Back Hill of the Star in which the hiding place was.

I give no nearer direction to the famous Cove Macaterick for the plainest reasons, though it is there to this day, and the herds ken it well. But who knows how soon the times may grow troubleous again, and the Cove reassert its ancient safety. But all that I will say is, that if you want to find Cove Macaterick, William Howatson, the herd of the Merrick, or douce, John Macmillan that dwells at Bongill in the Howe of Trool, can take you there — that is, if your legs be able to carry you, and you can prove yourself neither outlaw nor King's soldier. And this word also, I say, that in the process of your long journeying you will find out this, that though any bairn may write a history book, it takes a man to herd the Merrick.

So in all good time we came to the place. It is half-way up a clint of high rocks overlooking Loch Macaterick, and the hillside is bosky all about with bushes, both birk and self-sown mountain ash. The mouth of the cavern is quite hidden in the summer by the leaves, and in the winter by the mat of interlacing branches and ferns. Above, there is a diamond-shaped rock, which ever threatens to come down and block the entrance to the cave. Which indeed it is bound to do some day.

Wat and I put aside the tangle and crawled within the black mouth of the cavern one at a time, till we came to a wider part, for the whole place is narrow and constricted. And there, on a pallet bed, very pale and far through, we found Auld Anton — who, when he saw us, turned his head and raised his hand by the wrist in greeting. His lips moved, but what he said we could not tell. So I crept back and made shift to get him a draught of water from a well upon the hillside, which flowed near by the mouth of the cave. The spring water somewhat revived him, and he sat up, leaning heavily against me as he did so.

Nevertheless, it was some time before he could speak. Wat and I looked at one another, and as we saw the condition of things in the cave, it became very evident to us that the lassies Kate and Maisie had either wandered from the road, or had been detained in some manner that was unknown to us. So Wat, being ever for instant action, proposed that he should go off and seek the lassies, and that I should bide and do my best to succour Auld Anton in his extremity.

To this I consented, and Wat instantly took his way with his sword, his pistols, and his gaily set bonnet — walking with that carriage which had been little else than a swagger in the old days, but which now was no more than the air of well-set distinction which marks the man of ancient family and life-long training in arms.

So I was left alone with the father of the lassie I loved. I have said it. There is no use of denying it any longer. Indeed, the times were not such as to encourage much dallying with love's dainty misunderstandings. We were among days too dark for that. But I owned as I sat there, with her father's head on my lap, that it was for Maisie Lennox's sake, and not altogether for the sake of human kindness, that I was left here in the wilderness to nurse Anton Lennox of the Duchrae.

As soon as he could speak, Anton began to tell me of his illness.

"I fell," he said, "from my pride of strength in one hour. The spirit of the Lord departed from me, and I became even as the mown grass, that to-day is and to-morrow is cast into the oven."

He lay back and breathed quickly for a moment. I entreated him not to speak, but he put my words aside impatiently with his hand.

"Thus it was. I was fleeing with a few of the people from before the persecutors, and as we came over the hip of the Meaull of Garryhorn, the horsemen rode hotly behind us. Then suddenly there came upon me a dwam and a turning in my head, so that I cried to them to run on and leave me to the pursuers. But to this the godly lads would in no wise consent. 'We will carry you,' they said, 'and put you in some hole in the moss and cover you with heather.' So they designed, but the enemy being very close upon us, they got me no further than a little peat brow at the lane-side down there. They laid me on a shelf where the bank came over me. Then I heard our people scattering and running in different directions, in order that they might draw the enemy away from me. So I lay still and waited for them to come and take me, if so it should be the will of the Lord. And over me I heard the horses of the soldiers plunging. One beast, as it gathered way for the spring over the burn, sent its hoof down through the black peat and the stead of its hoof was on my bonnet's brim. Yet, according to the mercies of the Lord, me it harmed not. But the soldier fell off and hurt his head in his steel cap upon the further bank, whereat he swore — which was a manifest judgment upon him, to tangle him yet deeper in the wrath of God."

So here I abode in the cave with Anton, and we spoke of many things, but specially of the lassie that was near to my heart and the pearl of his soul. He told me sweet simple things of her childhood that warmed me like well-matured wine.

As how that there was a day when, her mother being alive, Maisie came in and said, "When I am a great girl and have bairns of my own, I shall let them stay all day in the gardens where the grosarts are, and never say, 'You shall not touch!'"

This Anton thought to be a thing wondrously sound and orthodox, and he saw in the child's word the stumbling stone of our mother Eve.

CHAPTER XXXIX.

THE BOWER OF THE STAR.

DAY by day I tended him as gently as I could, till in the cave our provisions were well-nigh spent. Then, one grey morning I took my pistol to go out on the hillside to see if I could shoot aught to eat. But because of my nervousness, or other cause, I could at that time do nothing. Indeed, not so much as a whaup came near me on that great, wide, dappled hill.

I saw a hill fox rise and run. He was a fine beast and very red, and held his tail nobly behind him like a flag. But, hardly beset as we were, we could with difficulty have eaten fox, even had I been able to shoot him, which I was not.

The day passed slowly, the night came, and it went sore to my heart that I was able to do so little for the friend of one I loved. I saw that he would have mended readily enough, if he had received the right nutriment, which, alas! it seemed far out of my power to obtain. Yet in the morning, when I went to the mouth of the cave, lo! there, immediately to the right of me, on a bare place, were two great whaup eggs, broad-buttocked and splashed with black. I never was gladder to see food. It was late for the whaups to be breeding; and, indeed, they had mostly left the moorland by that time. But, nevertheless, it was manifest that Providence had bidden some bird, perhaps disappointed of an earlier brood or late mated, to come and lay the eggs before our door.

I bade Anton take the eggs by the ancient method of sucking — which he made shift to do, and was very greatly strengthened thereby. So every morning as long as we remained there, the wild bird laid an egg in the morning, which made the Covenanter's breakfast. This is but one of the daily marvels from the Lord which attended our progress. For whensoever those that have been through the perilous time come together, they recount these things to one another, and each has his like tale of preservation and protection to tell.

But that minds me of a strange thing. Once during the little while when I companied with the Compellers, it was my hap to meet with clattering John Crichton, that rank persecutor. And what was my surprise to hear that all his talk ran upon certain providential dreams he had had in the night time, by which there was revealed to him the hiding place of many of the "fanatics." Aye, and even the very place pointed out to him in the dream where it would be most convenient to compass their capturing. And this in due time he brought about, or said he did. But, for all that, I do not think that the company he was among set great store by his truthfulness. For after each wondrous story of adventure and second-sight they would roar with laughter, and say: "Well done, Crichton! Out with another one!"

After a day or two of this lack of food, it came suddenly to me what a dumbhead I was, to bide with an empty belly in a place where at least there must be plenty of fish near at hand. So I rose early from off my bed of heather tops, and betook me down to the river edge. It is nothing but a burn which they call the Eglin Lane, a long, bare water, slow and peaty, but with some trout of size in it. Also from the broads of Loch Macaterick, there came another burn with clearer sparkling water and much sand in the pools. There were trout in both, as one might see by stealing up to the edge of the brow and looking over quickly. But owing to the drought, there was water only in the pools of Eglin, and often but the smallest trickle beneath the stones.

I had a beauty out in a few moments; for so eager was I that I leaped into the burn just as I was, without so much as waiting to take off any of my garments. So in the pool there was a-rushing and a-chasing till I had him out on the grass, his speckled sides glinting bonny on the heather as he tossed himself briskly from side to side. I followed the burn down to the fork of the water that flows from Loch Macaterick, and fished all the pools in this manner. By that time I had enough for three meals at the least; or perhaps, considering the poor state of our appetites, for more than that. I put those we should not want that day into a pretty little fish-pond, which makes a kind of backwater on one of the burns springing down from the side of the Rig of the Star. And this was the beginning of the fish-pond which continued to supply us with food all the time we abode there.

While I was in the river bottom, it chanced that I looked up the great smooth slopes of the opposite hill, which is one of the range of Kells.

There is a little shaggy clump of trees on the bare side of it, and I could have sworn that among the trees I saw people stirring.

I could only think that the people there were wanderers like ourselves, or else spies sent to keep an eye on this wide, wild valley between the Garryhorn hill and the Spear of the Merrick.

So I came back to the cave no little dashed in spirit, in spite of my great successes with the trout. I said nothing about what I had seen to Auld Anton, for he was both weak and feverish. And though certainly mending, he was not yet able to move out into the sunshine and lie among the bracken, a thing which would have done him much good on these still warm days.

But I made a fire with heather and the roots of ancient trees, which in that strange wild desert stick out of the peat at every step. There I roasted the trout, of which Anton Lennox ate heartily. I think they had more relish to a sick man's palate than whaup eggs, even though these came to him as it were in a miraculous manner; while I had guddled the trout with my boots and breeks on.

When the meal was over, I bethought me that I should make an excuse, and steal away over to the side of the Meaull, to see what it might be that was stirring on that lonely brae-face. For save the scraggy scrunts of the rowan trees and birks that surround the cave, there was not a tree within sight, till the woods at the upper end of Loch Doon began to take the sun.

I carefully charged my pistols and told Anton how I proposed to go out to shoot mountain hares or other victual that I could see.

He did not say a word to bid me stay, but only advised me to keep very close to the cave. Because, once off the bosky face of the cliff, there was no saying what hidden eyes might spy me out. For Lag, he said, was certainly lying in hold at Garryhorn at that time, and Claverhouse himself was on the borders of the country. Concerning this last I knew better than he, and was much desirous that we could get Anton well enough to move further out of the reach of his formidable foes.

I started just when the heated haze of the afternoon was clearing with the first early-falling chill of even. The hills were casting shadows upon each other towards the Dungeon and Loch Enoch, where, in the wildest and most rugged country, some of the folk of the wilderness were in hiding.

As I went I heard the grey crow croak and the muckle corbie cry "Glonk," somewhere over by the Slock of the Hooden. They had got a lamb to themselves or a dead sheep belike. But to me it sounded like the gloating of the dragoons over some captured company of the poor wandering Presbyters. It seemed a strange thing for me, when I came to think of it, that I, the son of the Laird of Earlstoun, my mother, that had long time been the lady thereof, and my brother Sandy, that was now Earlstoun himself, should all be skipping and hiding like thieves, with the dragoons at our tail. Now this thought came not often to us, who were born during the low estate of the Scottish kirk. But when it did come, the thought was even more bitter to us, because we had no sustaining memories of her former high estate, nor remembered what God's kirk had been in Scotland from the year 1638 down to the weary coming of Charles Stuart and the down-sitting of the Drunken Parliament in the Black Year of Sixty.

But for all that I thought on these things as I went. Right carefully I kept the cover of every heather bush, peat hag, muckle grey granite stone, and waving clump of bracken. So that in no long space, by making a wide circuit, I came to look down upon the little clump of trees, where I had seen the figures moving, as I guddled the trout for our dinner in the reaches of the Eglin Lane.

Now, however, there seemed to be a great quietness all about the place, and the scanty trees did not so much as wave a branch in the still air of the afternoon.

Yet I saw, as it had been the waft of a jaypiet's wing among them, when I came over the steep rocks of the Hooden's Slock, and went to ford the Gala Lane — which like the other water was, by the action of the long dry year, sunken to no more than a chain of pools. But as I circled about and came behind the trees, there was, as I say, a great quiet. My heart went up and down like a man's hand at the flail in a barn. Yet for my unquiet, there was no great apparent reason. It might be, indeed, that the enemies had laid a snare for me, and that I was already as good as setting out for the Grassmarket, with the ladder and the rope before me, and the lad with the piebald coat at my tail. And this was a sore thought to me, for we Gordons are not of a race that take hanging lightly. We never had more religion than we could carry for comfort. Yet we always got our paiks for what little we had, on which side soever we might be. It is a strange thing that we should always have managed to come out undermost whichever party was on top, and of this I cannot tell the reason. On the other hand, the Kennedies trimmed their sails to the breeze as it blew, and were ever on the wave's crest. But then they were Ayrshiremen. And Ayr, it is well kenned, aye beats Galloway — that is, till it comes to the deadly bellyful of fighting.

Thus I communed with myself, ever drawing nearer to the clump of trees on the side of the Meaull, and murmuring good Protestant prayers, as if they had been no better than Mary's beads all the time.

As I came to the little gairy above the trees, I looked down, and from the verge of it I saw the strangest contrivance. It was a hut beside a tiny runlet of water — a kind of bower with the sides made of bog-oak stobs taken from the edges of the strands. The roof was daintily theeked with green rushes and withes, bound about with heather. Heather also was mingled with the thatching rushes, so that from a little distance the structure seemed to be part of the heath. I lay and watched to see what curious birds had made such a bower on the Star in the dark days. For such dainty carefulness was not the wont of us chiels of the Covenant, and I could not think that any of the rough-riders after us would so have spent their time. An inn yard, a pint stoup, and a well-cockered doxie were more to their liking, than plaiting the bonny heather into a puppet's house upon the hillside.

CHAPTER XL.

MARDROCHAT THE SPY.

THEN even as upon the hillside I watched and waited, I saw one come out and go round about the bower. It was a figure in woman's garments. I knew the form at the first sight. It was Kate McGhie of the Balmaghie. I had found our lost maids. So I gave a whistle that she knew with my bird call, such as every lad of the heather carried, from old Sandy Peden to young James Renwick. At the first sound of it, she started as though she had been stung. At the second peep and whinny she came a little way on tiptoe. So I whistled with a curious turn at the end, as Wat, my cousin, was wont to do. Whereupon she came a little further, and I could see her eyes looking about eagerly.

Then I stood up and came running down the side of the gairy till she saw me. She gave a little cry and put her hands to her heart, for I think she had not expected to see me, but some other — Wat of Lochinvar, as I guess. But for all that she held out her hands as if she were mightily glad to see me.

"Ye canna send us back now!" she cried out, before even I came near to her.

"Ye deserve to get soundly payed for this misdemeanour," I answered. "Did ye ever think of the sore hearts ye left behind ye?"

"Oh, my father," said Kate lightly, "he would just read his book, bless King Chairlie, walk the avenue, and say 'Kate, Kate — deil's in the lassie! The daft hizzie has tane the hill again!'"

"But will not he be angry?"

"Angry, Roger McGhie? Na, na; I bade Mally Lintwhite make him potted-head, and gie him duck aff the pond to his supper, stuffed with mushrooms; and atween that and his claret wine he will thrive brawly."

Then Kate McGhie seemed suddenly to remember something, and we went down the hillside among the stones.

"Bide ye there!" she commanded, halting me with her hand as John Graham halts a squadron. And I did as I was bidden; for in those days Kate had most imperious ways with her.

She stole down quietly, stooped her head to raise the flap which made a curtain door for the bower, and went within. I watched with all my eyes, for I was eager to see once more Maisie Lennox, my dear sometime comrade and gossip. In a little she came forth, but what a leap my heart gave when I saw how pale she looked. Her hand and arm were bandaged, and she leaned lightly on Kate's shoulder.

Do you wonder that my desire went out to her greatly, and that all in a moment I sprang down the rickle of stones as if they had been a made road?

"Maisie, Maisie, wha has done this to ye, my lassie?" I cried, or something like that (for I do not mind the words very well). And with that she fell to the greeting — the lass that never grat whatever was wrong, so that I was fair beside myself to see her. And Kate McGhie pushed me forward by the shoulder, and made signs frowningly, which I could not understand. I thought she meant that I was to go away till Maisie had somewhat recovered herself.

Very obediently I made to do so, and was for stealing away up the hill again, when Kate stamped her foot and said suddenly, "If ye daur——!" So I abode where I was, till it seemed to me that Maisie was about to fall, being yet weak. So I went to hold her up, and as soon as I did so,

Kate McGhie slipped out of sight. Now, I think she did this of intention, for when she convoyed me a little down the hill, when I went in the evening, she rallied me very sorely.

"Man William Gordon," she said; "I e'en thocht I wad hae to pit your airms aboot her, and tell ye what to say. Ye maun be a queer make o' men up about the Glenkens. I thank a merciful Providence that we have another kind o' them about the headend o' Balmaghie!"

But when she left us I needed no instruction. With the best will in the world I fell to comforting Maisie; and though I put not down the matter of our discourse (which concerned only ourselves), I can vouch for it that speedily we were at one. And for a long season I sat on the grey bowder stones of the gairy and made much of her in another fashion than that of a comrade.

Then after this our first pleasuring was by-past, she told me how that Kate and she had come away to seek for her father, because of the report that had come of his danger and illness; but that an accident had befallen them upon the way, and they had failed of their errand. What the accident was she would not tell me, saying that Kate McGhie would be fond enough to give me the story. Then they had built this bower by the burnside, where ever since they had remained safe and unmolested.

I asked how they got their provender.

"O," she said, "Hughie Kerr brings it over the hill from the howe of the Kells. We have had no want of good meal."

Then when we had talked and I had told her of her father and his welfare, I bethought me to urge her to bide where she was, for that night at all events, saying that perhaps in the morning she might come over to see him. For I desired, seeing that the place was no longer safe (if, indeed, the persecutors did know where Anton was hid, which I believed not), to have him shifted as soon as he could bear the journey. But yet I was loath to do it, for there is no hold in all the high hill-lands so commodious as Cove Macaterick above the loch of that name.

When Kate McGhie came again to us, methought she looked more approvingly upon me than before — but indulgently, as one that passes an indifferent piece of work, which yet she herself could better have performed.

As soon as she came near, I began to ask her of Maisie's accident and the cause of it.

"Has she not told you herself? I am not going to heat cauld porridge for you twa to sup," she said, in the merry way which never deserted her. For she was ever the most spirity wench in the world, and though a laird's daughter, it pleased her often to speak in the country fashion.

But when I had advertised her that Maisie had not said a word about the matter, but on the contrary had referred me to herself, Kate McGhie made a pretty mouth and gave a little whistle.

"After all, then," she said, "we are not round the corner yet!"

Then she began to tell me of their journeying in the night after Pherson, the serving-man, had left them.

"We cam' over the heather licht foot as hares," said Kate McGhie. "The stars were bonny above. A late moon was rising over the taps by Balmaclellan, and the thocht that I was out on the heather hills set a canty fire in my breast.

"A' gaed richt till we cam' to the new brig across the Water o' Dee, that was biggit a year or twa syne wi' the collections in the kirks. When we cam' to it we were liltin' blythe and careless at a sang, when oot o' the dark o' the far side there steps a muckle cankersome lookin' man in a big cloak, an' stan's richt in the midst o' the road!

"'Whaur gang ye sae late at nicht by this road withoot the leave o' Mardrochat?' says he.

"'Sang,' says I. 'Wha's midden's this? And wha's Mardrochat that his barn-door cock craws sae croose on til't?'

"For," said Kate McGhie, looking at me, "as ye ken, I hadna been learned at the Balmaghie to thole snash frae onybody."

At which I smiled, for well I knew Kate's reputation with her tongue.

"'This is Mardrochat's road, and by the King's command his business is to question all comers. But it's not ill-gi'en words that he wad use wi' twa sic bonny lassies!' says the loon in the cloak.

"'Dear sirs,' says I, 'fifty puddin's on a plate! Mardrochat maun be a braw lad. Is he the King's hangman? It's an honourable and well-considered office nowadays, they tell me.'

"'Satisfy me whar ye are gaun sae late,' says the ill-contriving chiel, 'an' maybes I'll convoy ye a bit o' the road. It shall never be said that Mardrochat left twa weel-faured lassies them-lane in the howe o' the nicht!'

"'Heighty-teighty,' I telled the man, 'oor coo's come hame, an' her tail's ahint her! Stand oot o' the road an' let decent folk to their beds!'

"'There's nae beds bena the heather that gate!' said the man. And faith, there he was in the right of it. There were no beds except the wanderers' beds in the moss-hags that road for twenty lang Scots miles.

"And all this time we were standing on the brig close to one another.

"'Let us gang by,' said I again.

"'Na,' said the long loon that had called himself Mardrochat, and wha I kenned for an ill-set informer that made his siller by carrying tales to Clavers and Lag, 'ye pass na this road. Ye maun e'en turn and come wi' me!'

"And I think he would have come forward to put his hand upon us. But I made to get past him at one side, crying to Maisie to try the other. For I thought that the two of us were surely a match for any black thief of the kind to be found in the Glenkens.

"But as I was running by, he grippit me with one hand and drew his windlestrae of a sword wi' the other — drew it on a pair o' lassies, mind ye. Then what think ye? Your bit lassie there, Missie Mim, she flew on him like a wullcat and gripped the blade atween her fingers till she drew it oot o' his hand. Then she took it across her knee and garred it play *snap* like a rotten branch. Syne ower it gaed intil the water. And that was the way she got the cut on her hand, poor thing."

Then I gave a great shout and clasped Maisie in my arms, yet not harshly, lest she should be weak. I was glad to hear this testimony to her bravery.

"That is of a better fashion," said Kate, like one who has store of experience. Then she went on with her story, for she had yet more to tell. "But the loon was dour for a' the want o' his sword, and we micht no' hae mastered him but that he tried to trip us and so got tripped himself. He fell so that the head o' him took the wa' and fair dang him stupid. So we e'en gied him a bit hoise an' ower he gaed intil the water——"

"Mercy on us," I cried, "ye didna droon the man?"

"Droon him," said Kate, "deil a fear! Yon chiel is made for the tow. He'll droon nane. The last we saw o' him, he was sitting on his hurdies in the shallows, up to his neck in the water, trying what banes war hale after his stramash.

"So," continued Kate, "we gaed our roads in peace,

and the chiel sat still in the water, thrawin' his heid aboot and aboot like a turnspit, as lang as we could see him."

Even thus Kate McGhie told her tale, making my lass dearer to me with every word. Of Mardrochat the informer, who had made bold to meddle with them, I had heard many times. He had been a Covenanter of zeal and forwardness till, at a meeting of the Societies, his double-faced guile had been laid bare. Ever since which day in the wilds of Friarminion, he had been a cunning, spying fox, upon the track of the hill-folk. But I knew how dangerous the man could be, and liked it ill enough that the maids should have crossed him so early on their pilgrimage. I doubted not that it was from him that the original information had come, which, being carried to the enemy by Birsay and overheard by me in the house of Balmaghie, had sent us all hiving to the mountains.

CHAPTER XLI.

THE HOUSE OF THE BLACK CATS.

HAVING bidden such good-e'en to the maids as was severally due to them, I crossed the Nick of the Gadlach and went whistling over the moor. I took a new road over the heather, and was just at the turning of the Eglin Lane, when, deep in the howe of the glen, I came on the strangest kind of cot-house. It was piled together of the rough bowder stones of the country, their edges undressed and gaping, the spaces between them filled in with faggots of heather and plastered with stiff bluish clay from the burn-sides. The roof was of branches of the fir trees long buried in the moss, and was thatched with heather. There was an opening in the middle, from which a smoke arose. And I heard a sound like singing from within — a sound that made my flesh creep.

I went to the door and with my knuckle knocked gently, as is our fashion in that part of the country, crying, "Are ye within, good wife?"

Whereat the strangest unearthly voice answered back to me, as it had been some one reading in the Bible and laughing at the same time — a horrid thing to hear in that still place and so near the defenceless young lassies in the Bower of the Star.

"The waters of Meribah — the waters of Meribah — for they were bitter!" it cried in a kind of wail. "Come ben and hae some brose!" And then the thing laughed again.

I took courage to look within, but because it was dark I

saw nothing. The whole interior was full of the smoor of reek, and strange things sped round and round, crossing each other and passing the door continually, like the staves and buckets of a water-mill running round.

"Come awa' ben," again commanded the voice. "Doon, Badrona! Peace, Grimalkin!" The command was addressed to a number of monstrous black cats, which had been speeding round the walls of the cot like mad things, to the music of the unearthly crooning song which I had heard from within.

I stepped across the threshold and found a red peat fire upon the hearth and a black pot hanging over it. I looked about for the person who had addressed me. At first I could see him nowhere. But as my eyes grew accustomed to the light I saw the queerest being—the sight of whom made my heart grow cold and my hand steal to the little pocket Bible, bound in two halves, that was in my inner pocket.

A small square object sat huddled up at the far side of the fire. Upon its head there was a turban, like those the travellers into the lands of the False Prophet tell us of. But this turban was of black bull hide, and the beast's dull eyes looked out underneath with a hellish suggestion. The figure was squat like a toad, and sitting thus sunk down upon itself, it seemed to be wholly destitute of feet and legs. But a great pair of hairy arms lay out upon the hearth and sometimes clawed together the fiery red peats, as though they had just been casten and were being fitted for drying upon the moss.

"Come awa' ben. Ye are welcome, honest stranger," again said the thing of the uncanny look, "I am nane bonny, truth to tell, but I'm nocht to my mither. It's a braw thing that ye are no' to meet wi' her the nicht. She has gane ower by to gather the Black Herb by the licht o' the aval moon. When the moon faas ower on her back like a sheep that canna rise, then is the time to gather the bonny Wolf's Bane, the Deil's Bit, wi' the berries by the water-side that nane kens whaur to seek, an' the Mandrake that cries like a murdered bairn when ye pu' it frae the moss. See ye here, there's three dead bairns aneath that hearthstane. Gin ye like I will let ye see the banes. She didna pit me there, for the deil's wife has aye a warm side to the deil's bairn. Sit ye doon and bide a wee. It's braw an' heartsome to see a face at Willie's Shiel in the howe o' the Eglin."

After the first horrid surprise of coming in upon such a place, I saw that the thing after all was human — an idiot or natural as I judged, with a monstrous twisted body and strange elricht voice like the crying of the night-wind in a keyhole. But I thought it best to sit down on a seat, even as he bade me, and so I drew a creepie stool carelessly nearer to me with one hand.

"Na, dinna sit on that — that's a stool that naebody can sit on but my mither."

And when I looked at the creepie in the red firelight, for it felt strange to my hand, lo! it was formed of three skulls set close together, and the legs of it were of men's leg bones.

Then it flashed to my mind that I had chanced on the house of Corp-licht Kate, the witch wife of the Star, who for many years dwelt alone on the flowe of the Eglin, with only her idiot son with her for company.

"Na," said the object, "nane can sit on that creepie but the minnie o' me — Corp-licht Kate o' the Star. It's weel for me, an' it's weel for you, that my minnie's no' here the nicht. But sit ye down and tak' your rest."

I arose to flee, but the monstrous figure by the red fire waved me down. And I declare that as I looked at him, he seemed to swell and glow with a kind of brightness like the moon through mist. He waved his arms abroad, and immediately about me there began the most affrighting turmoil. Black forms that had been crouching in the corners came out and began to circle round us, as it appeared by some devilish cantrip, skimming round the house breast-high, without ever touching the floor or the walls. They seemed like an army of cats, black and unearthly, all flying in mid air, screeching and caterwauling as at a witch's festival. I began to wonder if the foul, human-headed, toad-like thing that squatted by the fire were indeed the black master of witches himself, to whom, for my sins, I had been delivered in the flesh before my time.

But with a wave of his hand the idiot stilled the turmoil, and the flitting demons came to the ground in the shape of a dozen or so of cats, black and horrid, with arched tails and fiery eyes — as wild to look at as though they had wandered in from the moor. These retreated into the dark corners of the room, whence we could hear them purring and spitting, and see their fiery eyes set on us in a circle out of the gloom, which was dense as night everywhere, save only immediately about the fire.

"I am nae deil, though ye think it, and maist folk says it," said the idiot, fixing his eyes on me. "Some says the daddie o' me was the deil, and some says Mardrochat. I kenna. There's no' muckle to choose between them. Ye can ask my mither gin ye like. I never speered her mysel'. Ye'll hae a sup o' my parritch. They are guid parritch — no' like my mither's parritch. I wad advise ye to hae nocht to do wi' my mither's parritch. Heard ye ever o' the Hefter o' the Star?"

I told him no, and sat down to see what might happen in this strange abode so near to the two places where dwelled those whom I loved best — the Bower of the Star and the Cave of Macaterick. But I loosened my sword and felt that the grip of my pistols came easy to my hand.

"Be na feared o' puir Gash Gibbie o' the Star Sheiling," cried the object, noticing the action; "he's as honest as he is ugly. But keep wid o' the mither o' him, gin ye wad scape the chiding of the channering worm."

The natural seemed to read the fears of my heart before I knew them myself.

"Na, ye'll no' dee like the Hefter o' the Star. He was an ill loon, him; he wadna let my mither be, when he cam to heft hoggs in the mid o' the year. He spied on us as he sat on a hill-tap to watch that his sheep didna break dykes. But ken ye what my mither did? She gaed oot to him wi' a wee drap kail broth. Tak' ye nane o' my mither's kail broth. They are no' canny. But the hefter, silly body, took mair o' them than he was the better o'. He took them doon in a bit hollow to be oot o' the wind, and when they fand him, he had manned it to crawl back to his watcher's hill-tap. But there the silly, feckless loon died like a trout on the bank. He didna like my mither's broth. Na, they didna gree weel wi' him!"

And Gash Gibbie went on yammering and grumbling, while I sat and gazed dumbfounded at him, and at the ugly grimalkins in the dark corners, which stared at me with shining eyes, till I wished myself well out of it all.

"An' ken ye what my mither said when the next hefter cam to see after his sheep on the hill?"

I shook my head.

"She said, 'Watna grand ploy it wad be gin this yin were to die as weel!' That was what my mither said."

"And did he die?" I asked.

Gash Gibbie moved his shoulders, and made a kind of *nichering* laugh to himself, like a young horse whinnying for its corn.

"Na, he was ower cunning for my minnie, him. He wadna bide here, and when my minnie gaed to him with the guid kail broo and the braxy sooming amang it, says the second hefter, 'I'm no' that hungry the day, mistress; I'll gie the hoodie craws a drap drink o't!'

"And so he did, and as fast as the craws got twa fills o' their nebs, they keeled ower on their backs, drew in their taes three times, cried *kraigh*, and tumbled heels up, as stiff as Methusala! Richt curious, was it na? She is a wonnerfu' woman, my mither!"

The thunder clouds which had been forming all through the heat of the afternoon, began to roar far away by Loch Doon, and as the place and the talk did not conduce to pleasant thoughts, I rose to go.

"What's your hurry?" cried Gash Gibbie, swinging himself round to my side of the fire, and lifting himself on his hands like a man that has no feet. "My minnie will no' be here till the mornin', and then we'll hae company belike. For she's gane to warn Mardrochat to send the sodgers to the twa run-awa' lassies up at the bit bouroch on the Meaull o' Garryhorn."

"To bring the soldiers?" I said, for the words made me suddenly afraid.

"Aye," said the natural, looking cunningly at me, "an' Gash Gibbie wad hae warned the bits o' lassies. But he's ower gruesome a tyke to be welcome guest in lady's bower. But Gibbie wishes the lassies no harm. They are clever, well-busked hizzies."

"I wonder if there are any more wanderers in hiding hereabouts," said I, thinking in my transparent guile to find out whether the Cove Macaterick were also known.

"Na, na, nane nearer than the Caldons in the Howe o' Trool. There's some o' Peden's folk there that my mither has put her spite on — but nane nearer."

The thunder and lightning was just coming on, as I passed the ring of cats in the outer darkness of the hut, and looked out. "Good night to ye, Gibbie," said I, "and thank ye kindly for your crack and the warming I hae gotten before the fire!"

"Guid-e'en to yoursel', bonny laddie, an' a guid journey to ye. It's gaun to be a coorse nicht, and Gibbie maun gang awa' ower the heather to see gin his bonny mither doesna' miss the road hame!"

CHAPTER XLII.

THE NICK O' THE DEID WIFE.

I WENT out, and the whole night seemed empty about me. The deep and wide basin between the hollow palms of the hills was filled with an eery leme of flame, flickering up from the ground.

I took my way with as great strides as I could compass, back to the bower under the trees. The thunder rolled continuously about and about. At times it seemed to recede far away, but always sounding from different places, as though many peals were running races one with the other. Then the lightning flickered, and keen little arrows sped hither and thither till the whole sky twanged like a harp.

It seemed a hundred miles to the shieling on the hill. And when I came near I was astonished and greatly affrighted to hear the sound of voices, and at least one of them the voice of a man. A strange fear came over me; hardly, I think, the fear of the King's men.

"I hae brocht wi' me my silver spune," said a voice that went to my heart; "I made siccar o' my silver spoon. Gin I hae to gang to the heather for the Covenant, at least I shall gang as a lady!"

It was my mother's voice, and I ran down to her, falling into her arms, and bidding her to be quiet in the same breath.

Wat had just arrived with my mother and little Margaret of Glen Vernock, who, winding herself about all our hearts, had become as her own child to my mother in the days of her loneliness. They were weary and in need of rest; but when I had told my news and the warning I had gotten from Gash Gibbie in the fearsome precincts of the hut of Corp-licht Kate, every one felt the need of at once forsaking the Bower of the Star and betaking ourselves to Cove Macaterick — which, if not so pleasant or commodious, was at least far more safe.

So we loaded us with Hugh Kerr's meal, and the little bits of things that the lassies had gathered about them or brought with them. My mother carried only an oaken staff in her hand, and in a satchel at her girdle her beloved silver spoon (with "Mary Hope" on it in antique letters), which her father had given her for her own when she learned to read, and first took her place at the table above the salt.

"O what wad he hae said, that was Lord President of Session in his time, gin he had seen his dochter Mary linkin' ower the heather wi' her coats kilted in her auld age?" my mother cried out once when we hurried her. For she had ever a great notion of her lineage — though indeed the Hopes are nothing to compare with the Gordons for antiquity or distinction.

"I think your father was 'at the horn' mair nor yince himsel', mither," said I, remembering certain daffing talk of my father's.

"Aye, and that is just as true," said my mother, reconciling herself to her position, "forbye it is weel kenned that the wife aye wears the cockade of her lord."

And at the word I thought of my Lady of Lochinvar, and hearkened to Wat talking low to Kate McGhie. But as for me I kept my mother by my side, and left Maisie Lennox to herself, remembering the fifth commandment — and knowing likewise that it would please Maisie best if I took care of my mother.

Thus we came to Cove Macaterick.

Now the cove upon the hillside is not wet and chill as almost all sea caves are, where the water stands on the floor and drips from every crevice. But it was at least fairly dry, if not warm, and had been roughly laid with bog-wood dug from the flowes, not squared at all, but only filled in with heather tops till the floor was elastic like the many-plied carpets of Whitehall.

There was, as I have said, an inner and an outer cave, one opening out of the other, each apartment being about sixteen feet every way, but much higher towards the roof. And so it remained till late years, when, as I hear from the herd of the Shalloch, the rocks of the gairy face have settled more down upon themselves, and so have contracted the space. But the cave remains to this day on the Back Hill of the Star over the waters of Loch Macaterick. And the place is still very lonely. Only the whaups, the ernes, and the mountain sheep cry there, even as they did in our hiding times.

We gave the inner (and higher) room to the women folk, and divided the space with a plaid hung up at the stone steps which formed a doorway.

We found Anton Lennox much recovered, but still very weak and pale. He sat propped up on his heather bed against the side of the cave. His countenance appeared stern and warlike, even when it was too dark to see, as it mostly was, his great sword leaning against the wall by his side.

I need not tell of the joy there was when Maisie Lennox greeted her father, and we that had been so wide scattered drew together once again. But as soon as I had told Wat of the happenings at the hut of Corp-licht Kate, nothing would serve him but we must set out and try to intercept the witch from fulfilling her mission. For if she brought the soldiers upon us, our trail from the bower among the trees was fresh and might be followed. Wat was determined at all costs to turn the witch; and, having brought her to her house, to keep a watch upon her there — at least till the rain had washed away our foot-prints down the mountain side, and confused them among the moss-hags.

So leaving most unwillingly the snug and sheltered place of Cove Macaterick, we stepped out into the gloomy and threatening night. The wild-fire still flickered, and the thunder rolled continuously; but the rain held off. The natural had mentioned that his mother was making over the hills toward Straiton, where for the time being Mardrochat, the informer, dwelt, and where was quartered a troop of horse for the overawing of the country.

We decided, therefore, that we should take our course in that direction, which led past Peden's hut, where the wanderer had abode so often. It was an uncanny night, but in some fashion we stumbled along — now falling into moss-hags almost to the waist, and now scrambling out again, and so on without a word of complaining. Wat's attire was not now such as that he had donned to visit my Lady Wellwood. It was but of stout hodden grey and a checked plaid like the rest.

So we mounted shoulder after shoulder of heathery hillside, like vessels that labour over endless billows of the sea against a head wind. The thunder cloud which seemed to brood upon the outer circle of the hills, and arch over the country of Macaterick and the Star, now grumbled nearer and louder. Not seldom there came a fierce, white, wimpling flash, and the encompassing mountains seemed ready to burn up in the glare. Then ensued darkness blacker than ever, and the thunder shaking the world, as though it had been an ill-built house-place with skillets and pans clattering on the wall.

T

We had been thus walking for some while, bearing breast to the brae all the time, and leaning forward even as a horse leans to its collar. We came in time near to the height of the pass. We could not see a yard before us. But suddenly we felt the ground begin to level in front; and lo! in a moment we were in the throat of the defile, with the hills black above us on either side. Suddenly there came a terrible white flash of lightning, brighter and longer continued than any we had seen. The very air seemed to grow blue-black like indigo. The thunder tore the heavens, galloping without ceasing. Flash followed rending flash. Immediately before us on a hillock we saw a wondrous sight. There sat Gash Gibbie, the mis-shaped idiot, crouched squat like a toad, at the head of a woman who lay with her arms straight at her sides, as though stretched for burial.

As we stood illumined against the murky blackness of the pass, the monstrous thing caught sight of us, and waved his hands, dancing meantime (as it seemed) upon spindles of legs. How he had come so far and so swiftly on such a night I cannot tell. But without doubt, there he was on the highest rock of the pass, with the dead woman stretched at his feet, and the fitful blue gleam of the lightning playing about him. And I warrant you it was not a comely or a canny sight.

"Come ye here," cried the idiot lad, wavering above us as though he were dancing in the reek of the nether pit, "an' see what Yon has done to my mither. I aye telled her how it wad be. It doesna do to strive wi' Yon. For Yon can gie ye your paiks so brave and easy. But my mither, she wad never hear reason, and so there she lies, dead streeked in the 'Nick o' the Deid Wife.' Yon has riven the life frae my mither!"

We were close at his side by this time, and we saw an

irksome sight, that shook our nerves more than the thunder. A woman of desperately evil countenance lay looking past us, her eyes fixed with an expression of bitter wrath and scorn upon the black heavens. Her face and hands were stained of a deep crimson colour, either by the visitation of God or made to seem so by the flickering flame of wild-fire that played about us.

CHAPTER XLIII.

THE VENGEANCE OF "YON."

GASH GIBBIE surveyed the sight with a kind of twisted satisfaction. He went hirpling about the body round and round. He squatted with crossed legs at its head.

"What think ye o' that?" he asked, "that's my mither. She's near as bonny as me, think ye no? Yon micht hae made her bonnier to look at, gin He was to be so ill to her."

And the monster crouched still lower, and took the terrible scarlet-stained face and neck on his knees.

"Mither! mither!" he wailed, "I aye telled ye it wad come to this — mockin' Yon disna do. A wee while, maybe, He lets ye gang on; but no for lang! Yon can bide His time, and juist when ye are crawin' croose, and thinkin' on how blythe and canty ye are — blaff! like a flaught o' fire — Yon comes upon ye, and where are ye?"

He took a long and apparently well-satisfied look at his mother.

"Aye, there ye lie, an' by my faith, ye are no bonny, mither o' mine. Mony is the time I telled ye what it wad be, afore Yon had dune wi' ye."

Small wonder that it chilled our blood to hear the twisted being cry out thus upon the mother that bore him. He seemed even no little pleased that what he had foretold had come to pass. So we stood, Wat and I, in silent amaze before him, as the storm continued to blare till the whole heaven above us appeared but the single mouth of a black trumpet.

Sometimes we seemed to be in a large place, ribbed and rafted with roaring sound, upholstered with lightning flashes of pale violet and blue. Then again the next moment we were shut within a tent of velvet blackness like a pall, with only the echoes of the warring midnight rolling away back among the hills. There seemed no God of Pity abroad that night to look after puir muir-wandered folk, but only mocking devils riding rough-shod on the horses of the pit.

"Come away hame, Gibbie," said I, "ye can do her little good. I fear she's by wi' it!"

"By wi' it!" quoth the natural, fleeringly. "Na, only beginning wi' it. D'ye no ken, hill-man-wi'-the-hirpling-leg, that Yon has gotten her. I can see her stannin' afore Yon, wi' her face like red fire, a black lie in her mouth and ill-intent in her heart. For as the tree falls, so doth it lie."

The imp seemed to have gotten the words at some field-preaching.

"Think ye I didna warn her?" he went on. "My braw chiels, ye hae gotten your warnin' this nicht! Meddle na wi' Yon, neither dare Him to His face lest He be angry. For juist like Gibbie killin' a speckly taed, Yon can set His heel on ye!"

He stroked the hair off the dead woman's brow with a hand like a hairy claw.

"Aye, an' ye were na sic an ill mither to me, though ye selled yoursel' to Ye-Ken-Wha! Whatna steer there is up there aboot the soul o' ae puir auld body. Hear till it——"

And he waved his hands to the four airts of heaven, and called us to hearken to the hills shaking themselves to pieces. "Siccan a steer aboot a puir feckless auld woman gaun to her ain ill place! I wonder Yon is no' shamed o' himsel'!"

And the twisted man-thing put his hands to his brow and pressed the palms upon his eyes, as if to shut out the unceasing pulsing of the lightning and the roar of the anger of God breaking like sea upon the mountains.

"Sae muckle squandered for sae little — an' after a' but little pleasure in the thing! I dinna see what there is in the Black Man's service to mak' siccan a brag aboot. Gin ye sup tasty kail wi' him in the forenicht, he aye caa's roond wi' the lawin' i' the mornin'!

"Losh! Losh! Sae muckle for sae little. I declare I will cut oot the three marks that my mither made on me, and gang doon to Peden at the Shalloch. I want na mair sic wark as this! Na, though I was born wi' the Black Man's livery on me!

"Preserve us!" he cried. "This is as fearsome as that year there was nae meat in the hoose, and Gash Gibbie brocht some back, and aye brocht it, and brocht it even as it was needed. And Kate o' the Corp-licht, she readied it and asked nae quastions. But only tearin' belly-hunger gied us strength to eat that awesome meat. An' a' the neighbours died o' starvation at Tonskeen and the Star an' the bonny Hill o' the Buss — a' but Gib an' his mither, their leevin' lanes. But yae nicht Yon sent Gibbie's sin to find him oot; or maybe the Black Thing in the Hole gat lowse, because it was his hour.

"And at ony rate puir Gibbie gat a terrible fricht that nicht.

"Wad ye like to hear? Aweel, puir Gibbie was lying on his bed up that stair, an' what think ye there cam' to him?"

He paused and looked at us with a countenance so blanched and terrible that almost we turned and ran. For the lightning played upon it till it seemed to glow with unholy light, and that not from without but from within. It was the most terrifying thing to be alone with such a monstrous living creature, and such a dead woman in the lonesome place he had called the "Nick of the Deid Wife." What with the chattering of our teeth, the agitation of our spirits, and the flicker of the fire, the old dead witch seemed actually to rise and nod at us.

"So Gash Gibbie, puir man, lay and listened in his naked bed, for he had gotten his fill that nicht, though a' the lave were hungry — an' that o' his ain providin'. But as he lay sleepless, he heard a step come to the door, the sneck lifted itsel', an' a foot that wasna his mither's came into the passage, *dunt-duntin'* like a lameter hirplin' on two staves!

"An' then there cam' a hard footstep on the stair, and a rattle o' fearsome-like sounds, as the thing cam' up the ladder. Gibbie kenned na what it micht be. An' when the door opened an' the man wi' the wooden feet cam' in — preserve me, but he was a weary-lookin' tyke.

"'Whaur came ye frae?' says puir Gash Gibbie.

"'Frae the Grave!' says he. He hadna muckle to say, but his e'en war like fiery gimblets in his head.

"'What mak's your e'en bones sae white an' deep?'

"'The Grave!' says he. He hadna muckle to say, but he spak' aye mair dour and wearisome than ever.

"'What mak's ye lauch sae wide at puir Gibbie?'

"'The Grave!' says he. He hadna muckle to say, but syne he steppit nearer nearer to the bedside.

"'What made that great muckle hole in your side?'

"'You made it!' cried the ghaist, loupin' at Gibbie's throat; an' puir Gib kenned nae mair."

And even as the monster shouted out the last words — the words of the spectre of his cannibal vision — Gash Gibbie seemed to us to dilate and lean forward to spring upon us. The wild-fire reeled about as though the very elements were drunken, and Wat and I fairly turned and fled, shouting insanely with terror as we ran — leaving the silent stricken witch with the face of blood, and the misshapen elf, her hell's brood progeny, raving and shouting on the hillside — these two alone at midnight in the "Nick of the Deid Wife."

"Aye, rin, rin," we heard him call after us. "Rin fast, and Yon will maybe no' catch ye — till it is your hour!"

And truly Wat and I did run in earnest, stumbling and crying out in our terror — now falling and now getting up, then falling to the running again without a single reasonable word. But as we came hot-foot over the Rig of Lochricaur, we seemed to run into the sheeted rain. For where we had been hitherto, only the blue dry fire had ringed us, but here we ran into a downpour as though the fountains of the deep of heaven had broken up and were falling in a white spate upon the world.

We were wet, weary, and terrified, more than we had ever been in our lives, before we reached the hermitage of the cave of Macaterick. There we found the women waiting for us, listening fearfully to the roar of the storm without, and hearkening in the lown blinks to Auld Anton Lennox praying — while the lightning seemed to run into the cave, and shine on the blade of the sword he held gripped in his right hand. So we stripped our wet clothes, and lay in the outer place all the night, where there was a fire of red peats, while the women withdrew themselves into their inner sanctuary. I could see the anxiety in their eyes when we came in, for they could not but discern the ghastly terror in our faces. But without any agreement between ourselves, Wat and I silently resolved that we should not acquaint any of the party with the hideous judgments of that night, to which we had been eye-witnesses.

CHAPTER XLIV.

A DESIRABLE GENERAL MEETING.

THE next morning dawned colder and more chilly. The catch of the autumn of the year was in the air, and it nipped shrewdly till the sun looked over the hills in the east. This was to be the great day of the Societies' general meeting, which had been summoned in the wilds of Shalloch-on-Minnoch.*

> *Now, because men so readily forget, I may repeat how that the United Societies had grown in strength since Ayrsmoss, and now needed only a head to make a stand for the cause. It was a strange way of the Providence of God, that it should come about that these little meetings for prayer in remote places of the land, should grow to be so mighty a power for the pulling down of strongholds. At this time, though every appearance in arms had been put down at Pentland, at Bothwell, and at Ayrsmoss, yet the Blue Banner itself had never been put down. And even now many a Malignant in the south and west trembled at the great and terrible name of the "Seven Thousand."
>
> The proclamations of the Societies, which were affixed to every kirk door and market cross in the south, caused many a persecutor and evil-wisher to quake and be silent. And the word that God was building for Himself a folk on the hills of Scotland reached even to the Low Countries, and kept the Prince of Orange and his counsellors watching with eager eyes those things which were done by the Remnant over seas, till the appointed hour should come. Heading and hanging would not last for ever, and such is the binding power of persecution that for each one cut off by prison, or the hangman's cord, ten were sworn in to do the will of the Societies. Till this present time most fatal dissension and division among themselves had been their undoing. But there was one coming, now a willow wand of a student of Groningen in Holland, who should teach the Societies to be a wall of fire about their faith and their land.
>
> To their conventions came commissioners from all parts of Scotland, but mainly from the southern and western shires, as well as from the Merse, and out of the bounds of Fife.

Though the morn had dawned caller, with a white rime of frost lying on the grass and for a little space making grey the leaves of the trees, the day of the great conventicle was one of great and lowering heat. My mother was set to go — and Kate McGhie also. Wat must needs therefore accompany them, and I had a letter from Groningen which I behoved to read. With Anton Lennox, stout of heart even in his sickness, abode my lass, Maisie Lennox — of whom (though I looked to be back on the morrow) I took leave with reluctance and with a heavy and sinking heart.

For us who were used to making a herd's track across the hills, it was not a long step over the moors from Macaterick to the foot of the Craigfacie of Shalloch, where the General Meeting of the Societies was to take place. But it was a harder matter for my mother.

She needed help over every little brink of a peat brow, and as we passed Tonskeen, where there is a herd's house in the wild, far from man and very quiet with God, I ran to get her a staff, which the shepherd's good wife gladly gave. For there was little that would be refused to a wanderer in these parts, when on his way to the Societies' Meeting.

Soon we left the strange, unsmiling face of Loch Macaterick behind, and took our way towards the rocky clint, up which we had to climb. We went by the rocks that are called the Rig of Carclach, where there is a pass less steep than in other places, up to the long wild moor of the Shalloch-on-Minnoch. It was a weary job getting my mother up the steep face of the gairy, for she had so many nick-nacks to carry, and so many observes to make.

But when we got to the broad plain top of the Shalloch

So grateful and inspiring were these gatherings, that many went to their death recalling the grace and beauty of these meetings — " desirable general meetings" — they were in deed and sooth, at least as I remember them. — (W. G., Afton, 1702.)

Hill it was easier to go forward, though at first the ground was boggy, so that we took off our stockings and walked on the driest part. We left the burn of Knocklach on our left — playing at keek-bogle among the heather and bent — now standing stagnant in pools, now rindling clear over slaty stones, and again disappearing altogether underground like a hunted Covenanter.

As soon as we came over the brow of the hill, we could see the folk gathering. It was wonderful to watch them. Groups of little black dots moved across the green meadows in which the farmsteading of the Shalloch-on-Minnoch was set — a cheery little house, well thatched, and with a pew of blue smoke blowing from its chimney, telling of warm hearts within. Over the short brown heather of the tops the groups of wanderers came, even as we were doing ourselves — past the lonely copse at the Rowantree, by the hillside track from Straiton, up the little runlet banks where the heather was blushing purple, they wended their ways, all setting towards one place in the hollow. There already was gathered a black cloud of folk under the rickle of stones that runs slidingly down from the steep brow of Craigfacie.

As we drew nearer we could see the notable Session Stone, a broad flat stone overhanging the little pourie burn that tinkles and lingers among the slaty rocks, now shining bone-white in the glare of the autumn sun. I never saw a fairer place, for the heights about are good for sheep, and all the other hills distant and withdrawn. It has not, indeed, the eye-taking glorious beauty of the glen of Trool, but nevertheless it looked a very Sabbath land of benediction and peace that day of the great Societies' Meeting.

Upon the Session Stone the elders were already greeting one another, mostly white-headed men with dinted and furrowed faces, bowed and broken by long sojourning among the moss-hags and the caves.

When we came to the place we found the folk gathering for prayer, before the conference of the chosen delegates of the societies. The women sat on plaids that had been folded for comfort. Opposite the Session Stone was a wide heathery amphitheatre, where, as on tiers of seats, rows of men and women could sit and listen to the preachers. The burnie's voice filled up the breaks in the speech, as it ran small and black with the drought, under the hollow of the bank. For, as is usual upon our moors, the rain and storm of the night had not reached this side of the hill.

I sat down on a lichened stone and looked at the grave, well-armed men who gathered fast about the Session Stone, and on the delegates' side of the water. It was a fitting place for such a gathering, for only from the lonely brown hills above could the little cup of Conventicle be seen, nestling in the lap of the hill. And on all the moor tops that looked every way, couching torpid and drowsed in the hot sun, were to be seen the sentinels — pacing the heather like watchmen going round and telling the towers of Zion, the sun flashing on their pikes and musket barrels as they turned sharply, like men well-disciplined.

The only opening was to the south-west, but even there nothing but the distant hills of Colmonell looked in, blue and serene. Down in the hollow there was a glint of melancholy Loch Moan, lying all abroad among its green wet heather and stretches of yellow bent.

What struck me as most surprising in this assembly was the entire absence of anything like concealment. From every quarter, up from the green meadows of the Minnoch Valley, over the scaurs of the Straiton hills, down past the craigs of Craigfacie, over from the deep howe of Carsphairn, streams of men came walking and riding. The sun glinted on their war-gear. Had there been a trooper within miles, upon any of the circle of the hills, the dimples of light could

A DESIRABLE GENERAL MEETING.

not have been missed. For they caught the sun and flecked the heather — as when one looks upon a sparkling sea, with the sun rising over it and each wave carrying its own glint of light with it upon its moving crest.

As I looked, the heart within me became glad with a full-grown joy. So long had we of the Religion hidden like foxes and run like hares, that we had forgotten that there were so many in the like case, only needing drawing together to be the one power in the land. But the time, though at hand, was not yet.

I asked of a dark long-haired man who stood near us, what was the meaning of such a gathering. He looked at me with a kind of pity, and I saw the enthusiasm flash from his eye.

"The Seven Thousand!" he said; "ken ye not the Seven Thousand upon the hills of Scotland, that never bowed the knee to Baal?"

"Pardon me, friend," said I, "long hiding on the mountains has made me ignorant. But who are the Seven Thousand?"

"Have ye indeed hidden on the mountains and ken not that? Did ye never hear of them that wait for the time appointed?"

I told him no.

"Then," said he, "who may you be that kens so little?"

I said that I was William Gordon, younger son of the persecuted house of the Gordons of Earlstoun.

"O, the Bull's brother!" said he, shortly, and turned him about to go away. But Spitfire Wat was at his side, and, taking the dark man by the elbow, presently halted him and span him round so that he faced us.

"And who are you that speaks so lightly of my cousin of Earlstoun?" he asked.

I think Wat had forgotten that he was not now among his

Cavalier blades — who, to do them justice, are ready to put every pot-house quarrel to the arbitrament of the sword, which is after all a better way than disputation and the strife of tongues.

The dark man smiled. "Ye are hot, young sir," he said bitterly. "These manners better befit the guard-room of Rob Grier of Lag than a gathering of the Seven Thousand. But since ye ask my name, I am poor unworthy Robin Hamilton, on whom the Lord hath set His hand."

Then we knew that this dark-browed man was Sir Robert Hamilton, who with my brother Sandy had been the Societies' Commissioner to the Low Counties, and who was here at Shalloch-on-Minnoch to defend his action. He was also brother of Jean Hamilton, Sandy's wife, and of a yet more sombre piety.

Then, though I knew well that he had been the rock on which the Covenant ship split at Bothwell, and a stone of stumbling in our counsels ever since, yet, because he looked so weary and broken with toils, travels, and watchings, my heart could not choose but go out to him.

As he looked and said nothing, a more kindly light came into his eye as he gazed at Wat. "Ye will be Black Bess of Lochinvar's son — a tacked-on Covenant man. But I doubt not a kindly lad, for all ye are so brisk with your tongue and ready with your blade. I have seen the day when it would have done me a pleasure to step out with you, in days that were full of the pride of the flesh. I do not blame you. To fight first and ask wherefore after, is the Gordon all over. But do not forget that this day, here on the wild side of the Shalloch-on-Minnoch, there are well-nigh a thousand gentlemen of as good blood as your own. Homespun cloth and herds' plaidies cover many a man of ancient name this day, that never thought to find himself in arms against the King, even for the truth's sake."

Robert Hamilton spoke with such an air of dignity and sadness, that Wat lifted his hand to his blue bonnet in token that he was pacified. And with a kindly nod the stranger turned among the throng that now filled all the spacious place of meeting.

CHAPTER XLV.

THE OUTFACING OF CLAVERS.

It was indeed a wonderful sight and made our hearts beat high only to look at it. Upon the Session Stone twelve men stood with heads bared to the fierce heat of the sun. All of them were grey-headed men, saving two only, a lad of a pale and girlish face with dark sweet eyes, and towering above him, the flecked raven locks of Sir Robert Hamilton. These twelve were the commissioners of districts, all ordained elders. At one side was a little table brought from the house of the Shalloch, and a man sat at it busily writing. By a curious sword cut across his cheek, I knew him for Michael Shields, presently the clerk, and afterwards the historian of the United Societies.

Behind upon the hillside was drawn up a guard of two hundred horse. And the tossing bits and jingling accoutrements made a pleasant sound to me that loved such things, which were mostly the portion of our enemies. The wide amphitheatre opposite to the Session Stone was occupied chiefly by the women and older men, who, as I have said, sat upon plaids spread upon the bank. Behind these again, and extending far up the gently sloping side of the Shalloch Hill, was a noble sight, that made me gasp for gladness. Company behind company were ranked the men whom Robert Hamilton had called the Seven Thousand. There were officers on their flanks, on whose drawn swords the sun glittered; and though there was no uniformity of dress, there was in every bonnet the blue favour of the Covenant. Their formation was so steady and their numbers so large that the whole hillside seemed covered with their regiments. Looking back over the years, I think we might have risked a Dunkeld before the time with such an ordered host.

I heard one speaking in the French language at my elbow and looked about me. Whereupon I spied two men who had been walking to and fro among the companies.

"But all this will do little good for a time," said one of the speakers. "We must keep them out of the field till we are ready. They need one to draw them into the bond of obedience. They are able to fight singly, but together they cannot fight."

"No matter," said the other, "they will stand us in good stead one day when the Prince sails over. The Seven Thousand shall be our mainstay in that day, not in Scotland only, but in Britain."

By this I guessed that these two were officers of the Prince of Orange sent over to see if the times were yet ripe.

Meanwhile the meeting proceeded to its end amid the voice of prayer and the solemn throb of psalmody. It was a great and gracious thing to hear the swell of praise that went up from that hillside, from the men who had worshipped only in the way of silence and in private, because they dared no other, for many weary months.

It was about the third hour of the afternoon, and we had not begun to wax weary, when, away on the hillside, we heard the sound of cheering. We looked about us to see what might be the cause. There came one riding slowly down upon a much tired horse between the ranks of the companies — a great tall man in a foreign coat and hat, whom at the first glint my mother knew for Sandy my brother.

As he came nearer the roar of greeting swelled and lifted. I declare I was proud of him. Even Robert Hamilton had

U

gotten no such greeting. I had not thought that our Sandy was so well-kenned a man. And I forgave him for flouting me.

"Mother," I said, "that is our Sandy they are cheering!"

"Think ye I kenned not that! Whaur has he come frae?" she said. "I wonder if Jean Hamilton kens."

It was like my mother to think first of others; but in a little she said,

"I trust I am not overproud, that my bairn is so honoured."

And indeed it made us all proud that Sandy was thus greatly thought of. So in a little he also took his place on the Session Stone, and made another young head among the grey beards. Soon he was called upon to speak, and in his sounding voice he began to tell of his message from the kirks of Holland, and to commend patience and faithfulness. They say that every man that stood to arms among the Seven Thousand heard him that day. Aye, and that even the watchers upon the tops caught many blessed words and expressions, which the light winds blew them in wafts. Saving Richard Cameron's alone, there was no such voice as Sandy's heard in Scotland during all his time.

Then Robert Hamilton rose and spoke, counselling that since there were so many present, they should once more and immediately fall to arms.

But one of the most venerable men there present, rose.

"Robin, ye are but one of the Council of Twelve, and ye know that our decision is to wait the man and the hour. It beseems you, then, either to speak within the order of the Society or to be silent."

Last of all the young man rose, he of the pale countenance and the clustering hair.

"It is young Mr. James Renwick, who is going abroad to

study and be ordained at Groningen in the Low Countries," said one near to me. And indeed he was mightily changed so that I had scarce known him.

The lad's voice was sweet and thrilling, persuasive beyond belief. In especial, coming after the mighty roaring of the Bull of Earlstoun (so they called Sandy) and the rasping shriek of Robin Hamilton, it had a great effect upon me. There came a sough from the people as his words ran over them, like a soothing and fanning wind blowing winningly among the trees of the wood.

So the day passed and the gladness of the people increased, till some of us felt that it was like the golden gates of heaven just to be there. For the passion of a multitude of folk with one heart's desire, thrilling to the one word and the one hope, had taken hold on us. The like was never seen upon the wild mountains of the south.

Then, as though to recall us to earth, from the green meads of the Minnoch side there came one running to pass the word that the enemy was in sight. Two companies of Strachan's Dragoons, with all Claverhouse's levies, were riding from Straiton as fast as their horses could carry them. Whereat, without haste and with due solemnity, the great and desirable General Meeting of the United Societies held on the wilds of Shalloch-on-Minnoch was brought to an end.

The women and aged men were placed behind the companies, and such as could reach home without passing the troopers' line of march were set upon their way. But when once we found ourselves without the lines of the companies, which stretched across from the black downthrow of rocks upon Craigfacie to the Rig of the Shalloch Hill, my mother would go no farther.

"Na," she said, "gang your ways back doon. This is the place for Kate and for an auld wife like me. But it shall never be said that William Gordon's wife grudged both her sons to the work of the Lord!"

So Wat and I went our ways down to where Sandy stood as chosen leader of the army of the Seven Thousand. He paid, indeed, but little attention to us, giving us no more than a nod, yet instantly setting us upon errands for him.

"Will ye fight?" said I, when I got a quiet moment of him.

"Alas!" he said, "there is no such good luck. Had I not the direct message of the Prince to abide and wait, I would even now strike a blow. As it is, we must just stand to our arms. I would to God it were otherwise!"

The companies of mounted soldiers rapidly approached, to the number of perhaps three hundred. But I think they were daunted, when from a knoll below the house of the Shalloch they first saw our great and imposing army. They say there were over two thousand under arms that day.

"The Seven Thousand will surely stay John Graham this day," said one at my elbow.

But Claverhouse was not a man easily feared.

Leaving his men, he rode forward alone, having but a trumpeter someway behind him. He held a white handkerchief in his hand, and waved it as he rode towards us upon his war-horse. I saw the trumpeter lad look about him more than once, as if he wished himself well out of it. But Colonel Graham rode straight at the centre of our array as if it had been his own. Sandy went out to meet him.

"Will ye surrender and lay down your arms to the King's troops?" cried Clavers as he came near. Since then I have never denied the man courage, for all his cruelty.

There came a gust of laughter from the nearer companies of our array when they heard his words. But Sandy checked the noise with his hand.

"Surrender!" he said. "It is you, John Graham, that

may talk of surrender this day. We are no rebels. We but stand to our arms in defence of our covenant rights."

"Keep that Whig garbage for the prayer-meeting, Earlstoun!" said Claverhouse. "I at least know you too well, Sandy Gordon. Do you mind the long wood of Dairsie by the Eden Water?"

What he meant I cannot tell, but I think his words daunted Sandy for a moment. For in his old unsanctified days they had been fast comrades, being of an age, and student lads together at Saint Andrews, where both were equally keen of the play upon the green; though ever since Sandy married Jean Hamilton he had turned him to new courses.

So having obtained no satisfaction, Claverhouse rode slowly back to the Dragoons. Then without a word, save the shout of command, he led them forward over the moor toward us.

"Sain my soul and body," said Wat, "is the Heather Cat going to charge an army in position?" And indeed it looked like it.

But as he came toward us, from the front rank where Sandy stood with a broadsword bare in his hand, and his horse brisk as though it had just been led from its stall, came my brother's voice.

"If ye set a horse's hoof over that burn, ye shall receive our fire. Men, make ready!"

Right up to the burn bank rode Clavers and his troop, and there halted. For a long minute he looked at us very contemptuously. Then he snapped his fingers at us.

"That for ye!" he cried. "Ye stand the day. Ye shall be scattered the morn. I ken ye brawly. Among a' your testimonies there is not one which any three of ye could read over and not fall out about. This day ye are on the brae-face. The morn ye'll be at the dyke back, with an ounce or two of his Majesty's excellent lead in ye. God save the King!"

And with that he waved his hand, cried to his men, and rode off like the steeve and dour persecutor that he was.

In the late evening we took my mother and Kate back again over the hill. My mother was very weary — so weary that at the house of Tonskeen we left her with the decent man and wife that abode there, with Kate to bear her company. She was not used to the life on the hills, and so for that time could flee no further. It was just grey day when we took the short way down the face of the gairy, that lifts its brow over the desolate moor of Macaterick. Being unencumbered with women folk, Wat and I now came down the nearest way, that which leads by the strange rocky hollow, steep on every side, which is named the Maiden's Bed. So, fleet of foot, we fled westwards.

As we looked, the sun began to rise over the Range of Kells and the tide of light flowed in upon us, gladdening our hearts. Wat was not so brisk as I, for he had left Kate behind; and though young men in times of danger have perforce to think of their skins first and of their maids after, yet it makes not the foot move so light when it must step out away from the beloved.

But all the same, it was a bright morning when we clambered down the steep side of the hill that looks toward Macaterick The feathery face of the rock above the levels of Macaterick, and the burn that flows from it by links and shallows into Loch Doon, glanced bright with the morning sun upon them. And there at last was the cave-mouth hidden under the boskage of the leaves.

I ran on before Wat, outstripping him, albeit that for ordinary he was more supple than I — so great was my desire to see Maisie Lennox, and assure myself that all had gone well with her father. I had not a thought but that she would be sitting safely within, with the cave garnished with fresh leaves like a bower, and her father watching her at her knitting through his bushy eyebrows.

Smiling, I lifted the curtain of birch leaves. Great God of Heaven! The cave was wholly empty, as I slid down into it. Maisie and her father had vanished!

I stood as one desperately amazed. There was no life or thought or soul left in me. I stood as one stands at the threshold of his home, before whom a gulf suddenly yawns fathomless.

CHAPTER XLVI.

THE FIGHT AT THE CALDONS.

Now that which follows is the telling of Toskrie Tam, who is now a gardener at Afton, but who, in the old days, being bitten by the worldly delight of soldiering, had ridden with Clavers and Lag in the tumultuous times. Tam is a long loose-jointed loon, for ever crying about rheumatism, but a truthteller (as indeed John Graham taught him to be), and one that his wife has in subjection. There is the root of the old man in Tam yet. For though he is an elder now, oftentimes I have come on him round a corner, using most uncovenanted language to his underlings. But he is a good gardener, and there is no service in being over gleg in the hearing with such. Besides, his wife clours him soundly enough when there is need.

Somewhat after the following manner Tam told his tale, a trifle unwillingly at first, but warming with the recollection as he proceeded.

"Aweel, Sir William, gin ye insist. No that I like to be speakin' aboot thae days; but as ye inform me that it is a' to be written doon, I'll tell ye it word for word. Weel, after the Conventiclers had outfaced us at the Shalloch-on-Minnoch, Clavers and Douglas rode south to the Minnoch Brig that looks to Loch Trool.

"'There's a dour pack o' Whigs up that glen,' says Clavers. 'Think ye we will take a turn and steer them?'

"'They will just be hiving hame frae the conventicle. We shall catch them as they run,' Douglas made answer.

THE FIGHT AT THE CALDONS. 297

"So without a word more, slack rein and go-as-you-please, we rode up Glen Trool. It was a bonny nicht and at a' times a bonny place, but the track was ill to keep, and we rode loose and scattering. Douglas was fair foaming with the affront of the Shalloch, and vowed, as he had often vowed before, that he would never more spare hilt or hair of the accursed breed.

"At the Caldons, a bit farmhouse set on a rig among trees at the foot of Loch Trool, Gib Macaterick and I were riding on ahead down by the water-side by the loch, when suddenly, without warning, we came on a little cloud of men all on their knees praying behind a dyke back. They were so busy with the supplications that they did not notice us. And we that looked for promotion over the head of the business, covered them with our muskets and called to them to surrender for traitors and rebels. But in a trice they were over the dyke and at us like wild-cats, gripping our horses and tumbling us off. They got Gib down, but I that was suppler, managed to jook among the young oak-trees and run what I was fit back to the troop.

"Douglas was in command, for Clavers had ridden on. He was a wild man when I told him that the rebels had taken Gib Macaterick.

"'Curse you and him both!' Douglas cried. 'Do I command a set of porridge-stuffed, baggy knaves that fall off their horses whenever they see a Whig tyke skartin' for fleas? I'll tan Gib's hide for him and yours too, my man, when we come to the post. Ye shall ride the timber horse with a bit musket at your heels to learn ye how siccarly to sit your beast.'

"Whereat he cried to wheel, and we went twos about down the Caldons road. The farm sits four square on a knowe-tap, compact with office-houses and mailings. There are the little three-cornered wickets in the walls.

As we came to the foot of the brae we found Gib Macaterick stelled up against the dyke, with his hands bound and a paper in his teeth — a printed copy of the Covenant. He was quite safe and sound. But when we loosed him, he could do nothing but curse and splutter.

"'Thou foul-mouthed Whig,' cried Douglas, 'hast thou also been taking the Covenant? Have him out and shoot him!'

"But Gib rose and made an end of the Covenant, by setting his foot upon it and crushing it into the sod. Then we moved forward, carelessly, thinking that the enemy would never stand against a troop, but that they would at once scatter to the hill which rises steep and black at the gavel end of the house.

"However, when we came within sight of the steading, half a dozen muskets cracked, and one of our company cried out with the pain of being hit. Indeed, the second volley tumbled more than one trooper from his saddle, and caused their horses to break ranks and run back, jingling accoutrements.

"So Colonel Douglas dismounted half his men, and sent the better part of a troop, under the Cornet of the same name, round to the high side of the farm to take the Conventiclers in flank. Which with all success they did, and came down at the charge upon the steadings, capturing half a dozen, mostly young lads, that were there with muskets in their hands. But there was one that threw himself into the lake and swam under water for it. And though our soldiers shot off a power of powder after him, we could get no satisfaction that he had been hit. We heard, however, that he was a Carsphairn man and that the name of him was Roger Dunn.

"So Douglas ordered a dismounted file to lead the young lads out into a dell a quarter of a mile from the house, where the noise of the shootings would not annoy him at his refreshment. So the Cornet took them out, well-pleased. For it was a job that suited him better than fighting, and there, in a little green hollow, he speedily laid the six featly in a row.

"'So perish all his Majesty's rebels!' said Colonel Douglas as he rode past, bung full of brandy and good mutton ham.

"'That's as bonny a kill o' Whigs as we hae gotten for mony a day. Rothes will be pleased with this day's work!' said the Cornet.

"It was growing dark by the time that we drew up from the loch and it was ill getting a guide. No one of us had ever been in the country, and there is no wilder in all the south, as I have cause to know. But we had not got to any conclusion, when one came running with the news that he saw a light. So we spurred on as briskly as we dared, not knowing but that we might again hear the whistle of musket balls about our ears.

"It was the little farm of Esconquhan, and only old Sandy Gillespie and his wife were at home — the lads no doubt being at the conventicle, or it may be among those who had fought with us in the yard of the Caldons, and now lay quiet enough down in the copsewood at the loch foot.

"Sandy Gillespie of Esconquhan was a shrewd old fox enough, and answered all Douglas's questions with great apparent readiness.

"'Hae you a Bible?' asked the Colonel.

"'Aye,' said Sandy, 'but it's gye and stoury. Reek it doon, guid wife! I misdoot I dinna read it as often as I should — aiblins like yoursel', Colonel.'

"Very biddably, the wife reached it down out of the little black hole over the mantelshelf, and the Colonel laughed.

"'It is indeed brave and dusty. Man, I see you are no' a right Whig. I doubt that bit book disna get hard wark!'

"Douglas's refreshment had made him more easy to deal with.

"'Nevertheless,' he continued, 'fettle on your blue bonnet and put us on the road to Bongill, at the loch-head. For there is a great Whigamore there of the name of Macmillan and he will no' get aff so easy. I warrant *his* Bible is well-thumbed!'

"'I canna rin wi' ye on siccan a nicht, and deed the road's no' canny. But you red-coats fear neither God nor deil!' said Sandy Gillespie readily.

"'Out on you, gangrel. Gin ye canna rin ye shall ride. Pu' the auld wretch up ahint ye,' said Douglas, ready to be angry as soon as he was crossed, like all men in liquor.

"And so we went over the hillside very carefully — such a road as beast was never set to gang on before.

"'Keep doon the swearin' as muckle ye can,' ordered Sergeant Murphy. 'Lord, Lord, but this is heart-breaking!'

"Sandy Gillespie, canny man, tried to dissuade him from going to Bongill that night. Which only made Douglas the more determined, thinking there was something or somebody that he might light on there, and so get great credit to himself.

"'Gin the road be as dour, crooked, and coarse as the Cameronian's road to heaven, I'll gang that road this night!' said Lag, who was pleased with the death of the six Whigs at the Caldons — though, as it might be, vexed that he had not been at the shooting himself.

"We were no more than clear of the loch-side path, when Douglas bade old Sandy tune his pipes to help the men along the easier road with a song.

"'A Whig's sang or a King's-man's sang?' asked the auld tod blythely.

"'Hoot, a Cavalier's song — what need hae we to tak' the Book here!' cried Douglas loudly.

"'More need than inclination!' said Claverhouse scornfully, who was now riding beside them.

"Sandy Gillespie, who was an exceedingly far-seeing old worthy, pretended that he was loth to sing, whereat Douglas ordered him with an oath to sing upon peril of his life.

"So the old man struck up in a high piping voice, but none so ill in tune:

> 'Our thistles flourished fresh and fair,
>   And bonny bloomed our roses,
> But Whigs cam' like a frost in June,
>   And withered a' oor posies.'

"As he went on the old man's voice grew louder, and in a little, half the command was cantily shouting the song, which indeed goes very well to march to.

"'And there's Bongill,' cried Sandy, suddenly stopping and dropping off his horse, 'an' guid e'en to ye!'

"And with that the old fellow slid off among the brushwood and copse, and we saw no more of him — which perhaps was as well for him.

"When we went into the little house of Bongill, we found an open door both back and front. Peats were blazing on the hearth. Great dishes of porridge sat on a table. Chairs and stools were overturned, and Bibles and Testaments lay everywhere.

"'Curse the old dog. He has sung them a' to the hill,' cried Douglas. 'Have him out and shoot him.'

"But Sandy was not to be seen. Only from the hillside, a voice — the same that had sung, 'Awa, Whigs, awa,' gave us 'Bonny Davie Leslie'; and then cried in mockery three times 'Good-night!'

"So the night being pit mirk and the hill unknown, we

took up our abode at Bongill till the morning. Sitting in the hole of the peat stack we found a strange object, a crazy natural, shapeless and ill-looking.

"But some of the men who had seen his mother, knew him for the idiot son of Corp-licht Kate, the Informer, of the Shiel of the Star. Douglas questioned him, for sometimes these naturals have much shrewd wit.

"'How came ye to be here?'

"'Weel, ye see the way o't is this ——'

"'Make a short story of it, if ye dinna want a bit o' lead through ye.'

"'A blaw of tobacco wad fit Gash Gibbie better — grand man in the reid coatie!' said the natural, with a show of cunning. 'I cam' to the Bongill i' the gloamin', an' faith the mistress would hae gien me a bed, but there was a horse in it already!'

"So being able to make nothing of him, Douglas let him go back to his dry peat coom.

"The next morning was bright and bonny as the others had been, for the autumn of this year was most favourable to our purpose — by the blessing o' the deil as Lag used to say in his cups, so that the track along the side of Curleywee to Loch Dee was dry as a bone. When we came to the ford of the Cooran, we saw a party coming down to meet us with prisoners riding in the midst. There was an old man with his feet tied together under the horse's belly. He swayed from side to side so that two troopers had to help him, one either side, to keep his seat. This they did, roughly enough. The other prisoner was a young lass with a still, sweet face, but with something commanding about it also — saving your presence, sir. She was indeed a picture and my heart was wae for her when some one cried out:

"'Mardrochat has done it to richts this time. He has gotten the auld tod o' the Duchrae, Anton Lennox, and his bonny dochter at the same catch. That will be no less than a hundred reward, sterling money!'

"Whereat Douglas cursed and said that a hundred was too much for any renegade dog such as Cannon of Mardrochat to handle, and that he could assuredly dock him of the half of it.

"So that day we marched to New Galloway, and the next to Minnyhive on the road by the Enterkin to Edinburgh."

This is the end of the Toskrie Tam's story as he told it to me in the garden house of Afton.

CHAPTER XLVII.

THE GALLOWAY FLAIL.

WHEN Wat and I found the cave empty, immediately we began to search the hill for traces of the lost ones. For some time we searched in vain. But a little to the right of the entrance of the cave the whole was made plain to us. Here we found the bent and heather trampled, and abundant stains of recent blood, as though one had been slain there and the body carried away. Also I found a silken snood and the colour of it was blue. It was not the hue, for that is worn by most of the maids of Scotland; but when I took it to me, I knew as certainly as though I had seen it there, that it had bound about the hair of Maisie Lennox. Though when Wat asked of me (who, being a lover might have known better) how I knew it for hers, I could not find words to tell him. But it is true that all the same, know it I did.

So we followed down the trail, finding now a shred of cleading and again the broken bits of a tobacco pipe such as soldiers use, small and black, till in our search we had rounded the hill that looks into the valley of the Cooran. Here at the crossing of the burn, where it was smallest, we found Anton Lennox's broad blue bonnet.

It was enough. Soon we were scouring the hilltops as fast as our legs could move under us. We travelled southward, keeping ever a keen watch, and twice during the day we caught sight of troops of dragoons, moving slowly over the heather and picking their way among the hags, quartering the land for the sport of man-catching as they went. Once they raised, as it had been a poor maukin, a young lad that ran from them. And we could see the soldiers running their horses and firing off white pluffs of powder. It was a long time ere the musket-cracks came to us, which must have sounded so near and terrible to the poor fugitive. But they hit him not, and for that time at least he wan off scot free. So presently we saw them come back, jeered at by their comrades, like dogs that have missed the quarry and slink home with their tails between their legs.

But neither one of our poor captives was among them. So we held fast and snell to the eastward, passing along the skirts of the Millyea, and keeping to the heights above the track which runs from the Glenkens to the Water of Cree. It was near to the infall of the road from Loch Dee that we first gat sight of those we sought. It was not a large company which had them in charge, and they marched not at all orderly. So that we judged it to be either one of the Annandale levies of the Johnstone, or Lag's Dumfries troop of renegades.

But as we came nearer, we marked quite clearly that they had two prisoners, tall men, one with some white thing about his head, and in the rear they had six or seven other men, mostly on foot. Coming nearer we could also see a figure as of a young maid upon a horse. Then I knew that the dear lass I had watched and warded so long, was surely at the mercy of the rudest of the enemy.

We were thus scouring along the moor, keeping a wary eye upon the troop and their poor prisoners, when Wat's foot took the edge of a moss-hag where the ground was soft. As it pressed the soil downward, we heard a sudden cry, a wild, black-a-vised man sprang up with a drawn sword in his hand, and pulling out a pistol ran at us. We were so taken aback at the assault that we could scarcely put ourselves upon the defence. But ere the man came near, he saw that we were dressed like men of the hills. He stopped and looked at us, his weapons being still pointed our way.

"Ye are of the people!" he said sternly.

"Ay," said we, for I think Clavers himself had owned as much, being taken unawares and unable to get at his weapons.

"I thought I saw ye at the General Meeting," he said.

"We were there," we replied; "we are two of the Glenkens Gordons."

"And I am that unworthy outcast James MacMichael."

Then we knew that this was he who, for the murder of the curate of Carsphairn (a mightily foolish and ill-set man), was expelled and excommunicated by the United Societies.

"I will come with you for company," he said, taking his bonnet out of the moss-bank into which Wat's foot had pressed it.

Now we wanted not his company. But because we knew not (save in the matter of Peter Pearson) what the manner of the man was, the time went past in which we could have told him that his room was more to us than his company. So, most ungraciously, we permitted him to come. Soon, however, we saw that he knew far more of heather-craft than we. Our skill in the hill-lore was to his but as the bairn's to that of the regent of a college.

"The band that we see yonder is but the off-scourings of half a dozen troops," said he, "and chance riders that Cannon of Mardrochat has gathered. The ill loon himself is not with them. He will be lying watching about some dyke bank. Ah, would that I could get my musket on him."

So we hasted along the way, keeping to the hills in order to reach the Clachan of St. John's town before the soldiers.

We went cautiously, Black MacMichael leading, often running with his head as low as a dog, and showing us the advantage of every cover as he went.

Nor had we gone far when we had proof, if we wanted such, of the desperate character of the man in whose company by inadvertence we found ourselves. We were passing through a little cleuch on the Holm of Ken and making down to the water-side. Already we could see the stream glancing like silver for clearness beneath us. All of an instant, we saw Black MacMichael fall prostrate among the rocks at the side of the cleuch. He lay motionless for a moment or two. Then, without warning, he let his piece off with a bang that waked all the birds in that silent place, and went to our hearts also with a stound like pain. For though Wat and I had both done men to death, it had been in battle, or face to face, when blade crosses blade and eye meets eye, and our foes had at least an equal chance with us. We had not been used to clapping at a dyke back and taking sighting shots at our foes.

As soon as Black MacMichael had fired, he lifted up his hand, cried "Victory," and ran forward eagerly, as one that fires at a mark at a wappenschaw may run to see if he has hit the target. Yet Wat and I went not down nor took part with him, but we held our way with sore hearts for the wickedness of this man.

Presently he came out and set after us. He cried "Hoy" many times for us to wait for him, but we tarried not. So he took to running and, being a powerful man and clever with his feet, he soon overtook us.

"What is the push?" he cried, panting. "I hit the skulker that watched for us from behind a rock. I keeled him over like a dog-fox on the hillside. See what he had upon him!" And he took from off his shoulder a very remarkable piece of ordnance which I shall presently describe.

"We want neither art nor part in your bloody deeds, James MacMichael," I answered him. "Take yourself away, till the Lord Himself shall judge you!"

He stood still as one astonished.

"Gosh," he said, "siccan a fash aboot killing an informer. I wad kill them a' like toads, for my son John that they hanged upon the dule tree of Lag. I would slay them root and branch — all the Griers of the wicked name. O that it had been Mardrochat himself. Then indeed it had been a fortunate shot. But he shall not escape the Black MacMichael!"

The murderer, for indeed I could not hold him less, clapped his hand upon his breast and looked up to heaven in a way that made me think him crazed.

"See here what I hae gotten aff him?" he cried again, like a child pleased with a toy.

It was the instrument known as the Galloway flail. It had a five-foot handle of stout ash, worn smooth like an axe haft with handling. Then the "soople," or part of the flail that strikes the corn on the threshing floor, was made of three lengths of iron, jointed together with links of iron chain, so that in striking all this metal part would curl round an enemy and crush his bones like those of a chicken.

"Stand off," I said, as he came nearer with the Galloway flail in his hand; "we want not to company with you, neither to share in your iniquity."

"I daresay no," he said, frowning on us; "but ye will hae enough o' your ain. But I'll e'en follow on for a' that. Ye may be braw an' glad o' the MacMichael yet, considering the errand ye are on."

Nor had we gone far when his words proved true enough.

We went down the cleuch, and were just coming out upon the wider strath, when a party of Lag's men, for whom no doubt the dead spy had been gathering information, beset us. There were only half a dozen of them, but had Mac-Michael not been at hand with his terrible weapon, it had certainly gone hard with us, if indeed we had not been slain or captured. With a shout they set themselves at us with sword and pistol; but since only one of them was mounted, the odds were not so great as at first they seemed. Wat was ready with his blade as ever, and he had not made three passes before he had his sword through his man's shoulder. But it was otherwise with me. A hulking fellow sprang on me with a roar like a wild beast, and I gave myself up for lost. Yet I engaged him as I best could, giving ground a little, yet ever keeping the upper hand of him. But as we fought, what was our astonishment to see MacMichael, whose company we had rejected, whirl his iron flail above his head and attack the mounted man, whose sword cracked as though it had been made of pottery, and flew into a hundred fragments, jingling to the ground like broken glass. The next stroke fell ere the man on horseback could draw a pistol. And we could hear in the midst of our warding and striking the bones crack as the iron links of the flail settled about his body. The next moment the man on horseback pitched heavily forward and fell to the ground. MacMichael turned with a yell of victory, and rushed upon the others. One stroke only he got as he passed at the dark, savage-like man who was pressing me — a stroke which snapped his sword arm like a pipe staple, so that he fell writhing.

"Stripe your sword through him! I'll run and do another!" cried the Black MacMichael.

But the others did not stand to be done (small blame to them), and soon all three were running what they could over the level holms of the Ken. One caught the riderless horse, running alongside till he could get a chance to spring upon the back of it, and so galloped back to the garrison at the Clachan of St. John.

MacMichael sat down, panting as with honest endeavour. He wiped his brow with calm deliberation.

"An' troth," he said, "I think ye warna the waur o' Black MacMichael an' Rob Grier's Gallowa' flail."

Yet there was not even thankfulness in our hearts, for we found ourselves mixed yet more deeply in the fray. Not that this broil sat on us like that other business of the dead spy behind the heather bush. For these men fell in fair fighting, which is the hap of any man. But we saw clearly that we should also be blamed as art and part in the killing of the spy, and the thought was bitter gall to our hearts.

CHAPTER XLVIII.

THE FIGHT IN THE GUT OF THE ENTERKIN.

ALL the next two days we were gathering for the rescue of Maisie and her father, finding, as we went eastward, men whose hearts were hot within them because of the oppression. But we found not place nor opportunity till the third day. It was the night of the second day that I stole down to the little village of Carron Bridge, which stands by the brink of a dashing, clean-running stream, where the troops were encamped. There I managed to get speech of Maisie Lennox. I clambered down one bank and up the other. And because the houses stood over the brawling of the stream, the soldiers on guard heard me not. I went from window to window till, by the good hap of love (and the blessing of God), I found the window of the room within which Maisie Lennox was confined.

I cried to her through the dark, low and much afraid. "Maisie May!" I called as in old days at the Duchrae, when I used to carry her on my back, and she in sportiveness used to run and hide from me.

She was not asleep, for I heard her say plainly, like one speaking from a bed:

"It is a dream — a sweet dream!" But nevertheless I knew that she sat up and listened.

"Maisie May!" I said again at the window, very softly.

I heard her move, and in a moment she came to the lattice, and put her hand on the sill.

"Oh, William!" she said, "is it indeed you and not a dream?"

"It is even William Gordon!" I said, sorry that I could not do more than touch her fingers through the thick bars of the guard-house.

"You must go away at once," she said; "there are three soldiers sleeping no further off than the door."

"We will rescue you to-morrow, Maisie," I said.

"And get yoursel's killed!" she said. "Do not try it, for my sake."

"Well, for your father's!" I said.

And at that she said nothing.

Then she told me that the young officer in command was a lad from one of the good families of the North, and that he treated them civilly. But that, having lost a prisoner on a former occasion, he might happen to lose his life if he let slip so noble a taking; which made him careful of his prisoners with a great carefulness. As well it might; for the Privy Council was not to be trifled with in those days.

There were nine of the prisoners altogether, including the minister of a Nithside conventicle that had been scattered that day. More I could not get from her. For, one of the soldiers stirring without, she prayed me so piteously to be gone, that I set off crawling down among the stones, though I was eager to hear how they had been taken at Cove Macaterick. But that I had to put off to another diet of hearing, as they say in the kirk.

On the morrow we came upon the man that was of all men the best fitted to give us aid in the matter of rescue. This was James Harkness of Locharben, "James of the Long Gun," as he was called. He had been a soldier, and was said to be the finest marksman in Scotland. Often had the King's party tried to win him back again to the troop, but James kept to the hills with his noted long gun ever at his back. For many years he had as companion his brother Thomas, called "Tam o' the Lang Hosen." But he had been killed in battle, so that often like a widowed Jack heron, James Harkness stood at gaze on some hilltop, leaning on his gun, and this was mostly his place at conventicles or meetings of the Societies.

Being an old soldier, it fell to him now to choose the place of the rescue and to command us in the manner of it. It was in the deep and narrow defile of the Enterkin that he posted us — a most wild and fearsome place, where the hills draw very close together. One of the places is called Stey Gail, and is so high that the sheep grazing on it are like flies but half way up, as my plain-spoken friend Mr. Daniel de Foe well remarked when he passed that way. On the other side there rises still higher, and almost as steep, the top of the Thirlstane Hill. There is one place at which the water runs down the cleft of the hills, and the place is perpendicular like a wall. It is so steep a place, as Mr. Foe saw it, that if a sheep die it lies not still, but falls from slope to slope, till it ends in the Enterkin Water.

The path passes midways on the steepest and most terrifying slope. Here, on the brow high above, we laid our ambush, and piled great stones to roll on the enemy if need were.

It was a dark, gloomy day, with black clouds driven by the wind, and scuffs of grey showers scudding among the hilltops.

Presently lying couched amid the heather we saw the dragoons come marching loosely two and two, with their reins slack on their horses' necks. At the entering in of the gorge we observed them fall to single file, owing to the narrowing of the path. We could see the minister riding first of the prisoners in his black clothes. Then after a soldier came Anton Lennox, sitting staid and sober on his horse, with a countryman to lead the beast, and to watch that, by reason of his wounds and weakness, he did not fall off.

Then followed Maisie, riding daintily and sedately as ever. Then came five or six other prisoners. Each man of these was held by a rope round his neck, which a trooper had attached to the pommel of his saddle. And at this he took an occasional tug, according to his desire, as other men might take a refreshment.

So these poor lads were being haled along to their fate in Edinburgh. And for a certain long moment, at least, I thought with more complacence on the stark spy behind the dyke, to whose treachery they owed their fate. But the next minute I was ashamed of my thought.

As I looked over I saw the whole party strung out along the steep and dangerous face of the precipice. Then while they were thus painfully toiling with their horses through the dangers of the way, James of the Long Gun rose to his height out of the bent, and sent his powerful voice down, as it had been out of the clouds. For as I said, it was misty and gloomy that day — as indeed it is seldom otherwise there, and to see the place well you must see it in gloom and in no other way.

"Halt, ye sons of Belial!" cried James of the Long Gun.

I could hardly help smiling, for he said it solemnly, as though it had been his idea of a civil salutation or the enunciation of an incontestable fact.

The young apple-faced officer answered, holding up his hand to stay the cavalcade behind him, and hearing some one call from the misty hill, but not catching the word.

"Who may you be, and what do you want?"

Then at the upward wave of James of the Long Gun's hand, twelve of us stood up with our pieces at the point.

This startled young Apple-Face (yet I would not call him that, for he was not uncivil to Maisie). For he thought of the Council's word to him, for he well knew that it would be kept, and that his life would stand for the prisoners'. So when he saw twelve armed men rise from the steep side of the Nether Pot, and more looking over the brow of the Crawstane Snout, he was shaken very greatly in his nerves, being young and naturally much in fear of his neck.

Then another officer, whom we afterwards knew as Sergeant Kelt (he has wrongly been called Captain, but no matter), took up the word and bade us to stand, for rebel loons.

But it was Long Gun that cried out to him:

"Stand yourself, Kelt. It is you that must do the standing, lest we send you to your own place at the bottom of the ravine, and with a dozen shot in you. Will you deliver your prisoners?"

"No, sir," cried Kelt, "that we will not, though we were to be damned!"

It was a soldier's answer, and I think none of us thought the worse of him for the expression he had at the close.

For indeed it was a hard case for all of them.

At which, quick as the echo of his oath, there rose one from the heather at our back and fired a musket at him. It was Black MacMichael.

"Damned ye shall be, and that quick! Tak' that," he cried, "an' learn no' to swear!"

And he fired his pistol also at the soldier.

Sergeant Kelt threw up his arms, shot through the head. His horse also fell from rock to rock, and among a great whammel of stones, reached the bottom of the defile as soon as its master.

Then every man of the twelve of us had our pieces to

our eyes, and each had picked his quarry, when the young officer held up his hand and desired a parley.

Indeed, the whole command was in great jeopardy, and so strung out like onions on a cord, that no man could either fight well himself or yet draw in to support his party. We had them completely at our mercy, there in the Gut of the Enterkin.

At this moment their fore-goer cried back to them, from the knoll whence he had gone to scout, that there appeared another band of armed countrymen on the top of the hill to their front. They were, indeed, but some merchant travellers who, seeing the military stopping the way, stood modestly aside to let them pass. But they did us as much good as they had been a battalion of the Seven Thousand.

At this the officer was even more afraid, though I think like a good soldier lad, more for his command than even for his own credit and life.

"Stand!" he cried. "A parley! What would ye have?"

So James of the Long Gun called out to him:

"We would have our minister."

For so they thought of ministers in those days. But I would have cried for certain others before him, being, as it were, a man prepared and ready to go. However, I tell it as James Harkness said it.

"Ye shall have your minister," said the officer.

"And the lass," cried I, striking in, for which James did not thank me.

"And the lass," the officer repeated, moving a little at hearing a new voice.

"And her father and the other prisoners," I added.

The officer hung a little on his words.

"Do you want them all? Must ye have them?"

"Aye, all — or we will take the lives of every one of you!"

"Then," said the officer, "my life is forfeit to the Council. Another shall surrender the prisoners and not I."

And with that he pulled a pistol from his holster and snapped it at his own head. Nevertheless it went not off, the lock being out of order, belike, or the poor lad's hand unsteady.

He was reaching down with his other hand to pull another pistol from the opposite holster, but ere he could draw it, the voice of the Covenanter, Anton Lennox, spoke, gravely and nobly, so as to be heard by all of us.

"Young man, face not in your own blood an angry God! Leap not thus quick to hell! Abide — and I, Anton Lennox, vow that I will not see you wronged. I am but an old and a dying man. My wounds can hardly let me live. What is my life any more? It is even at your service. I will go with you to the Council!"

And at the word he looked up to the dark heaven, the sunshine wafting after the shower caught his head, and lo! there was a kind of glory about it, as of one that sees mysteries unveiled.

Then we cried out to him to come with us, but he denied. And Maisie, his daughter, fleeched and besought him, but he would not even for her tears.

"Go thou, my lassie," he said, "for I am spent. When I set my sword to the hilt in the breast of Mardrochat, of a surety I also gat my dead stroke. Now I am no better than a dead man myself; and perhaps if I give my life for the life of this heathen man, the Lord will not see the blood of the slain on my hands."

It happens not often while men are yet in the struggle, that they seem to live to the height of their profession. But as Anton Lennox made his renunciation he was lifted, as it were, to the seventh heaven, and we common men gazed silently at him, expecting to see him vanish out of our sight.

Then he gave the orders as one with authority among the soldiers, even the officer not taking the words from his mouth.

"Loose the minister and let him step up the hill!"

And they did it. And so with the other prisoners till it came to his daughter, Maisie Lennox.

Then Anton, being sore wounded, bent painfully from his horse, and laid his hands on her shoulders.

"My lassie," he said, "daughter of the Covenant and of mine old age, do not weep or cry for me. Yea, though I dwell now by the waters of Ulais, whose name is sorrow, and drink of the springs of a Marah that cannot be made sweet, I am the Lord's man. He hath chosen me. My Master gave Himself for a thief. I, a sinner above most men, am willing to give myself for this persecutor that he may have time to repent."

And Maisie bent herself pitifully upon his hand, but she gave forth no voice or tear, and her little hands were still bound before her.

"Daughter of the Covenant," her father said again, "thou dost well. Kiss me once, ere, with all my garments red I come up from Bozrah, going to the sacrifice as a bridegroom goeth to his chamber. If it please the Lord, in the Grassmarket, which is red already with the blood of the saints, I shall witness a good confession and win worthily off the stage. It has been my constant prayer for years."

So without further word the troop filed away. And Anton Lennox, Covenanter and brave man, sat his horse like a general that enters a conquered city, not so much as looking behind him to where, by the side of the path, Maisie Lennox stood, bareheaded, her hands yet bound, for none had remembered to loose them. No tear was upon her pale face, and as each rude soldier man came by her, he saluted as reverently as though she had been King Charles Stuart himself.

And we, that were twelve men, stood at gaze on the hill above, silent and afraid. There was no word in our mouth and no prayer in our heart. We stood as though the place had been the Place of a Skull — the place wherein there is a garden, and in the garden a new tomb.

CHAPTER XLIX.

THE DEATH OF MARDROCHAT.

Now we knew that this affair would of a surety cause a great disturbance, and that the neighbourhood would be searched as a herd searches a hill for sheep. So with all haste we came back to Galloway, and though we could not return to the cave on the Star Hill, we continued due west that we might see how my mother and Kate McGhie were bestowed all this time, at the little house of Tonskeen in the howe of the hills.

Maisie was wondrous quiet. She had hardly uttered a word ever since we watched her father out of sight, sitting erect like a warrior upon his horse. It was indeed not a time for complaints. Women had to take sorrows as they came, as I was reminded of in an old letter which Jean of the Shirmers, my kind entertainer of the Garpel, had once written to Jean Hamilton upon Sandy's first taking. How I came by it I forget, if, indeed, I ever clearly knew. But at all events here it is: "You are not the first" (so the letter ran) "that hath had dear and tender husbands prisoners for Christ. Yea, blessed be God, not the first of the many hundreds that have lost them as to the world in Scotland in our day. Suppose that should happen which you cannot tell. Suppose that it should come even to that, we pray you, Jean Hamilton, tell us in whose hands the keys of the prison are. We rather desire to believe in your free resignation of all that was yours, especially of all that you love greatly. Will you dare to seek it back from Him now, as if He could not guide and keep and manage, what you have committed to Him? Far be from you this, or the like of this. Bless God that you have had a husband, if it were only to propine Him with."

Was there ever such consolation sent in any nation to the wife of a man condemned to torture and to death? Yet this and no other is the nature of our Scots Barnabas when he goes a-comforting. Like the three that came to Job of old, they ever tell you that you must take all the ill that comes to you thankfully, and at the back of it expect yet more and worse.

This is indeed more than enough about Jean Hamilton's letter. But it appeared to me so like our nation and our Cameronian folk, that I put it away in my case of despatches.

I did not trouble Maisie as we went with questions, knowing full well that when she felt the need of speech, she would come and tell me of her own accord. Till then, I was content to be silent, though I yearned to know the truth of the taking of the cave and all her adventure.

It was about the gloaming of the third day of our retreat, and we had come to the little house of the Nether Crae, where we were to bide. Maisie Lennox was within doors, and, as usual, we men folk hid behind the mow. The Nether Crae is a pleasant spot, but it looks down on the Duchrae. And from the door one can see the green fields and broomy knowes where Maisie and I had played so long. But now the soldiers had turned the steading out, the barn and byre were burned, and the stock driven away.

So, unable to bear the desolation, Maisie and I sat out on the fair green playing-croft that looks up to the hillside, and gazed sadly away from one another, saying nothing. It began to be dark. I waited for her.

Y

Suddenly she laid her head on my shoulder and began to sob very bitterly.

"My faither! O my faither!" she said, labouring with her breath.

I said not a word, but only gently clapped and stroked her hand and arm. For indeed I knew not what to say and the hand was near me.

"He saved me — he took me," she cried. "Then he gied himsel' for another."

I thought she meant for the soldier laddie, but still I said nothing, soothing her only.

It was coming now. I saw that she wanted to tell me all. So I said nothing.

"It was in the gloaming, as it is now," she began, "and my sweet lass, Margaret Wilson and I, had gone ower by to Tonskeen for some victual that the kind guidwife hid every day in a hollow of the turf-dyke for us. And as we came over the hilltop we heard the baying of hounds. But we thought that it would be but the herd's dogs at a collie-shangie, tearing at one another. So we came down the hill, stepping lightly as we could with our load, when of a sudden there leapt on us three evil men. Two of them took hold of me by the arms, and one gripped at Margaret.

"'Now take us to your faither, my bonny woman, or it will be the waur for ye!' said the greatest in stature, a black-a-vised, ill-natured rascal.

"But I was so astonished that I knew not what to say. The three were manifestly no soldiers — that I could see at once — but just the scourings of the Dumfries stables, that had taken to the informer's trade.

"Then when we came near, we saw that a great number of the crew had dogs, and were drawing the rocks for my father, as though they had been drawing a badger. And my heart leapt with anger to know that he was their quarry."

But the mouth of the cave was too high among the rocks for even a dog to get into at that time.

Indeed, there is something about it, whether the smell of the occupancy of man or not, that makes dogs not keen to enter it even now.

And this was the matter of Maisie's tale. I give it simply as she told it to me without "he-saids" or "she-saids."

She was sitting close by my side the while, now stilling her sobs that she might tell it exactly, and anon weeping freely upon my shoulder that her heart might have ease.

"When they had brought us by force to the face of rock and copse where, as you know, the cave is," Maisie went on, "they asked us again and again to take them to the Whigs' hiding-place. When we refused they uttered the most horrid threatenings, swearing what things should befall us. But they were not able at all to shake us, though we were but two maids and at their cruel will. And of themselves they were not able to find the mouth of the cave in that mile of tangled gairy face.

"So the cruellest and fiercest of all, the stark, black-a-vised man whom they called Mardrochat, the same that stopped us by the ford when first we fled from Balmaghie ——"

"O cursed Mardrochat," I cried, striking my hands together, "wait till I come to a settlement with you!"

"Nay," said Maisie, solemnly, "all is settled and paid already with Mardrochat. So they threatened till they were weary, and the night was coming on. Then Mardrochat turned about to his gallows thieves:

"'Must we go back empty-handed? Let me try my way with the lassies,' he cried. 'They shall be complaisant to tell where the old fox lies, or else suffer that which shall serve us as well.'

"With that he came near and put his hand upon me in the way to hurt me. Notwithstanding, with all the might that was in me, I strove to keep from crying out, lest my father should hear, which was what they counted on. But as God is my witness, I could not. Then, the fear being upon me and the pain of a woman, I cried out in my agony, as I had never before done in this world."

"O thrice accursed Mardrochat, die not till I meet thee," I cried again, beating and bruising my naked hand upon a rock in the impotence of hate.

Maisie went quietly and evenly on with her tale, without heeding my anger.

"But when I cried the third time in my extremity, even like a lion out of the thicket came my father forth, springing upon them suddenly with his bright sword in the gloaming. Never was there such striking since the world began. He struck and struck, panting and resting not, roaring in fierce anger, till they fairly fled from before the face of him. And the first he struck was Mardrochat — he that then held me, and the blood spurted over me. Thus it was," she went on calmly, as though she had been telling of the kye coming home at e'en, "my father clave him to the teeth, and he fell forward on that which had been his face. Then plucking his sword to him again, my father swung it hither and thither like lightning, and pursued them over the moor as a flock of sheep is hunted on the hill. And he smote and slew them as he ran. My father, Anthony Lennox, did all that alone. But, alas! in the valley, though we knew it not, there was a troop of horse encamped about a fire, the same whom he of the Long Gun halted and took us from in the midst of Enterkin. Now my father, running and smiting blindly, tripped over a halter and fell headlong in the heart of them. Thus they took Anton Lennox, who had never been taken before. They took us two maids also; but the dragoons being officered by gentlemen, there was no more ill-usage. Now though he had killed the informers and spies, the soldiers liked my father none the less for that, despising those who were employed on such service. Rather they gave my father honour and not dishonour, as one that was mighty at their own trade. And to me the babe-faced officer was both kind and courteous."

After this she was silent quite a while, sitting by me on the mossy seat by the old playing-green of the Nether Crae, and looking up as one that dreams, to the heather on the hillside.

"Is it not a noble thing," she said musingly, "to have a father that will render up his life for you as if it were a little thing?"

Now I thought within myself that he need not have given it also for a peony-faced officer boy. But I uttered not the word aloud, lest I should be shamed.

CHAPTER L.

THE BREAKING OF THE THIEVES' HOLE.

So on the morrow, early in the morning, we fared on into the hills; and when we came to Tonskeen in the wilds, we found my mother and Kate there. They were both well in health and glad to greet us, though my mother was doleful because of the news of Sandy's taking, which had just been brought to her. Yet all of us did our best endeavours to be cheerful, as was the custom in Galloway at that time, when there was hardly a family that had not some cause of mourning and sorrow. Though I do think that there was not one so deep in the mire as our unfortunate house of Earlstoun.

At Tonskeen also we found Thomas Wilson, brother of our sweet little Margaret. He brought us sad news of her. She had been separated from Maisie and her father after the capture, and taken to Wigtown instead of accompanying them toward Edinburgh.

The lad told us that his sister was now confined in the Thieves' Hole at Wigtown. He told us of her sham trial, and, spite of our sore hearts, he almost made us laugh with his account of the indictment which Winram and Coltran — in their cups, as I presume — had laid against her. Along with our Margaret had been tried her little sister of thirteen named Agnes. Both these young things had been most barbarously treated by the noble judges of Wigtown — Sheriff Davie Graham, Lag, Strachan, and Winram. Worst of all was Davie Graham, for having his hands upon the fines, he desired above all to amerce Gilbert Wilson, the tenant of Glen Vernock in the parish of Peninghame. Gilbert was a man well to do, keeping a good stock both of nolt and sheep upon a large ground, and so the more apt to be fined. He was a quiet, thewless, pleasantly conforming man, that was willing to let his hearing of the curates keep his head. But he could not help his children, as alas! who can? For years he was harassed with having to go to Wigtown every court day. He was near eaten out of house and home with having soldiers constantly quartered upon him. And all because his children had chosen to endure hardship cheerfully for the good cause, and to serve under the blue banner that has the cross upon it — at least so far as young bairns may. So from a child Margaret Wilson had companied with those that spoke and loved the truth. She had spent much of her time, ever since she was a lassie of ten, with my sober Maisie Lennox at the Duchrae. And afterwards, when she grew to be of age when lassies think of the lads, Margaret, for the sake of her faith and for naught else, lived on the wild mountains, in the bogs and caves of the hillsides.

To me Margaret Wilson ever seemed the stillest of quiet maids; but, as our Maisie used to say, she was terribly set in her opinions when once she had taken her stand. Now at eighteen she was grown to a tall maid, with a great blowing mass of lint white hair that shone like gold with the sun on it. Well might she have been spared to be some man's delight, had she not been (as she said when the lads speered her) trysted to another lot. The first party of soldiers to whom she was delivered, pitying her youth, let her go to her own home from the crossing of the water at Cree. But by misadventure she travelled on to the town of Wigtown — where with the little lass Agnes in her hand, she was resting in a friend's house, when drunken Winram, ever keen of scent for an ill-conditioned deed, got track of her being in the town. He sent soldiers to take her on the spot, together with her sister of thirteen years, and bade thrust them into the Thieves' Hole that was in the Tolbooth of Wigtown, where they put only the most notorious malefactors.

All this and more Thomas Wilson told us — how that his sisters and an aged woman were confined there and guarded by most brutal soldiers — yea, had already been doomed to be drowned within the tide mark in a very short space of time — though the day of their death as yet he knew not.

Whereat our brave Maisie Lennox was eager to go down to Wigtown and try for a rescue, if we could raise those that would help us. But we could not suffer her to go, though most ready to adventure ourselves. The good folk of Tonskeen were very willing to let my mother and the maids abide with them; for since the taking of Anton Lennox no soldiers had been seen in the district. And the slaying of wicked Mardrochat had feared the ill-set informing people greatly, so that for a long season there was no more of that.

It seemed strange, yet so it was, that Maisie Lennox, who had seen her father pass, as it were, to his death without a tear, wept constantly for her friend and gossip, Margaret of Glen Vernock.

"They cannot condemn Margaret. They will not condemn little Margaret!" she said over and over, as women use.

"Ay, but condemned her they have!" said her brother Thomas, "for they libel it against her and Agnes that they were guilty of rebellion at Bothwell Brig and Ayrsmoss——"

"'Tis plainly impossible," I said; "the judges cannot mean aught to their hurt. Why, at Bothwell, Margaret was but twelve, and little Agnes a paidling bairn of seven years. And as for Ayrsmoss, the poor bairns were never within twenty miles of the place in their lives."

But Thomas Wilson, a quiet, plainfaced lad, only mistrustfully shook his head.

"It is even true," he said, "they mean to make them suffer if they can. But we will hae a thraw at it, to see if we canna break through the Thieves' Hole and draw the lassies forth."

So it was set for the following night, that we should make the attempt to break the Thieves' Hole. The morrow, when it came, proved to be a clear day and fine overhead, which augured not well for our attempt. We would rather have had the blackest and wildest night for our venture. But we had little time, and so we set off to travel by the road the weary miles to Wigtown. We hid all the afternoon in a wood at Machermore, and laid our plans. It was about eleven of the clock that we went down into Wigtown, with the breaking tools which Thomas had gotten from his father's farm, as we passed down through Peninghame.

At the door of the little hostelry in the town we heard a great rioting and crying, which was, as we understood, the soldiers of Winram and some of Strachan's officers drinking late with the Wigtown lawyers, as was their custom. A big, important-looking man went by us, swaying a little unsteadily. He made a great work with his elbows as he went, working them backward and forward at his sides as though he was oaring a boat. This, Thomas Wilson whispered, was Provost Coltran, going home to his town house, after he and David Graham had had their nightcap together. Very evidently the Provost was carrying his full load. For in the midst of the ill-kept square of Wigtown, where certain tall trees grow, he paused and looked upward among the leaves to where the crows were chattering late among their younglings.

"Crawin' and splartin' deils," he said, shaking one fist up at them, and holding to a tree with the other. "I'll hae ye brocht afore the Toon Cooncil and fined — aye, an' a' your goods and gear shall be escheat to the Crown. Blood me gin I dinna, or my name is no Provost Cowtran! David Graham will be glad to hear o' this!"

So saying, he staggered away homeward, there to underlie the ill tongue of his wife for coming home in such a condition — albeit not much worse than was usual with him.

About the Tolbooth it was very quiet, and all was still also in Lag's lodging, whose windows looked down upon it. We got close to the window of the Hole, and crouched to wait for the deepest darkening behind some low ill-smelling sheds, in which pigs were grunting and snoring.

But even at this time of year it is very light at night, and especially in such a place as Wigtown — which sits not among the hills, but as it were on a knowe under a wide arch of sky, making it little and lonely under all that vastness.

Thomas Wilson was to gather a few trusty lads (for there were still such about the place), who should attempt to burn down the door of the Hole. While Wat and I with our crowbars or gellecks, our mallets and chisels, were to try our best with the window. What galled us most was the light in the west, which remained strangely lucid and even, as though the sky itself were shining clear in the midst of the night — a thing which I had never seen in my own hill lands, but often upon the flats of Wigtown.

Our hearts were beating, I warrant, when we stole out to make our attempt. This we did at eleven by the town clock, and there was no better or more kindly darkness to be looked for. It was silent in the Square of Wigtown, save for the crows that Provost Coltran had shaken his fist at. As we stole to the window, which indeed was no more than a hole wide enough, the bars being removed, to allow a man's body to pass through, we heard the praying of the prisoners within. It was the voice of our little Margaret Wilson. When last I heard that voice, it was in sweet and womanly converse with Maisie Lennox, concerning the light matters of which women love to speak, but are immediately silent about when a man comes by — aye, even if that man be their nearest. For this is the nature of woman.

At the first rasp of the chisel, there was silence within, for the prisoners knew well that only friends would try to enter in that way. We could hear the lads piling faggots at the outer door, as had been done once before with great success, when the bars were burnt through within half an hour. But, since the fire would assuredly bring the soldiers, it was put off till we had made our attempt upon the window.

Wat was stronger than I when it came to the forcing aside of the bars, and he it was that set his strength to mine, and with the long iron impelled out of its binding mortar the great central bar. Then after we had broken the lesser one above and below with much less stress, the window lay open. It seemed a practical enough breach. It came my time to mount and enter to see if I could help the women out, an enterprise which needed much caution.

Wat had scaled the roof to see if there was aught there that might be advantageous. I was up and scrambling with my toes against the rough wall, half of my body within, when I heard a scuffle and a sudden cry of warning from the other side of the tower. I heard Wat leap down with a shout, and I would have followed, but I received a mighty push which sent me headlong through the prison window into the Thieves' Hole. Here I sat, very astonished and dazed, with my head having taken the wall, till the door was opened and a figure, booted and spurred, cloaked also from head to heel, came in, and with a lantern bearer behind him, stood looking at us. The two young lassies, Margaret and Agnes, sat in a corner clasping one another's hands, and a very old woman sat near me with her head clasped in her hands. She never looked up so long as I saw her, and seemed to have quite lost both interest and hope.

I knew that the big man with the cloak was the Laird of Lag, for once with my father I had seen him on the street at Kirkcudbright, when he spoke us fairly enough — the matter one of cattle and crops belike.

"Whom have we here," he said, "coming so late by the window to see the lassies? Young Whiggie, this is not proper wark; but who may you be?"

I sat and said nothing.

"Stell him up," he said, "and let us see what like this breaker of maidens' chambers may be."

But I stood up of my own accord, with my hand on the prison wall.

Then he appeared to recognise me, for he said sourly:

"Ye'll be an Earlstoun Gordon, nae doot — ye favour the breed — though there's mair of the lawyer Hope nor the fechtin' Gordon aboot you. I hadna thocht ye had as muckle spunk."

Then he ordered two soldiers to stand guard over the hole on the outside, and, setting a double guard on the Tolbooth, he cried, "Have young Gordon forth to my quarters." Which when they did, he entertained himself for several hours telling me how he would send me with the utmost care to Edinburgh, and of the newly imported tortures that would be inflicted on Sandy and myself. He said that Sandy was to be tortured and that he had seen the precept from London with the order.

"So ye'll juist be in time to try on the new 'boot.' There's a fine braw new-fangled pattern wi' spikes, and I hear that the new thumbikins are excellently persuasive. Faith, they hae widened many a Whig's thrapple already, and made it braw and wide in the swallow!"

Then, adding all the time cup to cup, he fell to cursing me and all our house, not letting even my mother alone, till I said to him:

"John Graham had not treated a prisoner so. Nor you, Robert Grierson, if you thought that my kinsman Kenmure was at hand to strike his sword through your body — as once he came near doing in the street of Kirkcudbright in the matter of bell of Whiteside!"

Now this (as I knew) was a saying which angered him exceedingly, and he was for having out a file of soldiers and shooting me there and then. But luckily Winram came in to say that the other assailants of the Tolbooth had gotten cleanly off, and that a soldier was invalided with a sword-thrust through and through his shoulder, in which very clearly I recognised Wat's handicraft.

CHAPTER LI.

THE SANDS OF WIGTOWN.

THE morning of the eleventh of May came as calm and sweet as the night had been, which had proved so disastrously clear for us. I slept little, as men may guess, thinking on the poor lassies; and sometimes also on the torture in the prison, and the death on the scaffold. For I knew that though there might be delay, there could be no such thing as pardon for one that had carried the standard at Sanquhar, charged the storming fray of Ayrsmoss, and sole of all in Cameron's muster had gotten clear away.

From early morning I could hear on the street the gathering of the folk from the country-side far and near. And then the soldiers came clattering by to their stations, laughing as they went like people going to look upon a show.

"There are but two of them to be 'pitten doon,' after all," I heard one of the soldiers say. "Gilbert Wilson has paid a hundred pound to get off his bit lassie Agnes."

And that was the first intimation I had that only the elder woman, Margaret Lauchlison, whom I had seen in the Thieves' Hole with her head on her hands, and our own sweet Margaret were to be drowned within the flood-mark of the Blednoch.

Black, black day! Would that I could blot it out of my memory. Yet that men in after times may see what weak maids and ailing women bore with constancy in the dark years, I set down that day's doings as I saw them — but briefly, neither altering nor suppressing, because of this matter I cannot bear to write at large. It was but half an hour before the binding of the women that Lag sent for me — in order that I might see the thing which was done, and, as he said, carry the word to Sandy and the rest of the saints at Edinburgh.

And this, as I told him, with all constancy I should be very fond to do.

Now the Blednoch is a slow stream, which ordinarily flows in the deep ditch of its channel, wimpling and twining through the sands of the bay of Wigtown. The banks are but steep slopes of mud, on which if one slips he goes to the bottom with a slide. Up this deep channel the sea comes twice every day, damming back the sluggish stream and brimming the banks at full tide. When Lag's men took me down to the water edge, I saw the two women already tied to stakes set in the ooze of the Blednoch bank. At the sight my heart swelled within me at once sick and hot. Margaret Lauchlison was tethered deepest down, her stake set firm in the bottom and the post rising as high as her head.

Nigh half way up the steep bank stood our little Margaret, loosely reeved to a sunken stob, her hands clasped before her. She still wore the gown that I remember seeing upon her when she dwelt with us among the hills. But even in this pass she was cheerful, and lifting her eyes with a smile she bade me be so likewise, because that for her there was no fear and but a short pain. Also she called me very sweetly "William," and asked me to commend her to Maisie Lennox — a thing which more than all went to my heart. For it told me by the way she said it, that Maisie and she had talked together of loves and likings, as is all maidens' wont. The women were not tightly tied to the posts, but attached to them with a running rove of rope, by which they could be pulled close to the stakes, or else, at the will of the murderers, drawn up again to the bank, as one might draw a pitcher from a well.

Already was the salt tide water beginning to flow upwards along the Blednoch channel, bearing swirls of foam upon its breast.

Margaret Lauchlison, being an aged woman of eighty years, said no word as the tide rose above her breast, where lowest in the river bed she stood waiting. Her head hung down, and it was not till the water reached her lips that she began to struggle, nor did I see her make so much as a movement. Yet she was determined to die as she had lived, an honest, peaceable, Christian woman of a good confession — not learned, save in the scholarship of God, but therein of high attainment and great experience. And all honour be to her, for even as she determined, so she died.

Then, when some of the soldiers were for fleeching with her to take the Test, Lag cried out (for he ever loved his devil's-broth served hot):

"Bide ye there! 'Tis needless to speak to the old besom! Let her go quick to hell!"

But Provost Coltran, sober enough this morning, and with other things to think of than the crows, come to the bank edge. And standing where his feet were nearly on a level with our little Margaret's head, he said to her:

"What see ye down there, Margaret Wilson? What think ye? Can you with constancy suffer the choking of the salt water when it comes to your turn?"

Now, though Coltran was a rude man, and pang full of oaths, he spoke not so unfeelingly. But to him Margaret replied, in a sweet voice that wafted up like the singing of a psalm, from the sweltering pit of pain:

"I see naught but Christ struggling there in the water in the person of one of His saints!"

Then the Provost came nearer still, and bending down

like an elder that gives counsel, said to her, "Margaret, ye are young and ken no better. We will give you your life gin ye pray for the King. Will ye say aloud 'God save the King'?"

"I desire the salvation of all men," Margaret said. "May God save him an He will!"

Coltran rose with a flush of triumph in his eye. He was none so bad a man, only dazed with drink and bad company.

"She has said it!" he cried, and from far and near the people took up the cry "She has said it, she has said it!" And some were glad and some shook their heads for what they counted the dishonour of the submission.

Now, Blednoch sands under Wigtown town were a sight to behold that day. They were black with folk, all in scattering, changing groups. There were many clouds of folk on the sands when the lassies were "pitten doon," and in every little company there was one praying. Through them patrolled the soldiers in fours, breaking up each little band of worshippers, which dissolved only to come together again as soon as they had passed.

Then the town officer, a cruel and ill-liked man, who never did well afterwards all his days, took his long-hafted halbert, and, standing on the verge of the bank, he set the end of it to Margaret Lauchlison's neck.

"Bide ye doon there and clep wi' the partans, Margaret, my woman!" he said, holding her head under water till it hung loose and the life went from it.

The elder woman thus having finished her course with joy, they unrove the nether rope and drew little Margaret up to the bank, exhorting her to cry aloud "God save the King!" and also to pray for him, that she might get her liberty.

For they began to be in fear, knowing that this drowning of women would make a greater stir in the world than much shooting of men.

z

"Lord, give him repentance, forgiveness, and, salvation!" she said fervently and willingly.

But Lag cried out in his great hoarse voice, "Out upon the wretch! We want not such oaths nor prayers. Winram, get the Test through her teeth — or down with her again."

But she steadfastly refused the wicked Test, the oath of sin. As indeed we that loved Scotland and the good way of religion had all learned to do.

"I cannot forswear my faith. I am one of Christ's children. Let me go to Him!" she said, being willing to depart, which she held to be far better.

"Back with her into the water!" cried Lag. "The sooner she will win to hell! 'Tis too good for a rebel like her!"

But Coltran said, "Ye are fair to see, Margaret, lass. Think weel, hinny! Hae ye nane that ye love?"

But she answered him not a word, being like one other before her, like a lamb led to the slaughter.

So they tied her again to the stake, where the water was deeper now and lappered on her breast, swirling yellow and foul in oily bubbles.

Her great head coverture of hair — which, had I been her lad, I should have delighted to touch and stroke — now broke from the maiden's snood, and fell into the water. There it floated, making a fair golden shining in the grimy tide, like the halo which is about the sun when he rises. Also her face was as the face of an angel, being turned upward to God.

Then they began to drive the folk from the sands for fear of what they might see — the beauty of the dying maid, and go mad with anger at the sight.

Whereupon, being in extremity, she lifted her voice to sing, calm as though it had been an ordinary Sabbath morning, and she leading the worship at Glen Vernock, as indeed she did very well.

It was the twenty-fifth Psalm she sang, as followeth. And when she that was a pure maid sang of her sins, it went to my heart, thinking on my own greater need.

> "My sins and faults of youth
> Do Thou, O Lord, forget;
> After Thy mercies think on me,
> And for Thy goodness great."

It was a sweet voice and carried far. But lest it should move the hearts of the people, Lag garred beat the drum. And as the drums began to roll, 1 saw the first salt wave touch the bonny maiden lips which no man had kissed in the way of love.

Then the guards plucked me by the arm roughly and dragged me away. The drums waxed still louder. But as we went farther away, the voice of the maiden praising God out of the floods of great waters, broke through them, rising clearer, besieging the throne of God and breaking down the hearts of men. I saw the tears hopping down many a rude soldier's cheek.

Nevertheless, they swore incessantly, cursing Lag and Winram back and forth, threatening to shoot them for devils thus to kill young maids and weakly women.

But once again in the pauses of the drums the words of Margaret's song came clear. Forget them shall I never, till I too be on my death-bed, and can remember nothing but "The Lord's my Shepherd," which every Scot minds on his dying day. These were the words she sang:

> "Turn unto me Thy face,
> And to me mercy show;
> Because that I am desolate,
> And am brought very low.
>
> "O do Thou keep my soul,
> Do Thou deliver me;
> And let me never be ashamed,
> Because I trust in Thee."

After the last line there was a break and a silence, and no more — and no more! But after the silence had endured a space, there arose a wailing that went from the hill of Wigtown to the farthest shore of the Cree — the wailing of a whole country-side for a young lass done to death in the flower of her youth, in the untouched grace and favour of her virginity.

CHAPTER LII.

THE MADNESS OF THE BULL OF EARLSTOUN.

How they carried me to Edinburgh I cannot stop to tell, though the manner of it was grievous enough. But in my heart all the way there remained the fear that while I was laid up in Edinburgh, Robert Grierson, the wild beast of Galloway, might come and take my mother and Maisie. And do so with them even as he had done with Margaret Lauchlison and our little Margaret of Glen Vernock. And this vexed me more than torments.

In Edinburgh they cast me into an inner den of the prison, where in the irons there were ten men already. Then when my name was made known, through the darkness and the fearsome stench of the place, where no fresh air had come for years, what was my joy to hear the voice of Anton Lennox bidding me be of good cheer—for that our Lord was a strong Lord, and would see me win with credit from off the stage of life.

At this I took heart of grace at the kenned voice and face, and we fell to discoursing about Maisie Lennox and how she did. He told me that to the honour of the King's service the soldiers had treated him kindly, and had given him the repute of being a man honourable above most. Nevertheless, the warrant for his execution was daily expected from London. He told me also that my brother Sandy was in Blackness Castle, but that it was reported again that he was soon to be examined by torture. Indeed there was a talk among the guard that I was to share this with him, which made them the more careful of me, as one whom the Council had an eye upon.

But it was not long before this matter was brought to a probation. About three of the clock on the following day, there came officers to the Tolbooth Port and cried my name, to which I answered with a quaking heart — not for death, but for torture. So they took me out and delivered me to the guard, who haled me by back ways and closes to a little door let into the side of a great hulk of grey wall.

Along stone passages very many, all dripping with damp like a cellar, they dragged me, till beside three doors hung with red cloth they stopped. Then instead of swearing and jesting as they had done before, the officers talked in whispers.

Presently a door swung open very silently to admit me, and I set my feet upon a soft carpet. Then, also without noise, the door swung to again. I found myself alone in a cage, barriered like the cage of a wild beast. It was at one end of a vast room with black oaken ceiling, carven and panelled. Before me there was a strong breastwork of oak, and an iron bar across, chin high. Beside me and on either hand were ranged strange-looking engines, some of which I knew to be the "boots" for the torture of the legs, and the pilniewinks for the bruising of the thumbs. Also there stood at each side of the platform a man habited in black and white and with a black mask over his face. These men stood with their arms folded, and looked across the narrow space at one another as though they had been carven statues.

The rest of the great room was occupied by a table, and at the table there sat a dignified company. Then I understood that I stood in the presence of the Privy Council of Scotland, which for twenty-five years had bent the land to the King's will. At the head sat cruel Queensberry, with a face louring with hate and guile—or so it seemed, seen through bars of oak and underneath gauds of iron.

Still more black and forbidding was the face of the "Bluidy Advocate," Sir George Mackenzie, who sat at the table-foot, and wrote incessantly in his books. I knew none other there, save the fox face of Tarbet, called the Timeserver.

When I was brought in, they were talking over some slight matter concerning a laird who had been complaining that certain ill-set persons were carrying away sea tangle from his foreshore. And I was not pleased that they should have other thoughts in their minds, when I was before them in peril of my life.

At last Sir George Mackenzie turned him about and said, "Officer, whom have we here?"

The officer of the court made answer very shortly and formally, "William Gordon, son of umquhile William Gordon of Earlstoun in Galloway, and brother of the aforementioned Alexander Gordon, condemned traitor from the prison of Blackness, presently to be examined."

"Ah!" said Mackenzie, picking up his pen again, "the Glenkens messan! We'll wait for the muckle hound and take both the lowsy tykes thegether!"

But Queensberry, as was his custom at Council, ran counter to the advocate in his desire, and commanded presently to interrogate me.

The Duke asked me first if I had been at the wounding of the Duke Wellwood.

I answered him plainly that I had. But that it was a fair fight, and that the Duke and his men had made the first onslaught.

"You have proof of that at your hand, no doubt," said he, and passed on as though that had been a thing of little import—as indeed, in the light of my succeeding admissions, it was.

"You were at Sanquhar town on the day of the Declaration?" he said, looking sharply at me, no doubt expecting a denial or equivocation.

Now it seemed to me that I must most certainly die, so I cared not if I did it with some credit. For the whiner got even less mercy from these men, than he that defied and outfaced them.

"I was at Sanquhar, and with this hand I raised the Banner of Blue!" I said.

"Note that, advocate," said Tarbet, smiling foxily. "The King hath a special interest in all that took his name in vain at Sanquhar."

Mackenzie glanced with a black, side-cocking look of interest at the hand I held up, as if to say, "I shall know that again when I see it on the Netherbow!"

"You were at Ayrsmoss, and won clear?" was the next interrogatory.

"I was one of two that broke through both lines of the troops when we came to the charge!" I said, with perhaps more of the braggart than I care now to think on.

Then all the Council looked up, and there was a sudden stir of interest.

"Blood of St. Crispin!" said Queensberry, "but ye do not look like it. Yet I suppose it must be so."

"It is so," said Sir George the Advocate shortly, flicking a parchment with the feather of his quill pen. He had the record before him.

"Is there anything more that ye were in? Being as good as headed already, a little more will not matter. It will be to your credit when the saints come to put up your tomb, and scribe your testimony on it."

"I am no saint," said I, "though I love not Charles Stuart. Neither, saving your honourable presences, do I love the way that this realm is guided. But if it please you to ken, I have been in all that has chanced since Bothwell. I was at Enterkin the day we reft the prisoners from you. I was in the ranks of the Seven Thousand when, at the Conventicle at Shalloch-on-Minnoch, the hillmen made Clavers and Strachan draw off. I was taken at the Tolbooth of Wigtown trying to deliver a prisoner, whom ye had reprieved. And had there been anything else done, I should have been in it."

The Council leaned back in their chairs almost to a man, and smilingly looked at one another. The President spoke after a moment of silence.

"Ye are a brisk lad and ill to content, but your sheet is gallantly filled. So that I think ye deserve heading instead of hanging, which is certainly a great remission. I shall e'en take the liberty of shaking hands with you and wishing you a speedy passage and a sharp axe. Officer, the prisoner is in your care till his warrant comes from London."

And to my astonishment Queensbury turned round and very ceremoniously held out his hand to me, which I took through the bars.

"I shall never again deny that Gordon blood is very good blood," he said.

Then they brought in Sandy, looming up like a tower between the warders. He had a strange, dazed look about him, and his hair had grown till he peered out of the hassock, like to an owl out of an ivy bush, as the proverb says.

They asked a few questions of him, to which he gave but mumbled replies. If he saw me he never showed it. But I knew him of old, and a sly tod was Sandy.

Then Sir George Mackenzie rose, and turning to him, read the King's mandate, which declared that, in spite of his underlying sentence of death, he was to be tortured, to make him declare the truth in the matter of Fergusson the plotter, and the treason anent the King's life.

Then, the black wrath of his long prisonment suddenly boiling over, Sandy took hold on the great iron bar before him and bent his strength to it — which, when he was roused, was like the strength of Samson. With one rive he tore it from its fastenings, roaring all the while with that terrible voice of his, which used to set the cattle wild with fear when they heard it, and which even affrighted men grown and bearded. The two men in masks sprang upon him, but he seized them one in each hand and cuffed and buffeted them against the wall, till I thought he had splattered their brains on the stones. Indeed, I looked to see. But though there was blood enough, there were no brains to speak of.

Then very hastily some of the Council rose to their feet to call the guard, but the door had been locked during the meeting, and none for a moment could open it. It was fearsome to see Sandy. His form seemed to tower to the ceiling. A yellow foam, like spume of the sea, dropped from his lips. He roared at the Council with open mouth, and twirled the bar over his head. With one leap he sprang over the barrier, and at this all the councillors drew their gowns about them and rushed pell-mell for the door, with Sandy thundering at their heels with his iron bar. It was all wonderfully fine to see. For Sandy, with more sense than might have been expected of him, being so raised, lundered them about the broadest of their gowns with the bar, till the building was filled with the cries of the mighty Privy Council of Scotland. I declare I laughed heartily, though under sentence of death, and felt that well as I thought I had borne myself, Sandy the Bull had done a thousand times better.

Then from several doors the soldiery came rushing in, and in short space Sandy, after levelling a file with his gaud of iron, was overpowered by numbers. Nevertheless, he continued to struggle till they twined him helpless in coils of rope. In spite of all, it furnished work for the best part of a company to take him to the Castle, whither, "for a change of air," and to relieve his madness he was remanded, by order of the Council when next they met. But there was no more heard of examining Sandy by torture.

And it was a tale in the city for many a day how Sandy Gordon cleared the chamber of the Privy Council. So not for the first time in my life I was proud of my brother, and would have given all the sense I had, which is no little, for the thews and bones to have done likewise.

CHAPTER LIII.

UNDER SENTENCE OF DEATH.

So waiting the arrival and the day of my doom, I continued to abide in the Tolbooth. Anton Lennox, also waiting, as he said, his bridegroom day of marriage and coronation, was with me. In the night alone we had some peace and quiet. For they had turned in upon us, to our horror, that wind-filled fool, John Gib — whom for his follies, Anton Lennox had lundered with a stick upon the Flowe of the Deer-Slunk.

With him was Davie Jamie the scholar, now grown well nigh as mad as himself. Sometimes the jailors played with them, and said, "John, this is your Sunday's meal of meat!"

Whereupon, so filled with moon-madness were they, that they would refuse good victual, because it had been given them upon a day with a heathen name. Or, again, the more ill-set of the prisoners made their game of them — for they were not all of them that suffered for their faith, who were with us in the Canongate Tolbooth. But many city apprentices also that had been in brawls or had broken their indentures. And, truth to tell, we were somewhat glad of the regardless birkies. For when we were dull of heart they made sport with us, and we were numerous enough to keep them from interfering with our worship.

So these wild loons would say:

"Prophesy to us, John Gib, for we know that thou hast the devil ever at thine elbow. Let us see thy face shining, as it did at the Spout of Auchentalloch, when ye danced naked and burned the Bible."

And whether it was with our expectant looking for it, or whether the man really had some devilry about him, certain it is that in the gloom of the corner, where in his quiet spells he abode, there seemed to be ofttimes a horrible face near to his own, and a little bluish light thrown upon his hair and eyes. This was seen by most in the dungeon, though, for my own part, I confess I could see nothing.

Then he would be taken with accesses of howling, like to a moonstruck dog or a rutting hart on the mountains of heather. And sometimes, when the fear of Anton Lennox was upon him, he would try to stop his roaring, thrusting his own napkin into his mouth. But for all that the devil within him would drive out the napkin and some most fearsome yells behind it, as a pellet is driven from a boy's tow gun.

This he did mostly during worship — which was held thrice a day in the Tolbooth, and helped to pass the time. At such seasons he became fairly possessed, and was neither to hold nor bind. So that for common they had to bring Anton Lennox to him with a quarter-staff, with which he threatened him. And at sight of old Anton, Gib, though a big strong man, would run behind the door and crouch there on his hunkers, howling grievously like a dog.

He was ordered into leg-irons, but his ravings pleased the Duke of York so much (because that he wanted to tar us all with the same stick) that he had them taken off. Also he bade give him and David Jamie as much paper and ink as ever they wanted, and to send him copies of all that they wrote, for his entertainment. But in time of worship after this, Anton Lennox ordered four of the strongest and biggest men to sit upon John Gib, streeked out on the floor, as men sit together upon a bench in the kirk at sermon-hearing. And we were glad when we fell on this plan, for it discouraged the devil more than anything, so that he acknowledged the power of the gospel and quit his roaring.

Yet I think all this rough play kept up our hearts, and stayed us from thinking all the time upon that day of our bitter, final testifying, which was coming so soon. To make an end now of Muckle John Gib, I heard that he was sent by ship to the colonies, and that in America he gained much honour among the heathen for his converse with the devil. Nor did the godly men that are there, ever discover Anton Lennox's weighty method of exorcism — than which I ween there is none better, for even the devil needs breath as well as another.

But for all this, there was never an hour that chimed, but I would wake and remember that at the sound of a trumpet the port might any moment be opened and I be summoned forth to meet my doom. And Anton Lennox dealt with me there in the Cannongate Tolbooth for my soul's peace, and that very faithfully. For there were not wanting among the prisoners those that made no scruple to call me a sword-and-buckler Covenanter, because I would not follow them in all their protests and remonstrances. But Anton Lennox warred with them with the weapons of speech for the both of us, and told them how that I had already witnessed a good confession and that before many witnesses. He said also that there would not be wanting One, when I had overpassed my next stage, to make confession of William Gordon before the angels of heaven. Which saying made them to cavil no more.

CHAPTER LIV.

ROBBERY ON THE KING'S HIGHWAY.

Now that which follows concerns not myself, but Maisie Lennox .and others that were at this time forth of the Tolbooth. Yet, because the story properly comes in here, I pray the reader to suffer it gladly, for without it I cannot came to my tale's ending, as I must speedily do. How I came to know it, is no matter now, but shall without doubt afterwards appear.

While Anton Lennox and I lay in the Tolbooth, those that loved us were not idle. Wat moved Kate and Kate moved Roger McGhie of Balmaghie. So that he set off to London to see the King, in order to get remission for me, and if need be to pay my fine, because there was nothing he would not do to pleasure his daughter. But though his intercession did good in delaying the warrant, yet my owning of the raising the flag at Sanquhar was too much for the King, and in due course my warrant sped; of which the bruit came north with a servant of Balmaghie's who rode like the wings of the wind. But indeed I was not greatly disappointed, for since my declaration to the Privy Council, I never expected any other end.

As soon, however, as the news came to the house of Balmaghie, Maisie Lennox betook herself to the woodside to think. There she stayed for the better part of an hour, pacing up and down more like an aged man than a young maiden. Then, as my informant tells me, she came in again with a face wonderfully assured.

"Give me a horse and suit of lad's clothes," she said to her who kept the drapery closets and wardrobes at the house of Balmaghie.

"Preserve us, lass, for what wad ye hae lad's claes?" said the ancient housekeeper. But without waiting to reply, Maisie Lennox went and got them.

"The lassie's gane wud!* There's nae reason in her," she cried out in amazement.

But indeed it was a time when men and women were not inclined to stand upon reasons. For each being supposed to have his neck deep in the tow, he had no doubt his own good logic for whatever he proposed.

So Mistress Crombie, housekeeper to the Laird of Balmaghie, without further question, fitted Maisie Lennox with a suit of lad's clothes, which (having taken off and again suitably attired herself) she strapped in a roll on her saddle bow and covered with a plaid. Then, dressed like a maid that goes to her first place and rides a borrowed horse, she took her way eastward. Now at that time, so important were the proclamations and Privy Council matters, that every week there rode a post who carried naught but reprieves and sentences.

It had been the custom of late, ever since the numerous affrays near the border of Berwick, that this messenger of life and death should ride by Carlisle and Moffat to Edinburgh.

Now this young maid, contrary to the wont of women folk, had all her life said little and done much. So when Maisie Lennox came to the side of the Little Queensberry Hill, having ridden all the way sedately, as a sober maiden ought, she went aside into a thicket and changed her woman's appearance to that of a smart birkie who rides to college. It was about the time when the regents call up such to the

* Mad.

beginning of their classes. So it was a most feasible-like thing, and indeed there were a good many upon the roads. But Maisie Lennox kept out of their company, for these wandering students are ever inclined to be goatish, and full of impish pranks, whether as I saw them at Groningen or in Edinburgh town.

So she (that was for the time being he) came riding into the town of Moffat, just when the London state messenger was expected. There my lass entered the hostelry of the White Hart, which was kept by a decent woman named Catherine Cranstoun. As a ruffling young gallant, she strode in, with her chest well out and one hand on the hilt of the rapier, which she held modishly thrust forward. But Maisie, when she found herself within, was a little daunted to see a great pair of pistols, a sword, and other furniture of a King's rider lie upon the table. While from within a little chamber, the door of which stood ajar, she heard the sound as of one who sleeps, and snores sonorously in his sleep.

"A good day to ye, Mistress Cranstoun," said Maisie boldly, and most like a clerkish student. "Will ye get me a drink of good caller water?"

"That," said the good wife shrewishly, turning her eyes scorningly across her nose, "is not good asking at a change-house. I warrant we do not live and pay our winter's oats by sellin' caller water to student birkies!"

"So, good madam," said our Maisie again; "but if you will get me a drink from your famous medicinal spring — a good fresh quart — most gladly I will pay for it — aye, as if it had been claret wine of the best bin in your cellar."

At hearing of which the landlady pricked up her ears.

"I will e'en gae bring it mysel'," she said in a changed voice, for such orders came not every day. "It is for a wager," she thought. "The loons are ever after some daft ploy."

As she went to the door she had a thought.

"Mind ye," she said, "meddle not wi' the pistols, for they belong to one on the King's service."

So she set out to bring the water in a wooden cogie with a handle.

As soon as she was fairly gone, Maisie stole on tiptoe to the door of the room whence the snoring proceeded. She peeped circumspectly within, and there on a rough bed with the neck of his buff riding-coat thrown open, lay the King's rider, a great clean shaven fellow with a cropped head, and ear-rings in his ears. The edge of the mail bag peeped from under the pillow, and the ribbons of seals showed beneath the flaps.

Maisie laid her hand on her heart to still its painful beating. Clearly there was no chance of drawing the bag from under the rider's head, for his hand was twisted firmly in the strap. It was with mighty grief in her heart that Maisie Lennox stepped back. But at sight of the pistols on the table, a thought and a hope sprang up together within her. She hasted to take them up and draw the charges, leaving only a sprinkling of powder in the pan of each.

And as she rode off, she bore with her the landlady's benediction, for the good wife had never been so paid for caller spring water before.

It was at the entrance to the wild place known as the Devil's Beef Tub, near the last wood on the upward way over the hills, that Maisie waited for the King's rider. There were, no doubt, many thoughts in her heart, but she did not dwell upon them — save it might be upon this one, that if the rider discovered that the charges had been drawn, it would certainly go ill with her and worse with those whom she had come out to save.

What wonder then if her maid's heart flew faster even than Gay Garland had done when he fled before the gypsy clan.

At last, after long waiting, she heard far off the clatter of a horse's feet on the road, and her courage returned to her. As the King's messenger came trotting easily down an incline, she rode as quietly out of a byway into the road and let him range alongside.

With a polite toss of the reins, as was then the modish fashion, she bade him good day.

"Ye are a bonny birkie. Hae ye ony sisters?" said the man in the Lothian tongue.

Maisie answered him no—an only bairn and riding to the college at Edinburgh.

"Ye'll be a braw student no doubt."

She told him so-so.

"I'se warrant ye!" said he, for he was jovial by nature, and warmed with Mistress Cranstoun's wine.

So they rode on in friendly enough talk till they were nearing the wood, when Maisie, knowing that the time had come, wheeled about and bade him "Stand!" At the same time she pointed a pistol at his head.

"Deliver me your mails," she said, "or I shall take your life!"

The man laughed as at a pleasant jest.

"Gae wa' wi' ye, birkie. Nane o' your college tricks wi' me, or ye may aiblins come to a mishap. I am no' a man to tak' offence, but this somewhat passes merrymaking!"

But when Maisie pulled the other pistol and levelled it also at his head, the rider hesitated no longer, but pulled out his own and took aim at her heart.

"Your blood be on your own head, then! I never missed yet!" he cried, and pulled the trigger.

But the powder only flashed in the pan. With an oath he pulled the other and did likewise with it, but quite as fruitlessly.

Then he leaped down and tried to grip Maisie's horse by the bridle, for he was a stark carle and no coward.

But her horse obeyed the guiding hand. With a swing to the left she swept out of his reach, so as to catch the bridle of the horse which carried the mails and which, fresh from the stable, was inclined to crop the herbage. Then she rode away leaving the man standing amazed and speechless in the middle of the road. He started to run after his assailant, but Maisie sent a bullet back, which halted him. For by chance it struck a stone among the red dust at his feet, and went through between his legs buzzing like a bumblebee. And this is indeed a thing which would have halted most folk.

It was with a fearful heart that Maisie Lennox, in the deepest shades of the wood, ripped open the bags. Almost the first paper she came upon was her father's death warrant. With trembling hand she turned over the papers to find mine also. But there were only Privy Council letters and documents in cypher. Over and over she turned them, her heart, I doubt not, hammering loudly. But there was not another warrant anywhere. It must have been sent forward by another hand. It might even be in Edinburgh already, she thought. Almost she had returned the letters to the bag and left them at the tree foot, when she noted a little bulge in the thickness of the leather near the clasp. In a moment she had her knife within, and there, enclosed in a cypher letter to the President of the Council, was a free pardon, signed and sealed, wanting only the name inserted. Without doubt it was intended for some of the private friends of Duke Queensberry. But at sight of it Maisie's heart gave a still greater stound, and without a moment for consideration she galloped off towards Edinburgh, upon the fresh horse of his Majesty's post rider. When she came to the first woods over the crown of the dreary hill road, she put off the lad's apparel and dressed again as the quiet maid upon her travels, whom none would suspect of bold robbery of his Majesty's despatches upon his own highway.

Then as she took the road to Edinburgh, consider what a turmoil and battle there was in her heart. She says that she saw not the road all the way for thinking, and I doubt it not. "My father or my lad —— " she argued with herself. "Which name shall I put in? It may not serve them long, but it will save them at least this day from death."

And in the clatter of her horse's feet she found no answer to her question.

Then she told over to herself all that her father had done for her since she remembered — the afternoons when it was the Sabbath on the pleasant green bank at the Duchrae loaning end, the words of wise counsel spoken there, the struggle at the cave when the cruel Mardrochat was sent to his account. She did not forget one. Other things also she owns that she thought of. "Whatever may happen to me, I must — I shall save my father!" she concluded.

She was on a lonely place on the moors, with deep moss-hags and holes in the turf where men had cut peat. These were now filled with black water. She stopped, took out the warrant for her father's execution, tore it into a thousand pieces, and sunk it carefully in the deep hag. The white horse of the King's rider meanwhile stood patiently by till she mounted again — I warrant as swiftly as she used to do in the old days at the Duchrae.

But the tearing of the warrant would only delay and not prevent her father's death. She saw that clearly. There came to her the thought of the free pardon. To inscribe a name in the blank space meant a release from prison and the chance of escape. She resolved to write it when she came to the next change-house.

But as she rode she fell to the thinking, and the question that surged to and fro in her heart, like the tide in a sea-cave, was — which name would be found written on that pardon when she rode to the Tolbooth of Edinburgh to deliver it into the hands of the Captain of the Guard.

As she thought she urged her horse the faster, so that the sooner she might come to the change-house and settle the question.

"He is my father," she said over and over, dwelling on all that her father had been to her. "I cannot — I will not think of others before him. It is my father's name I will write in the pardon — I must, yes I must!"

And the name of another did she not mention at all, as I have been informed. At last she came to the door of the change-house, and, throwing her reins over the tieing post at the gate, she went in boldly.

"Bring me an inkhorn and a goose-quill!" she cried to the dame of the inn, forgetting that she had donned her maid's clothes again, and speaking in the hectoring voice of the birkie student. She threw a silver coin on the table with a princely air that suited but indifferently with the sober fashion of her maiden's dress. And among the mutchkins on the ribbed and rimmed deal table, she squared herself to write in the name upon her free pardon.

She set her pen to the parchment bravely. Then she stopped, took a long breath and held it, as though it were the dying breath of one well-beloved which she had in her keeping. With sudden access of resolve she began a bold initial. She changed it. Then she wrote again hastily with a set face, but holding her hand over the writing, as though to shield the words from sight. Which being done, she looked at what she had written with a blanched and terror-stricken countenance.

No sooner was the ink dry, than bending again to the

paper, she began eagerly to scrape at it with her finger-nail, as though she would even yet change her thought.

But as she rubbed the parchment, which was very fine and soft, part of it curled up at the edge into a tiny roll like a shaving of bark when one cuts a white birch. Instantly Maisie discerned that there were two parchments instead of one.

With a light and cunning hand she separated them carefully. They had been secretly attached so as to look like one. Casting her eyes rapidly over the second parchment, her heart leaped within her to find that it was another pardon, the duplicate of the first, and, like it, duly signed and sealed. It was a moment's work to write in the other name upon this great discovery. Then throwing, in her joy, a gold piece upon the table beside the shilling, she mounted at the stance, and rode away in the direction of the capital.

"My word!" said the good wife of the change-house, gazing after her, "but that madam doesna want confidence. I doot she will be after no good!"

"She doesna want siller," quoth her husband, gathering up the money, "and that's a deal more to the point in a change-house!"

But Maisie Lennox has never told to any — not even to me, who have some right to know her secrets — that name which she first wrote when she had to choose between her father's life and her lover's.

She only says, "Let every maid answer in her own heart which name she would have written, being in my place, that day in the change-house!"

And even so may I leave it to all the maidens that may read my history to let their hearts answer which. For they also will not tell.

CHAPTER LV.

THE RED MAIDEN.

THE great day which we had been expecting dawned, and lo! it was even as any other day. The air was shrewdly cold when I awoke very early in the morning, just as I had awaked from sleep every morning since I can remember. It was my custom to begin to say the little prayer which my mother had taught me before I was fairly awake. This I did when I was but a boy, for the economising of time; and I continued the practice when I put away most other childish things. I declare solemnly that I was past the middle of the prayer, before the thought came to me that this was the morn of the day on which I was to die. Even then, by God's extreme mercy, fear did not take me utterly by the throat.

I had dreamed of the day often, and shivered to think of that awaking. But now that it was here, it seemed to me like any morn in the years, when I used to awake in the little sunlit tourelle at Earlstoun to the noise of the singing of birds, and turn my thoughts upon riding to the Duchrae by the Grenoch side to see Maisie Lennox—little Maisie May, whom now I should see no more.

So by the strengthening mercy of God I was enabled to finish my mother's prayer with some composure. And also to remember her and Maisie, commending them both to the gracious care of One who is able to keep.

Then came the Chancellor's Commissioner to tell us that by the high favour of his master, we were to be headed in the early morn. And that, too, in the company of the great Earl of Cantyre, who, after lying long in prison, was that day, for rebellion in the Highlands and the Isles, condemned to lose his head. No higher favour could be granted, though it seemed not so much to me as doubtless to some, that I should lay my head beside an Earl's on the block of the Maiden, instead of setting my neck in a rope at the hands of the common executioner in the Grassmarket.

But there is no doubt that all Scotland, and especially all the clan Gordon, would think differently of the matter — ay, even my mother. And to Wat such a death would seem almost like an accolade.

They read me my warrant in my death dungeon by the light of a dim rushlight. But that of Anton Lennox they read not, for a reason that has already appeared, though they told us not of it at the time. Yet because the messenger was expected to arrive every moment with it, Anton, who shared my favour of execution, was to accompany us to the scaffold.

When they ushered us forth it was yet starlight, but the day was coming over the Forth. And the hum and confused noise of rustling and speech told us of the presence of a great multitude of people about us. They had indeed come from far, even from the wild Highlands, for such a heading had not been known for years. Our keepers gave us a good room, and an excellent breakfast was ready for us in a house contiguous to the scaffold. When we came in, the Earl was at the head of the table, and the gentlemen of his name about him, Anton and I standing apart by ourselves. Then the Dean of Edinburgh, Mr. Annand, came and asked us to be seated. Anton would not, but went to the window and stood commending himself to the God in whose presence he was so soon to appear. However, since it seemed to be expected of a gentleman to command his spirit before death, for the honour of his party and cause, I sat me down with the others, and ate more heartily than I could have expected, though the viands tasted strange, dry, and savourless. They gave us also wine to wash them down withal, which went not amiss.

When they saw that it was growing lighter, they put out the candles, and we were brought down the stairs. When I came to the outside and heard the murmur of the crowd, suddenly and strangely I seemed to be breathing, not sweet morning air, but water chilled with ice. And I had to breathe many breaths for one. There seemed no sustenance in them.

Now Cantyre, being a very great man, was allowed his chief friends to be with him. Eight of them attended him in full mourning to the scaffold, chiefly Montgomeries of Skelmorly and Campbells of Skepnish and Dunstaffnage — all noble and well-set men. And Anton Lennox and I were permitted to walk with him without any disgrace, but with our hats on our heads and in our own best attire, which the Chancellor had allowed to be provided for us. At least so it was with me. For Anton Lennox would have none of these gauds, but was in an ordinary blue bonnet and hodden grey. But for me, though I was to die for the faith, I saw no reason why I should not die like a gentleman.

As we went by the way, the people hushed themselves as we came, and many of them sank on their knees to give us a parting prayer to speed us on our far journey. The Dean and other Divinity men of the ruling party approached, to give us what ghostly counsel they could. But, as I expected, Anton would have none of the Dean or indeed of any other of them. But I was not averse to speak with him, at least as far as the natural agitation of my spirits would permit.

As for prayers, I leant on none of them, except my mother's, which I had repeated that morning. But I kept saying over and over to myself the Scots version of the twenty-third Psalm, "The Lord's my Shepherd," and from it gat wondrous comfort.

The Dean asked me if I had my "testimony" ready written. I told him that testimonies were not for me.

"What," he said, "do you not hold the covenants?"

"I held a sword for them so long as I could. Now, when I cannot, I can at least hold my tongue!"

Even with the scaffold looming out down the vennel, it pleased me to say this to him, for such is the vanity of Galloway, and especially of a Galloway Gordon. Besides, I had once played with the Dean at golf upon Leith Links, and he had beaten me foully. Not twice would he outface me, even though it were my death day.

Mr. Annand was a very pleasant-spoken man, and I think a little grateful that I should speak complacently to him. For he was abashed that Cantyre would have nothing to say to him — no, nor for that matter, Anton Lennox either.

He asked me what affair had brought me there, which vexed me, for I had supposed the whole city ringing with my braving of the Council, and the Chancellor's shaking hands with me.

"I have done God's will," I made him answer, "at least as I saw it, in fighting against Charles Stuart, for his usage of my country and my house. Were I to escape, I should but do the same thing again. It is his day, and Charles Stuart has me on the edge of the iron. But not so long ago it was his father's turn, and so, in due time, it may be his."

"God forbid!" said the Dean piously, thinking no doubt, poor man, that if the King went that way, certain others might also.

"God send him as honourable a death. 'Twere better than lolling with madams on Whitehall couches, that he should honourably step forth from the window of the banqueting hall as his father did!" I made him answer.

"You are a strange Whig, Mr. William Gordon," he said; "do you even give that testimony to them from the scaffold. It will be a change from their general tenor."

I said, "You mistake me. I believe as much and as well as any of them, and I am about to die for it, but testimonies are not in my way. Besides, somewhere my mother is praying for me."

"I would the King could have spared you," he said. "There is need of some like you in this town of Edinburgh."

"When I was in Edinburgh," I replied, "I had not the spirit of a pooked hen, but holding the banner at Sanquhar hath wondrously brisked me."

All this while I could see the lips of Anton Lennox moving. And I knew right well that if I had little to say at the last bitter pinch, he would deliver his soul for the two of us — ay, and for the Earl, too, if he were permitted.

It was just at this moment that we came in sight of the Maiden, which was set high on a platform of black wood. There was much scaffolding, and also a tall ladder leading thereto. But what took and held my eye, was the evil leaden glitter of the broad knife, which would presently shear away my life.

CHAPTER LVI.

THE MAID ON THE WHITE HORSE.

THEN slowly a rim about my neck grew icy cold till it ached with the pain — as when, on a hot day, one holds one's wrists over-long in a running stream. Nevertheless, my southland pride and the grace of God kept me from vulgarly showing my fear.

Yet even the Earl, who came of a family that ought by this time to have grown accustomed to losing their heads, was shaken somewhat by the sight of the Maiden. And, indeed, such present and visible death will daunton the most resolute courage. Therefore he caused bind the napkin upon his face, ere he approached nearer, and so was led upon the scaffold first. I went next, schooling myself to go firmly and saying only, "It will soon be over! It will soon be over!" Then I would fall to my twenty-third Psalm again, and specially to the verse about "death's dark vale," which did indeed strengthen me·so that I feared none ill, or at least not so very much. But at such times one goes on, winning through unshamed, more by the mechanical action of one's body and the instinct of silence, than by the actual thing which men call courage.

But when at last we stood upon the scaffold, and looked about us at the great concourse of people, all silent and all waiting to see us die, more than everything else I wished that they had thought to put a rail about the edge. For the platform being so high, and the time so early in morning, I walked a little as though my legs had been the legs of another and not mine own. But in time this also passed off.

Then they read Cantyre's warrant, and asked him if he had aught to say. He had a long paper prepared, which, standing between his two friends, who held him by either arm, he gave to the Dean. And very courteously he bade us who were to die with him farewell, and also those that were with him. He was a most gallant gentleman, though a Highlandman. They made us stand with our backs to the Maiden, and rolled the drums, while they set him in his place. But for all that I heard louder than thunder the horrible crunch as of one that shaws frosty cabbages with a blunt knife. Methought I had fainted away, when I heard the answering splash, and the loud universal "Ah!" which swept across the multitudes of people.

Yet as they turned me about, because my time had come, I saw quite clearly beneath me the populace fighting fiercely one with another beneath the scaffold, for the blood that drippled through the boards, dipping their kerchiefs and other linen fabrics in it for keepsakes. Also I perceived the collapsed body, most like a sack that falls sideways; and the tall masked headsman holding up the poor dripping head. For the napkin had fallen away from the staring eyne, and I shuddered at the rasping echo of his words.

"This is the head of a traitor!" he cried, as the custom is.

Again the people cried, "Ah!"—They cried it through their clenched teeth. But it was more like a wild beast's growl than a human cry.

Then I was bidden speak if I had aught to say before I died.

So I took off my hat, and though for a moment I stood without strength, suddenly my voice was given back to me, and that with such surprising power that I never knew that I had so great an utterance.

"I die (so they recorded my words) in the faith my father taught me, and for which my father died; neither for King nor bishop will I change it. Neither for love nor lands will I recreant or swear falsely. I am a Gordon of Earlstoun. I die for the freedom of this land. God do so to me and more also, if ever I gave my back to a foe, or my shoulder to a friend all the days of my life! That is all my testimony. God have mercy on my sinful soul, for Christ's sake. Amen!"

"Lord, that is no Whig word!" cried one from the crowd — a soldier, as I think.

"'Tis a pity he is a rebel," said another. I heard them as though they had spoken of another, and not of myself. And all the time I had been speaking, I was watching the headsman wiping his broad sliding blade with a fragment of fine old linen, daintily as one may caress a sweetheart or other beloved possession.

Then the Dean began the praying, for because I had played with him upon the Links of Leith at our diversion, I could not reject his ministrations. And also, as I said, he was a pleasant, well-spoken man. But he had hardly said many words, or indeed gotten fairly into the matter of his prayer — which being an Episcopalian, it took him a long time to do — when his voice seemed to be drowned in the surging murmur which rose from the people far down the spaces of the Grassmarket. The sound we heard was as that of a mighty multitude crying aloud; but whether for joy or hate, I could not tell. The Dean went on praying with his book open. But none, I think, minded him, or indeed could have heard him if they had. For every eye in all that mighty throng was turned to the distance, whence came the cheering of the myriad throats.

The soldiers looked one to the other, and the officers drew together and conferred. They thought, doubtless, that it was the messenger of death with the other warrant of execution, that for Anton Lennox. Yet they marvelled why in that case the people shouted.

The commander bade the drums beat, for the voices of those about the scaffold-foot began to take up the shouting, and he feared a tumult. So the kettle drums brayed out their angry waspish whirr, and the great basses boomed dull and hollow over all.

But in spite of all, the crying of the whole people waxed louder and louder, and the rejoicing came nearer and nearer, so that they could in no wise drown it with all their instruments of music.

Then, in the narrow Gut of the West Port I saw a white horse and a rider upon it, driving fiercely through the black press of the throng. And ever the people tossed their bonnets in the air, flecking the red sunrise with them. And the crowd fell back before the rider as the foam surges from the prow of a swift boat on Solway tide.

And lo! among the shouting throng I looked and saw, and knew. It was my own lass that rode and came to save me, even while the headsman was wiping the crimson from the bloody shearing knife to make it ready for me. In either hand she waved a parchment of pardon, and the people shouted: "A pardon! a pardon! God save the King!"

Without rein she rode, and the people opened a lane for her weary horse. Very pale was her face, the sweetest that ever the sun shone on. Very weary were the lids of her eyes, that were the truest and the bravest which ever God gave to woman. But when they were lifted up to look at me on the scaffold of death, I saw that through the anxiety, which drew dark rings about them, they were joyful with a great joy!

And this is what my Maisie Lennox did for me.

FOLLOWETH

The conclusion of the author to the reader.

BUT our perils were not yet wholly over. We were in fear that at any hour the messenger might arrive, having gotten another horse, even in that lonely place where Maisie left him. But having pardons in the King's hand, our foes themselves were eager to be rid of us. They knew that Roger McGhie had been busy on our behalfs, so that the Council showed no surprise that he had prevailed, knowing how great he was with John Graham, and also with the Duke of York. But they ordered us all, Maisie Lennox, her father, and I, forth of the kingdom upon the instant. So within an hour we went, right well content, along with the officers on board a ship at Leith, that waited with anchor weighed and sails backed in the Roads for the Council's permit to proceed. Which being obtained by the same boat that brought us, they drew away with us on board upon the instant. And it was as well, for, as our friends afterwards advised us, the plundered messenger came in during the night; and with the earliest break of morn there was a swift vessel on our track. But by that time we were well-nigh half over, with a good ship and a following wind. So that there was no vessel in Scotland that could catch us. .

In due time we landed at Rotterdam with great joy and rejoicing. Now, there remains many a story that I might tell concerning our life there — how I took service in the Scots regiments of the Prince, how poor we were and how happy. Indeed, if I be spared and keep my wits, I may write it one day. For, to my thinking, it is a good tale, and infinitely more mirthful than this of the killing time, which presently it has been my lot to tell, though Sandy had no part in it, seeing that he abode until the coming of the Prince in the stony castle of Blackness, yet not greatly ill-done to, being tended there by his wife.

Also in it there should be commemorated how my mother came to us, and concerning Wat and Kate, and all that sped between them. Also, for a greater theme, how we went back and helped Renwick and Cleland to raise again the Seven Thousand, and how we stood in the breach when the Stuarts were swept away. Especially I would joy to tell of the glorious Leaguer of Dunkeld. That were a tale to attempt, indeed, with Maisie Lennox at that tale's ending, even as she has been the beginning and middle and end of this. Only by that time she was no more Maisie Lennox.

Concluded in my study at Afton, December 2, 1702.

W. G.

FINIS.

MAD SIR UCHTRED OF THE HILLS.

By S. R. CROCKETT,

AUTHOR OF "THE RAIDERS," "THE STICKIT MINISTER," ETC., ETC.

16mo. Buckram. $1.25.

"Mr. Crockett is surely the poet-laureate of Galloway. The scene of his latest tale ('Mad Sir Uchtred') is laid among the hills with which we became familiar in 'The Raiders.' It is a brief tale, not a novel, and it can be read through in an hour; indeed, if one begins it, one must read it through, so compelling is the charm of it. The Lady of Garthland makes a gracious and pathetic figure, and the wild and terrible Uchtred, the wrong done him, the vengeance which he did not take, — all these things are narrated in a style of exquisite clearness and beauty. Mr. Crockett need not fear comparison with any of the young Scotsmen who are giving to English literature just now so much that is fresh, and wholesome, and powerful." — *Boston Courier.*

MACMILLAN & CO.,

66 FIFTH AVENUE, NEW YORK.

THE STICKIT MINISTER,

AND SOME COMMON MEN.

BY

S. R. CROCKETT.

12mo. Cloth. $1.50.

"Mr. Crockett has given us a book that is full of strength and charms. Humour and pathos mingle with delightful effect. . . . It is hard to imagine that any lover of literature could be altogether wanting in appreciation of their quaint homeliness and pleasant realism. To come across a volume like this is indeed refreshing. No wailing pessimism mars our enjoyment with its dreary disbelief in humanity; every page exhibits a robust faith in the higher possibilities of our nature, and the result is distinctly successful. Amongst the gems of the collection we may indicate 'The Heather Lintie,' a simple sketch, instinct with quiet, penetrating pathos; whilst as a specimen of acute and kindly humour, 'A Knight-Errant of the Streets,' with its sequel, 'The Progress of Cleg Kelly,' would be hard to surpass. . . . The author has constructed stories full of grace and charm. Those to whom humanity in its most primitive and least complex aspect is interesting will find real pleasure in studying Mr. Crockett's strong and sympathetic presentment of Scottish peasant life." — *The Speaker.*

MACMILLAN & CO.,
66 FIFTH AVENUE, NEW YORK.

A New Novel by the Author of "The Stickit Minister."

THE RAIDERS.

Being Some Passages in the Life of John Faa, Lord and Earl of Little Egypt.

BY

S. R. CROCKETT,

AUTHOR OF "THE STICKIT MINISTER, AND SOME COMMON MEN."

12mo. Cloth. $1.50.

" . . . The things that befell us in those strange years when the hill outlaws collogued with the wild freetraders of the Holland traffic, and fell upon us to the destruction of the life of man, the carrying away of much bestial, besides the putting of many of His Majesty's lieges in fear. . . .

"It was with May Mischief that all the terrible blast of storm began (as indeed most storms among men ever do begin with a bonny lass, like that concerning Helen of Troy, which lasted ten years and of which men speak to this day). The tale began with May Mischief, as you shall hear. I keep the old name still, though the years have gone by, and though now in any talks of the old days, and of all our ancient ploys, there are the bairns to be considered. But it is necessary that ere the memory quite die out, some of us who saw these things should write them down." — *The Foreword.*

MACMILLAN & CO.,
66 FIFTH AVENUE, NEW YORK.

www.ingramcontent.com/pod-product-compliance
Lightning Source LLC
Chambersburg PA
CBHW030358230426
43664CB00007BB/653